Mysterious Ways

Mysterious Ways

True Stories
of the Miraculous

Editors of **GUIDEPOSTS**

Revell
a division of Baker Publishing Group
Grand Rapids, Michigan

© 2016 by Guideposts

Published by Revell
a division of Baker Publishing Group
P.O. Box 6287, Grand Rapids, MI 49516-6287
www.revellbooks.com

Printed in the United States of America

Previously published by Guideposts

Library of Congress Cataloging-in-Publication Data is on file at the Library of Congress, Washington, DC.

ISBN 978-0-8007-2876-2

17 18 19 20 21 22 23   7 6 5 4 3 2 1

Contents

Part 3:   The Writing on the Wall

Part 4:   Right Place, Right Time

Introduction

For years, *Guideposts* magazine readers have been sharing stories of those unexpected and miraculous moments when a loving power reaches into their lives, moments that are surely more than coincidence. We call these stories "Mysterious Ways." When we began publishing these startling and unforgettable accounts thirty-five years ago, we immediately knew we had struck a spiritual sweet spot with our readers, and nothing was more convincing than the thousands of stories sent in, which left them—and us—breathless with wonder at the goodness of God. "Mysterious Ways" soon became the most popular feature in *Guideposts*, so popular that it eventually became a magazine itself, packed with stories that send shivers down your spine and bring tears to your eyes.

This book is a collection of the absolute best stories we've published over the last five years, plus more than fifteen classics from our archives—the most wondrous Mysterious Ways that have come across our desks. These true, personal experiences prove what our hearts know: everything happens for a reason, and that reason is often made clear to us in amazing and life-changing ways—ways that fill us with awe and gratitude and deepen our trust in the Almighty.

I like to say, "Mysterious Ways are the intersections in life where God is directing traffic."

You're in for a treat: more than ninety unforgettable moments when the curtain of heaven was drawn back for a shining instant. Each will remind you that we do not pass through this world unaided. This is a book you'll experience in your soul. It will inspire, nourish, and even, I believe, change you.

Edward Grinnan
Editorial Director, *Guideposts* magazine

PART 1

A Very Present Help

God is our refuge and strength,
a very present help in trouble.

PSALM 46:1

The Bilge Pump

ALINE ALEXANDER NEWMAN

The sun sparkled on the water, the fragrance of pines filled the air, the sky was a vibrant blue. My husband, Neil, and I had just opened our summer cabin in the Adirondacks, and it was the perfect day for the one chore that remained—retrieving our old motorboat from winter storage.

I loved taking the boat out, and every year for the past fifteen years, I'd piloted it the fourteen miles through a picturesque chain of lakes to our cabin, while Neil drove our car. It was virtually a tradition. Now, though, as we got close to the boat launch, I suddenly got nervous.

"What's wrong, honey?" Neil asked.

"I don't know," I said. "I just feel so apprehensive." I looked over our boat, a six-seater built for water-skiing with a seventy-five-horsepower outboard motor. It had served us well over the years, though the turquoise-and-white paint job was worn away near the waterline. Still, it had cruised fine last summer. It was just how we'd left it. So why was I feeling so skittish?

"Want me to drive the boat this time?" Neil offered. "I'll meet you at the cabin."

"Deal," I said, relieved.

Neil climbed in, fired up the motor, and putt-putted away. I got into the car and headed for our cabin. The boat couldn't go as fast as the car—too many waves and narrow channels. So I was the first to arrive. Then the minutes ticked away. After waiting for almost half an hour for Neil, I panicked. *Oh, Lord, what if something went wrong?* I ran out on our dock and looked out over the water.

Finally, the boat appeared around the bend. *Whew*, I thought. Then I noticed . . . the boat didn't look right. It rode way too low in the water. Neil was at the helm, waving frantically. He barely made it to the dock.

"What happened?" I asked, helping him out. His pant legs were soaked.

"The boat sprung a leak," Neil said. "I wouldn't have made it at all if it weren't for that battery-operated bilge pump."

"What bilge pump?"

"I got it on a whim last summer. Guess I forgot to tell you about it. Good thing it was me driving the boat today. You wouldn't have even known the pump was there."

Or known how to operate it if I had.

About That G in GPS . . .

SHARI SEVERINI

Four hours from our destination—that's what the GPS said. At least that's what it said before we smelled a caustic odor and pulled our forty-foot RV off the highway in Chicago. The whole family—my husband, V.J., our four kids, and I—were traveling from our home in Michigan to an annual family reunion in Wisconsin Dells, an outdoorsy vacation area. We'd left a week early to camp out and sightsee. Now it seemed we'd never get there. "I think it's the back brakes," V.J. said, checking out the left rear wheel.

"Now what do we do?" I asked.

"We need to find a Freightliner garage. We can't take her just anywhere," V.J. answered. Our RV was a Winnebago with a custom Freightliner chassis—one solid piece of forged steel that gave us enough power and stability to tow our Chevy behind us. A selling point had been the four hundred locations nationwide that could service us on the road. We weren't far from O'Hare Airport. "There might be a Freightliner garage nearby," I said.

"Open on a Sunday?" V.J. said. "We'll probably be stuck here. Maybe even for days if they have to order parts."

Ugh. This would ruin our vacation.

"I'll type Freightliner into the GPS," V.J. said. "See what it comes up with."

V.J. located a Freightliner garage only ten miles away. *Thank God for that GPS*, I thought. How on earth did we ever get along without it?

We followed the prompts. Left turn here. Go 1.5 miles. Make a right. Our RV limped along. Something about the route, however, didn't seem right. We left the busy highway, turning down a traffic-free road through an industrial complex seemingly devoid of people. *Is this really the way to the garage?* The GPS indicated that we'd arrived at our destination. We were at an anonymous-looking building. No garage in sight.

The kids were restless. V.J. and I were confused. "Guess we can't trust the GPS after all," V.J. said. "I don't want to take the RV back out on the road unless we know where we're going."

I scanned the area. Not far from us, a lone man stood by a car. What was he doing there so late on a Sunday evening? We told the kids to stay in the RV while V.J. and I asked the stranger for directions. As we walked over, I saw the man grab something from his trunk—a toolbox.

"Hello," I said. "We're looking for a Freightliner garage. Is there one around here?"

"Miles away," he said. "What's your trouble?"

V.J. explained the situation, and the man went over to our RV. He rolled up his sleeves and opened his toolbox. Kneeling down near the back tire, he quickly diagnosed the problem. "One of your S-cam brakes is frozen," he said. "That's what caused the burning smell. I'm going to take it off. That still leaves you with three good brakes. You'll be fine for now. Just make sure to have this replaced when you get home."

How did he know all this? He must have seen the astonishment on my face. "Trust me," he added. "I'm just here doing a side job. Monday to Saturday, I'm a Freightliner mechanic."

Our GPS still had a perfect track record. But this location couldn't have been programmed in. A different GPS must have taken over. My family calls it God's Protection Service.

Someone's in Trouble!

JOHN AND ELIZABETH SHERRILL

It was a hot summer morning. Hermano Pablo (missionary Paul Finkenbinder) and four other Christian ministers climbed into Pablo's ancient Chevrolet to travel through the foothills of El Salvador. For several days, they'd been conducting revival meetings out in the country; now they were headed for San Salvador, the capital city.

The trip over the narrow, twisting roads was hazardous even under good weather conditions. But conditions that morning were far from good. Summer is the rainy season in El Salvador, and in many places the dirt road had already turned to mud. Worse, none of the five men in the car knew this region. They did not know that about 150 miles ahead of them, around a deceptive curve, lay the tracks of a railroad.

The same morning, many miles away in the city of Santa Ana, an Indian housemaid was having trouble settling down to work. Angela Mancia kept stopping in the middle of her chores.

Angela worked for a missionary couple, Ralph and Jewel Williams. She knew Hermano Pablo well—he always stayed with the

Williamses when he was in Santa Ana—and Angela often prayed for him and his work. But she was not thinking about him that morning. Indeed, she was aware only of a vague uneasiness, a mounting sense of fear.

Hermano Pablo was driving with one eye on the thunderclouds massing in the east. His friends—Israel Garcia beside him in the front seat, Juan, José, and Fernando in the back—watched the approaching storm as they talked.

About eleven o'clock, the tropical storm reached them, the rain lashing the windshield faster than the wipers could sweep it clean. Pablo leaned forward, straining to see ahead.

Angela was struggling with unaccountable tears when Jewel Williams walked into the kitchen. "Angela! What on earth's the matter?"

"I don't know, señora," Angela insisted. "Except . . ." and all at once she was sure of something. "Someone's in trouble! I know it! Do you think . . . do you think I should go to the church and pray?"

"Of course!"

So Angela started up the muddy street to the little church where she and the Williams family worshiped.

Ordinarily, it took about ten minutes to climb the hill. But that morning it took Angela half an hour because she stopped to talk to every Christian friend she met. To each she described the strange uneasiness, the growing sureness that God was telling her to pray for someone.

"Won't you come with me?" she asked each one. Half a dozen women agreed. And so it was that morning that a handful of Indian Christians walked through the door of the little Assembly of God church, sat down, and began to pray without knowing what it was they were praying about.

At about one o'clock, the five ministers stopped for lunch. The rain continued. Outside, the road was growing more slippery every minute. They climbed back into the old car and went on.

In Santa Ana, the pendulum clock on the wall of the church read 1:30. The women prayed without stopping to eat, unaware of hunger, unaware of anything except the urgency that now gripped them all. "Lord, somewhere one of your children is in trouble. You know who it is, Lord Jesus. Put your hand where the need is."

It was like driving inside a drum, Pablo thought—with the rain hammering on the roof. It was nearly as dark as the inside of a drum too, although it was only two in the afternoon. Pablo decided to stop until the storm was over. But where? Up ahead he made out a curve. Just beyond it, perhaps, there'd be a place to pull over.

"Help your child, Lord, wherever he is!"

"Look out!" Israel Garcia cried.

The headlight of a train shone through the storm, coming fast. Pablo jerked the wheel and slammed on the brakes, but the car kept sliding over the slick mud.

They heard the frantic scream of the whistle. Then the locomotive hit them. The car spun around, and the train hit it again. The right-hand door flew open; Garcia was hurled out. The car rose into the air, came down on its top, and turned over.

"Help him, Lord!"

Pablo opened his eyes. He was lying on the ground, and the rain had stopped. Beside him was a tangle of metal that only gradually he recognized as his Chevy.

Now he realized that he was delirious, because it seemed to him that a crowd of people was standing around him and that among them were his four friends—all alive and all talking to a policeman, who was making notes in a little book. The engineer of the train was there too, staring at them.

"The time?" the policeman was asking him.

The engineer drew a watch from his pocket, still staring at the four. In the voice of one dazed, he replied, "It's two thirty." Slowly, shakily, Pablo got to his feet. "It's not possible," the engineer began. Pablo was embracing his friends. At the policeman's orders, they started for the ambulance, walking away from the circle of gaping passengers, away from the still-throbbing locomotive, away from the sound of the engineer's voice saying, "How can it be? No one could have walked out of that car! It isn't possible!"

Far away in Santa Ana, the long prayer vigil was over. A sudden silence fell over the church. Angela opened her eyes and looked around. The haunting feeling was gone. The other women felt it too. They knew that whatever they had been called to do was now finished.

Angela's voice was a little tired as she spoke. Almost in a whisper, she suggested they sing a hymn of praise and thanksgiving. "I'd like to sing 'How Great Thou Art,'" she said—and then for the first time, she remembered the work waiting for her back at the house.

Angela glanced at the pendulum clock and was astonished to see how late it was. The clock's hands stood at 2:30.

21

The Billboard in the Snow

RUTH SCHENK

Twelve hundred miles to go, I thought, pulling onto the highway in Indiana, my seventy-five-year-old mother-in-law in the passenger seat. My oldest daughter was getting married in San Antonio, Texas, in a few days, and we were anxious to get down there. It was a beautiful, sunny March day, light-jacket weather, and barely any traffic. We'd get to Texas in no time at all, I figured.

Wrong. The lamblike weather quickly turned into a lion. Flurries began to fall before we even hit the Illinois state line. By the time we got to Joplin, Missouri, we were in a blinding snowstorm. I couldn't see past the hood of the car.

I glanced at my mother-in-law. Mom had heart problems and high blood pressure, one reason we'd driven instead of flown. To avoid the stress, supposedly. Pulling over and waiting it out wasn't an option. We could get stuck. I couldn't risk that with Mom in the car. I kept going, slowly and carefully. Mom kept her eye on the shoulder of the road, making sure we were headed straight.

"We've got to stop somewhere," I finally said. It was too dangerous to keep driving.

"Where?" Mom asked.

Up ahead, amid the swirling snow, I could just make out a shadowy shape. A billboard: "Holiday Inn, Next Right."

We exited onto a narrow country lane, skidding slightly at the turn, and then drove through thick woods for almost a mile. *We're lost*, I thought. Our situation was getting desperate.

Then I saw it: a one-story building that looked like a motel, with a parking lot. No sign, but it had to be the place the billboard had advertised. We parked next to a cement mixer and walked to the front. A decal was plastered on the door: Holiday Inn.

The woman at the front desk looked surprised to see us. "Can I help you?" she asked.

"We'd like a room for the night," I said.

"I'm sorry, we're not open yet. We're actually still under construction." Then she looked at Mom and glanced outside at the weather. "But we do have a few rooms ready with beds. You are more than welcome to one."

By noon the next day, the sky and the roads were clear. I went to the front desk to return the key. "You're lucky you weren't stranded on the highway last night," the woman said.

"I saw your billboard, thank God."

The woman looked confused. "We don't have a billboard," she said. "We haven't even put up our sign here yet. Only the decal on the door . . ."

Bulletproof

EVAN MILLER

Something bad had gone down. That was clear. Police and emergency vehicles jammed the parking lot outside the Fort Worth, Texas, McDonald's. Officers took statements from traumatized witnesses. People huddled together. Parents held their children, weeping. Detectives searched for evidence. Shell casings. How many shots had been fired? An APB was blasted out to every unit in the area. Man in a white shirt and black jeans. On foot. A crazed gunman. Still on the loose.

The scene was all too familiar. A reminder of how fragile life can be. One moment everything's fine, boring even; the next, total chaos, ending in unimaginable tragedy.

Or was it? Davage Armstrong's statement told a different story. Five shots inside the restaurant. At least two more fired outside. But, as he told the skeptical detectives over and over, they wouldn't find what they expected at the scene.

Go back just a few minutes earlier. An ordinary September evening, McDonald's crowded with people enjoying a meal out. A young couple grabbing free refills at the soda machine. Teenagers sitting around laughing, devouring Big Macs and fries. Everyone blissfully unaware of the nightmare about to unfold. Davage and his seven-year-old son were in line to order toward the back of the restaurant. The two of them went there all the time for a quick bite before Davage went to work.

Davage was talking on his cell phone, his son tugging on him, hungry for a hot apple pie. Davage noticed the man in the white T-shirt by the door—pacing, agitated—but the guy wasn't hassling anybody. Davage pressed the phone against his ear, trying to hear what his older brother was saying on the other end.

"You're right," Davage said. "But I think things are finally coming together." He hadn't always made the best decisions in life. But he was thirty now, more mature, holding down a good job as a home health aide. And his son? This past year they'd grown a lot closer. Still, he appreciated his brother's encouragement. Just a few years before, their other brother had been killed by an armed robber. That, maybe more than anything, had straightened out Davage.

"Hold on, I've gotta order," Davage said into the phone.

"Welcome to McDonald's," the cashier said. "What can I get you?"

There was a commotion over by the soda machine. Davage looked to his left. The man in the white T-shirt . . . he was brandishing a black pistol. "Give me your money!" he shouted. No one moved. Then the gunman turned and charged directly at Davage, waving the gun in his face.

"You think I'm playing?" the gunman said.

He leveled the pistol directly at Davage's head. All around him people started crying, backing away slowly, hiding behind tables, anything they could find. Some bolted for the door. But for Davage and his son, there was no escape.

There was only the gun, inches away, aimed right between Davage's eyes.

Davage watched the gunman's finger squeeze the trigger. *I'm dead*, he thought. *It's over.*

Click.

The gun didn't fire. Davage didn't think, just reacted. He motioned for his son to run. The boy dashed for the bathroom. Davage surged forward, grabbed the gunman by his shirt, and pushed him against a wall. Hard. The men struggled. The gunman's arms flailed. Davage couldn't get the gunman down, couldn't hold him. The barrel of the gun swung toward his head. Davage ducked. This was his only chance to get away. He turned and ran. Any second he expected to hear the gunshot and feel the bullet explode through his back.

Click.

Run. Just keep running.

Click. A third misfire.

He saw a door in front of him. He opened it, ducked inside what looked like the manager's office, and pushed the door tight behind him with all his weight. What good would it do though? The gunman would just fire through it. The door was flimsy, no better than paper against a large-caliber bullet.

Was his son okay? The thought filled Davage with fear. Anguish. He heard people screaming. He strained to hear his son's voice. Then, nothing. Silence. What was happening out there? He couldn't take it. He had to get to his son.

He inched open the door. The dining room was nearly empty, just a few people pressed against a wall, peeking around the corner. Where was the gunman? Davage left the office and moved toward the front door.

Crack!

Now that was a gunshot. The sound made his blood curdle. Then again.

Crack!

The gunman was outside. Shooting wildly in the parking lot. Whatever problems the gun had had before the gunman had fixed. He was ready to take out real targets. He swung around and stared through the glass door at Davage, his eyes smoldering.

Davage backed away. The gunman walked to the door, swung it open, aimed. Davage wanted to run, but his legs were like lead.

The gunman pulled the trigger.

Click.

He shook the gun and aimed it again at Davage's head. Davage threw his arms in the air. "Please, I'll give you anything—money, my car," he said. "Anything."

The gunman wasn't listening. He was in a fury, his face contorted with rage, hate, frustration. Davage closed his eyes and prepared to die, to meet the Lord.

Click.

The gunman threw his hands into the air, incredulous. He turned and fled the restaurant, this time for good.

Davage found his son in the bathroom, huddled inside a stall, trembling, sobbing. He looked at his father as if he was seeing a ghost. "I thought you were dead," he cried.

Davage took the boy into his arms. For the longest time, they stayed in the bathroom, terrified the gunman would return. Finally, they made their way out to the parking lot with the others. The wail of police sirens filled the night. Help was coming. But all Davage could think about was how many times he'd heard the sound of the gun misfiring. One by one he counted them. Five shots in all. At close range.

The detectives raised their eyebrows. They asked time and time again if Davage was sure. But then the other statements came in, backing him up. The surveillance tape showed the gunman's finger on the trigger—pulling it once, twice, three times more. When the police finally caught the man, they examined the gun and the magazine. Nothing wrong with it that they could see. Enough ammo left to have made the McDonald's a bloody, deadly scene.

In the months since, Davage has struggled to make sense of what happened to him, to all the folks whose lives were spared that night. He's often thought of his brother, who hadn't been so fortunate. For Davage, there's no simple explanation. "Maybe God just needed to show me that miracles still happen, that life is a precious gift not to be wasted," he says. "I'm going to do my best with the second chance I've been given."

The Cross in the Water

EROS M. SAVAGE

One cold early evening many years ago, my wife, Bartie, and I set out in our cabin cruiser for a picnic dinner on southern San Francisco Bay. We waved to a college crew team heading out for a practice row, then proceeded down the channel toward the San Mateo Bridge. The choppy water soon turned into huge waves.

At the drawbridge, I signaled to the bridge tender to let us through. He shook his head, pointing to the whitecaps on the water ahead. We were about to take our pitching craft home when in the distance, near some mud flats, we saw a ruby-colored light glowing, shimmering in the shape of a cross. Bartie and I were mesmerized. We turned our craft in its direction. It was irresponsible of me—in shallow, muddy water, an engine might suck up mud that can destroy it—but I felt compelled to follow the cross. Soon mud was coming from the exhaust pipe, and the temperature of our engine had risen into the danger zone, but the light drew me on.

Then we came up to it only to find that the light was merely a buoy reflecting the red sunset. Bartie and I felt foolish; we had actually risked our boat to chase a mirage.

"Look, the water is full of coconuts," Bartie said. But they weren't coconuts at all; they were the men from the rowing crew, whose shell had crashed into the bridge and sunk. One by one we pulled them aboard. They had been in the water for over an hour. Facing death, gulping the icy salt water, they had come to a point of desperation and had prayed together for rescue.

And that was when the cross began to shine for me.

False Alarm

DENNIS O'KEEFE

A misfire of the number-two cylinder," the mechanic at the auto shop off California's Highway 15 read from my truck's diagnostic computer. So that's what the "check engine" light meant. "You just had this vehicle serviced at our shop in San Diego?" he asked.

I nodded toward the camper trailer hitched to the back. "I always do before one of these excursions," I told him. I was on my way to the northern Sierras for a solo camping trip far off the beaten path.

I'd loved the great outdoors since my childhood in Ottawa, when I explored the gorgeous Gatineau Hills. But it was only after I retired that I was able to spend serious time getting back to nature. My wife wasn't the outdoorsy type and hated long road trips. So we compromised. She would fly to a city near where I was camping, and we'd spend time sightseeing before I headed off on my own. I was fine with that, but my wife was always concerned. "What if something happens to you when you're all alone? What if you get stranded?" We both prayed about that.

I took every precaution. Had the truck checked over. Packed extra supplies. Kept a first-aid kit and other emergency gear. Most important, I had a thirty-gallon water tank that hung underneath the trailer. That was a must in dry conditions.

But today, one hundred miles from home, the engine over-revved and the warning light came on. At least the auto shop would honor its affiliate's work and fix the problem for free. "I'll rev the engine and see if the cylinder misfires again," the mechanic said. He started it up and hit the gas. The engine's roar made the truck tremble.

Boom! What was that? Not the truck. It came from the camper trailer. The two-hundred-pound water tank had broken free and crashed to the ground!

The mechanic shook his head. "If that had fallen off on the highway, it could've gotten you or others killed. It's lucky you came in. Your engine's just fine. A false alarm."

Luck? A false alarm? My wife and I know the real explanation.

Protected by the Word

Adam Hunter

Body armor. Advanced combat helmets. Steel cladding. These things keep our soldiers safe. You might find the suggestion odd, then, that a book could serve as a shield. Marksmen have demonstrated that a hardcover tome can't stop anything more powerful than a .22 caliber. Yet soldiers have experienced the lifesaving power of Bibles on the battlefield as far back as the First English Civil War, in 1643, when a young parliamentarian escaped a battle unscathed only to find a lead slug wedged in the sixteen-page pamphlet of Bible verses in his vest pocket.

The Good Book has saved lives in warfare—and we have the pictures to prove it.

The Civil War

During the Civil War, the American Bible Society distributed pocket-sized New Testaments to fighters on both sides of the conflict, most likely in the hopes of saving souls rather than lives. The Bible of Union soldier Charles Merrill helped do both when, at the Battle of Chancellorsville, it absorbed a musket ball that was headed for his heart. His family was so impressed that they sent the damaged Bible to President Lincoln. He sent back a new Bible with his signature inside. Today both Bibles are displayed at the Peabody Essex Museum in Merrill's hometown of Salem, Massachusetts.

World War I

British bombardier George Vinall sent a battered Bible and three pieces of shrapnel home from France. His bunker had come under enemy fire, he wrote. "The shell burst outside. . . . We ran for a trench nearby." Afterward, he discovered two of the shrapnel pellets embedded in the bunker he'd fled. "The third was in the pocket of my tunic, stopped by my Bible. The eighth verse of Isaiah 49, where the bullet stopped, contains these words, which caught my eye: 'I will preserve thee' (KJV)" Vinall demonstrated his gratitude after the war—by translating Bibles in Japan.

World War II

With the advent of modern weaponry, the US Army field Bible was given an important upgrade—a steel cover. One of these "Heart-Shield Bibles" saved infantryman George Ferris. On April 10, 1945, he was shot by a German sniper. "The medics showed me the Bible that my oldest sister sent me. . . . There was a bullet hole in it," Ferris told the 87th Infantry Division Legacy Association. "The medics said that the bullet had been slowed and deflected, so it went across my body . . . and out the other side instead of through my heart."

Vietnam War

On March 14, 1967, infantryman Jack Fulk of Albion, Indiana, walked into an ambush near the Cambodian border. Hit four times, he could hear North Vietnamese soldiers celebrating the kill. But he wasn't dead. He crawled to safety and made a stunning discovery. "The day before we went out, the chaplain . . . was handing out pocket-sized New Testaments. I had taken one and put it in my left shirt pocket, not thinking much about it," he told his hometown paper. "When that last bullet went through my arm, it hit me right over my heart." Fulk found the bullet—sixty-four pages deep in his little Bible.

A Cry of Help

KARIN ASBRAND

My minister-father believed that God walks beside you day by day, lending you a hand whenever you need it. He shared this faith with his four children.

I remember one summer night about nine o'clock when we were all returning from a day's outing in the family jalopy. Suddenly, a car with glaring headlights swerved around the bend and sideswiped our car. My father, blinded by the headlights, veered off the road. We crashed through a fence and came to a sudden stop. Our car was leaning precariously toward the right.

"Don't anyone move," Dad warned. "We don't know what's below us. Just sit still until someone comes to help. God is with us." We scarcely dared to breathe. We were even afraid to call for help. Dad said the noise might make the car lean still further. My baby sister slept in Mother's lap. Time dragged on. Cars whizzed by us on the highway. Nobody stopped even though our headlights were on.

When my little brother began to whimper, Dad said quietly, "Just hang on. Help will come. All of you pray."

Soon the baby woke up and started to scream. Mother couldn't quiet her. We heard a car drive by slowly, slam on its brakes, and stop. Our ears strained as a car door opened and then footsteps approached.

"Great guns," a man exclaimed when he saw all of us in the car. "I'll go get help. There's a garage nearby." The tone of his voice frightened me as he added, "Don't anyone move!"

He disappeared but soon returned with another man and a tow truck. In no time at all, we were safely back on the road. "You're lucky to be alive. There's a river about thirty feet below that fence you crashed through," the garage man explained. "One little move in the wrong direction and you all would have been pitched right into it."

"If your windows hadn't been open," said our benefactor, "I never would have heard that baby and figured something was wrong."

"The Lord was with us," said my father.

That night, and for many nights, our family prayers were words of gratitude to God for watching over us.

Last Leap

KEVIN HINES

Every year thousands flock to San Francisco to walk across that fabled vermilion span, the Golden Gate Bridge. They come for the sweeping views of the city, the fog-wreathed hillsides abutting cold, gray waters. The bridge rises 220 feet above the bay. Below, sharks and sea lions swim and dangerous currents churn. Tourists crowd the walkway, braced against the wind, snapping photos.

On a cool, foggy September afternoon, I boarded a bus to the Golden Gate Bridge. I wasn't a tourist. I didn't care about the view. I was going to jump.

I sat at the back of the bus, nervously eating a packet of Skittles I'd stolen from a drugstore. In my backpack, I carried a one-paragraph note I'd written to my family and friends. I wiped tears from my cheeks, half hoping someone might ask what was wrong. No one did.

I was nineteen. Recently diagnosed with bipolar disorder. But this was more than a mood swing. My biological parents were drug addicts. I had been taken away from them when I was just a toddler. My father later died during a drug bust. I had been adopted by a good family and given a loving upbringing. But my adoptive parents divorced when I was in high school, undermining my sense of security. My high-school drama teacher, who'd been like another father to me, inexplicably committed suicide. My older sister, Libby, also adopted, had been hospitalized for anorexia.

My life was collapsing around me, and I was collapsing with it. I had horrifyingly real visions of demons shouting that I deserved to die. Paranoid delusions, I knew, but so real I couldn't take their abuse anymore. I wrote my note, tiptoed into my dad's room while he was still asleep to whisper good-bye, and then left the house, stopping at my college to drop my classes so no one would have to hassle with it after I was gone.

I got off the bus and walked slowly toward the midpoint of the 1.7-mile span, where I would leap and be free, dead the second I hit the water. *Die! You must die!* the demon voices shouted, impatient. But my legs felt heavy. Some small part of me yearned to live. *If one person, just one person, asks if I'm all right, I won't jump.* I looked furtively at the faces I passed. Didn't anyone see me, cowering from the tormenting voices?

Someone approached! A beautiful young woman in a stylish outfit waved at me. My heart soared.

"Excuse me. Will you please take my picture?" she asked in a European accent. She posed beside the guardrail and smiled.

Numbly, I took her camera and snapped a few shots. I barely heard her thank me before she walked away. Tears rolled down my face. I didn't even try to hide them. "No one cares!" I shouted into the wind.

I braced myself. Running light and fast, I reached the guardrail and vaulted over it. My feet found a ledge, where I could have perched and waited for someone—a cop, maybe a concerned passerby, anyone to talk me back over the rail.

I didn't wait. I jumped.

Rushing air screamed in my ears, drowning out even the demonic voices. I plunged headfirst, fast as a speeding car. The green, churning water raced toward me. All of the problems, the depression, the loneliness, the helplessness, and the confusion that had driven me over the side of the bridge—all of it suddenly felt inconsequential compared with ending my life.

What have I done? Oh, my God, what have I done?

The air tore at me like shards of glass. The bay rushed closer and closer. All I wanted was to live. My only chance was to go in feet first. I threw my head back and cried, "God, please save me!"

Maybe it was my head jerking back or the wind, but my body twisted in midair until my feet pointed down. I held my breath. A second later, I hit the water.

The impact traveled up through my feet, my legs, my torso, like I'd landed on pavement. My spine shattered, piercing my internal organs.

All at once I realized that somehow I was still alive. I was sinking below the surface. I couldn't kick my legs or tell which way was up. I moved my arms—excruciating. The light from the surface faded. Darkness engulfed me.

My eyes bulged and my head spun. Everything went blurry. I flailed my arms, reaching for that faint light above. It seemed impossibly far.

Suddenly, I burst to the surface. I tried to heave a huge breath. All that came out was a strangled noise. My rib cage was crushed.

I treaded water, every movement a spasm of pain. This wasn't supposed to happen. I was supposed to be free from the hurt. And yet I realized that the demonic voices in my head were silent. I had one desire: to live. If I could get out of the water.

I turned my head. A concrete pillar was about twenty-five yards away. I swam weakly toward it, but the bay's powerful current was carrying me away. I turned in the other direction and saw a buoy. I aimed for it, but the buoy moved away even faster. *Please, God, don't let me die after all. Not now. Not when I want to live more than I've ever wanted to in my life!*

Something warm and rubbery bumped my legs. Sharks lurked in these waters. Great whites. I waited for a pair of massive jaws to close around me. Instead, I was lifted up. Almost out of the water completely. I was lying on top of whatever it was. When I started to sink, it pushed me back to the surface. It felt solid and incredibly, unbelievably strong. It held me afloat while far above a crowd gathered at the bridge railing, pointing and yelling.

At that moment, in my pain and exhaustion, I felt a wave of calm so profound that I suddenly knew for certain I would live. My life was a gift that was being miraculously returned to me. It was as if whatever was beneath me was just a manifestation of something so large and loving and powerful that I could never hope to comprehend it. All I could do was lie there, feeling safe. Just floating. Feeling at peace. Feeling, at last, love.

Minutes later, I heard the throb of an engine. A Coast Guard boat pulled up beside me. Two men jumped in the water and hoisted me over the side. I was strapped onto a stretcher. As the boat raced off, one of the Coast Guard officers put a hand on my head and gave me a searching look. "Do you have any idea how many corpses we pull out of these waters?" he asked. "You're a miracle, kid."

I don't think I'm the miracle. But I know a miracle happened that day. It took many years before my battle with mental illness turned a corner. Only recently have I been able to settle into life as an activist for suicide prevention. I don't want anyone to do what I did: discover too late that nothing, no matter how unbearable, has to be faced alone. That even within the deepest abyss there is more reason to live than to die.

What was that creature that lifted me out of the water? A man on the bridge that day later told me he saw a sea lion circling beneath me. To me, it doesn't matter. It matters only that I emerged from those turbulent waters a man made new.

911 at the Parsonage

NANCY BROOKS

There was a loud knock at the door of the parsonage. Odd. It was a weekday afternoon, not a time people usually dropped by. We didn't have any church activities scheduled. I was the only one there. Probably a parishioner. I opened the door without even asking who it was. Standing before me was a stranger, a hulking man, rough around the edges. "Pastor, I need money," he said. "Can I come inside?"

The parsonage was tucked behind the church in a small yard below street level, surrounded by shade trees. "It's a beautiful day," I said. "Why don't you sit at the picnic table and I'll fetch us some cold water? Then we'll talk."

It wasn't uncommon for transients to find their way to historic Union Congregational Church in Buffalo, Wyoming. Our town had only four thousand residents, but in the summer and early fall, that number more than doubled. Buffalo sat at the junction of two busy interstates in the foothills of the Big Horn Mountains. Recent years had brought all manner of folks looking for work in the booming natural-gas industry. Local churches had developed a program to refer those in need to the police department, who would check them out before we provided vouchers for room and board.

I came outside with two glasses of water and explained the program. The man grew agitated. "I've been on the road for twenty-five years," he declared, his voice rising. "I'm not going to the cops. I need money, and you're gonna give it to me!"

I tried to calm him, but he just got more enraged. No one could see me here behind the church. I didn't have any cash to give the man. Who knew what he'd do to me if I tried to run away?

Suddenly, someone came around the corner of the church. A policeman. I bolted into his arms. Moments later, five more officers arrived and subdued the stranger.

"You okay?" my hero asked. "We got a 911 hang-up call from the parsonage."

"Impossible," I said. "I'm the only one here, and I didn't make that call."

The officer smiled. "Well, pastor, somebody certainly did."

Protected

HENRY MUNGLE

The President of the United States of America, authorized
by Act of Congress, takes pleasure in presenting the Silver
Star to Henry H. G. Mungle, United States Army, for gallantry
and intrepidity in action against an opposing armed force while
serving as Crew Chief of a security platoon, 560th Military Police Company, 93rd Military Police Battalion in the 2nd Military
Region, Republic of Vietnam.

"On the morning of June 12, 1971, at approximately 0900
hours, a truck convoy was attacked by an NVA company. Sergeant
Mungle, commander of a V-100 armored vehicle, quickly directed
his vehicle driver to go to the rescue of the convoy. . . . Sergeant
Mungle's heroic actions in first thwarting the enemy attack, and
then risking his life by shielding a wounded soldier with his body,
administering lifesaving first aid and assisting in his evacuation,
showed rare and extraordinary courage and reflect great credit
upon himself, his unit, and the United States Army."

Department of the Army citation
December 31, 1974

That's how the government tells the story of my Silver Star. But there's another dimension to the story that you will never find in any citation. It began on my first tour of duty in Vietnam, a sweltering night in February 1969. I sat in the driver's seat of a military jeep and scanned the streets of Bien Hoa. Another soldier and I had set out for our overnight shift, patrolling the bustling South Vietnamese city. I took it all in—modern concrete buildings next to makeshift shanties, asphalt roads that trailed off into dirt paths, so unlike the cities back home.

I was twenty-one and had never been in battle, though I'd been around the military all my life. My father had served in World War II and Korea. I felt a mix of anticipation and fear. That afternoon intelligence reports had picked up on massive movements of enemy troops in our sector. At midnight, the radio crackled. My commanding officer. "Yellow alert!" Attack was imminent. Our orders were to inspect a neighborhood at the edge of Bien Hoa and gather intel.

We arrived around 1:00 a.m. at an eerily silent quarter. No one, not even a stray dog, in sight. Clink! A metallic echo came from a nearby alleyway. My partner and I listened for a few moments. Nothing more. I climbed out to investigate. At the entrance to the alley, I pointed my M16 rifle. The cavernous space was dark except for a few dim lights in the windows above. I advanced slowly, my eyes adjusting to the shadows. All at once a voice shouted, "Get out!"

I flinched and tightened my finger on the trigger. Where had that come from? It was a male voice, very close by. I swiveled around, but there was no one. It hadn't come from the windows. They were too far away. I took two steps forward.

"Get out!" The voice came again, louder, harsher. I stopped midstep. The hair on my arms stood up. I backed slowly out of the alley, keeping my weapon trained on the darkness. "Everything all right?" my partner asked. I didn't say a word. I just hopped behind the wheel of the jeep and sped to the base.

46

The North Vietnamese Army unleashed an onslaught on our company. It lasted forty-eight hours until finally the enemy retreated. I'd survived my first battle. Days later, I learned that the NVA had set up headquarters at the end of a long, dark alley. The same alley I'd almost blundered into.

My family had never been religious, never talked about God. But what really happened there in the alleyway? The enemy wouldn't have shouted a warning; they would have shot me on sight. Something—someone—had kept me from walking into certain death. Somehow, I'd been protected.

I didn't forget that when I returned to Vietnam two years later, to the mountainous jungles of the Central Highlands. I was put in charge of a V-100 armored car with two soldiers operating under my orders, protecting supply convoys.

The morning of June 12 we sat at the top of the An Khe Pass, an area along the QL19 highway well-known for enemy ambushes. I scanned the road with my binoculars. "All clear," I radioed. The convoy, trucks and jeeps laden with ammunition, began moving. It hadn't gone far when an explosion shook the ground. The NVA had been lying in wait. It was a trap.

"Get down there!" I ordered my crew. The V-100 leaped forward.

A barrage of machine-gun fire and rocket-propelled grenades came at us. By the time we got to the road, four trucks and a gun jeep had been destroyed. I spotted a soldier lying beside the smoking shell of his vehicle, bleeding, his leg mangled.

I popped the hatch. "Sarge, where are you going?" one of my soldiers yelled. Grenades exploded, bullets whizzed by, the noise deafening. For an instant, I debated staying put. I couldn't save that soldier. . . . I'd get killed myself. But I remembered the alley. The mysterious voice that kept me from walking to my death. I said a quick prayer, climbed out, and stepped on to the road.

That's when I felt it: something tangible, an overwhelming sense as strong as the one I'd felt in the alley, only now I felt safe. Secure and calm. As if a physical barrier separated me from the danger of the battlefield.

I rushed to the injured soldier. He was bleeding badly. I crouched and dressed his wounds. "Hang in there, buddy," I told him. I ran back to the V-100 to call in a chopper. With every step, bullets buzzed past my head. One struck the ground between my legs. I kept moving.

I returned to the soldier and shielded him with my body, returning fire with my rifle. A bullet passed beneath my raised arm. Nothing hit me. It felt like nothing could. The chopper arrived and evacuated the injured soldier. I got back in the V-100 and gave orders to pick up as many of the wounded as we could. We rescued two Republic of Korea soldiers, five South Vietnamese soldiers, and three civilians. It was hours before reinforcements and artillery pushed the NVA back.

When the fight ended, I didn't have a scratch. My men joked that I was invincible. But I knew how mortal I was. In my mind, I replayed every brush with a bullet. The force that shielded me hadn't come from within. I'd felt it descend from above.

Today my Silver Star sits in a glass case with other honors I earned during my twenty years in the military and twenty-seven more in the CIA (that's a whole different story). But what I treasure most can't be kept in a glass case. It's a connection I first forged as a scared kid thrust into battle, when a Force pulled me from a dark alley to safety.

The Embankment

Carole Murphy

Night driving made me nervous. I usually left it to my husband. Just before my sister's anniversary party, though, Bob was called away by one of his parishioners. A pastor's emergency. I couldn't miss the party, so I took our eighteen-month-old granddaughter, whom we were babysitting, and went without him. *I'll just make sure to leave while it's still light out*, I thought. But I lost track of time showing off the baby to everyone. Before I knew it, it was nine o'clock. I said good-bye, buckled my sleepy granddaughter into her car seat, and took off.

Willeo Road is notorious for its tight curves, tracing the path of the Chattahoochee River. More than a few drivers have taken a turn too fast and met a tragic end in the water. But it was the shortest way home.

I kept my eyes on the winding road, my high beams barely penetrating the darkness. *We'll be home soon*, I told myself, gripping the wheel.

There was a sharp bend ahead. I must have been going faster than I thought. The van slid, tires shuddering beneath me. I panicked and slammed on the brakes. The van fishtailed. I fought the wheel, but it was no use. *I'm going off the road . . .*

"Oh, God, help me!" I cried.

Oof. A jarring stop. The seatbelt dug into me. It took a minute to get my bearings. We'd hit an embankment. I stared at the thick tangle of trees hugging the edge of the road. If it hadn't been for that embankment, we would've crashed right into them. I could see my granddaughter in the rearview mirror, still snug and secure. I took a deep breath, reversed, and then eased back onto the road.

At home, I told Bob what had happened. He pulled me close. "Around nine I had this strong urge to pray for your safety," he said. "Now I know why."

The next day we went back to Willeo Road. Bob was curious to see where he'd almost lost us. "There!" I shouted. Our van's skid marks were clearly visible, veering off toward the trees. Beyond them, now that it was daylight, I could see a steep drop . . . and the fast-flowing Chattahoochee. No embankment. Nothing to stop anyone from going over the edge.

PART 2

Heaven's Healing

"As long as I am in the world, I am the light of the world." When He had said these things, He spat on the ground and made clay with the saliva; and He anointed the eyes of the blind man with the clay. And He said to him, "Go, wash in the pool of Siloam" (which is translated, Sent). So he went and washed, and came back seeing.

JOHN 9:5–7

A Bloom in the Dark

DAWN BURNS

Nothing anybody did made any difference. Nobody could cure me. I was hopeless. In and out of the hospital four times, a graduate of five rehab programs. I'd come out and get drunk and high as soon as I could. They said I needed to trust in a Higher Power. Turn my will over. Well, I believed in God. I just wasn't sure he believed in me. Why was he letting me kill myself? Why wasn't he stopping me? It was clear I couldn't stop myself.

That November day I was alone at our house in the mountains. My husband was at work, and I'd gone on another binge. Crack and booze. All at once I could feel myself slipping over the edge. I couldn't breathe. *This time you really are going to die.* I grabbed my cell phone and dialed my parents, hoping they'd pick up. Wouldn't have blamed them if they hadn't. They'd bailed me out enough and seen me steal from them, break into their house, take money from their bank account for another fix, another binge.

They found me collapsed on my kitchen floor, as good as dead. Dad did CPR. Mom took my phone and dashed down to the end of the drive, the only place she could get a signal. An ambulance rushed me to the hospital one more time. Or one last time. How many more times did I have?

They had to strap me down in detox, then took me up to the third floor and put me in a room, IVs flooding my veins. My body was a mess, my liver damaged, my temperature sky-rocketing, my blood pressure stratospheric. My fingernails had fallen out, and I was bruised all over.

The nurses came in every hour, checking the IV and all the monitors I was hooked up to, checking to see if I had a chance of surviving.

I tossed and turned, asking God the same questions I'd asked him a thousand times: *Why did you let me do it? Why didn't you stop me?* As if it was his fault and not my own. If I could kill myself like this, maybe there wasn't a God at all. No Higher Power. Maybe those twelve steps were all based on some fairy tale. My parents and husband visited, telling me what a miracle it was that I was alive. "We're so grateful," they said. I wasn't buying it.

One visitor, though, I didn't recognize. It was early one morning, just a hint of sunlight slipping in through the shades. I woke up to see a little blonde girl with glasses peering over the foot of my hospital bed. In her hand she was carrying a balloon flower, with a red balloon center, a green stalk, and orange petals.

They should know better than to let little kids run around here, I thought, *among the hopeless and the doomed*. I turned away, expecting her to leave, but she came over to the side of my bed. "Here," she said, "I want you to have this."

I took the balloon flower from her. "Thanks," I said. I wanted to know who she was, where she had come from, but I was still so tired. I dozed off.

The next thing I knew the nurse was waking me to check my temperature. I asked her if she knew who had come by earlier.

"The little girl with the glasses. Maybe part of some Brownie troop that visited the hospital?"

The nurse frowned. "No kids are allowed on this floor. Are you kidding? We'd never permit it. I've been at the nurses' station all day. Nobody's been here."

"But . . ." I sputtered. But what? Of course, it had been nothing but a hallucination. Another one of my fevered brain's attempts to flush out the chemicals I'd fed it.

"Where'd you get that?" the nurse asked. She reached over me, picked up something from the side of my bed, and held it aloft. The colors shone in the pale light.

I left that hospital a changed woman. Never took a drink or touched a drug again. I no longer wondered if God really cared about me. If that little girl had never visited, why was the balloon flower still there?

Walking Miracle

EVAN MILLER

The answer must be in the Bible, Joel Haler's father told him. Of course, the minister's son was used to that response—he'd heard it often in his twenty years, though what he read didn't always make sense to him. Still, Joel rolled his wheelchair up to the kitchen table and flipped the pages of his Bible to the book of Job, chapter 23: "Then Job replied: 'Even today my complaint is bitter; his hand is heavy in spite of my groaning'" (v. 1 NIV).

Joel read through the chapter twice, considering every word. A bitter complaint? He knew all about that. Yet it wasn't the answer he was seeking. His father urged him to keep looking, searching for the meaning of the message Joel believed he'd been sent, the mysterious code that seemed to offer Joel the promise he'd walk again: J23.

It was January 2014, three months since a freak accident in a college gym class had left Joel paralyzed below the waist. For three months, he'd hoped for a miracle. Every week at his father's church, members of the congregation told Joel they were praying for him. Still, nothing had changed. He'd been to four hospitals, seen specialists, had all kinds of tests. MRIs. Spinal taps. The doctors offered no hope that he would walk again.

Ever since he had been a little boy, his father had told him that God had a plan. But was it God's plan for him to spend his life in a wheelchair? Or was life just random?

Then came the dream. Joel was inside the Fieldhouse in New Castle, Indiana, the biggest high-school basketball arena in the country, where he had once played for the New Castle Trojans. That night the place was rocking, the fans—nine thousand strong—stomping and clapping like this was the state championship game. Joel, surrounded by teammates, ran through the entrance tunnel to the court. A giant paper banner covered the opening. Suddenly, his perspective changed. He was inside the gym, staring directly at the banner. It was stark white, printed with a letter and a number: J23. Joel saw it for only a second before the Trojans burst through it.

Joel's eyes flew open. He was lying in bed, in the dark. He tried again to move his legs. Nothing. J23? What was that supposed to mean?

The answer wasn't in the book of Job. Joel turned to Jeremiah, but that was no help either. Neither was chapter 23 in Joshua. Those were the only J books with 23 chapters.

"This is pointless!" Joel closed the Bible with a thud and pushed away from the table.

In the days that followed, Joel looked elsewhere. The crossword puzzle. Google. License plates. Nothing. Maybe J23 had no meaning. Maybe it was just something random, like life.

That Sunday at the end of the church service, one of the children, a four-year-old boy, came up to Joel, who was sitting in his wheelchair at the back of the sanctuary.

"You're going to walk on a Thursday," the boy announced, his voice filled with youthful confidence.

The boy's mother looked on uncertainly. Three months earlier, she explained, her son had told her that God had given him a message to share with Joel. She'd dismissed it, but he had insisted.

First J23, now this. Joel and his family puzzled over the boy's prediction. Which Thursday? Were Joel's dream and the boy's message connected?

At home, Joel asked his dad to get the calendar. They opened it to June. The twenty-third was a Monday. July 23 was a Wednesday.

"What about January?" his dad asked.

Joel flipped back to the first page. January 23 was a Thursday—four days away. Impossible. After three months in a wheelchair, his legs were so atrophied that he would need months of physical therapy. He had only just begun sessions strapped into a robotic harness that moved his legs. He was nowhere near strong enough to stand, much less walk.

Wednesday night arrived. Joel couldn't sleep. There was nothing he could do but wait.

Midnight came. January 23 began. Joel's legs were still dead weight. An hour passed. Then two more. Joel stared down at his paralyzed limbs. It was hopeless. He dropped his head into his hands.

He barely felt it at first. Like a feather stroking his ankle. Ever so slowly the feeling spread up his legs, growing into an intense pain. He couldn't take it. He wiggled his toes, then pinched his arm to make sure. No, he was definitely awake.

He swung his legs off the bed. He could bend his knees! Cautiously, he lowered his feet to the floor and stood. He took a step. Then another. He didn't stumble.

Outside his parents' room he called out, "Mom! Dad! Look!"

A rocket ship couldn't have propelled the Halers out of bed any faster. "You're walking! You're walking!" they said over and over. Joel didn't need to worry about falling. His parents had never hugged him tighter.

There was no medical explanation. Perhaps swelling from his injury had subsided, and any damage to his spinal cord had been minor. But that wouldn't explain his walking after three months in a wheelchair.

Nothing could account for it. Except J23.

Today Joel visits churches around the country, sharing an experience he himself cannot completely explain. Not a verse in the Bible but a glimpse of a plan. Not randomness but goodness.

I Saw the Hand of God Move

JOE STEVENSON

I've always believed in God. But over the years, my beliefs about who God is—and what he can do—have changed. It wasn't until my son was gravely ill that I learned you can believe in God and yet not know him at all.

Know. Knowledge. Logic. When I was younger, those were the words I wanted to live by. As a child, I contracted scarlet fever, and this illness ruled out my ever playing sports or roughhousing around. The only real adventures I could go on were adventures of the mind. I read books with a vengeance—Great Books of the Western World, the volumes of Will and Ariel Durant, and literally thousands more—and out of my reading I formed my strongest beliefs. I believed in logic, in the mind's ability to put all creation into neat, rational categories.

At the same time, I was growing up in a strong Christian family, and so I believed in God. But I insisted—and my insistence caused a lot of arguments—that God himself was also a Being bound by logic and his own natural laws. I guess I pictured God as a great scientist. Miracles? No, God couldn't and wouldn't break laws in that way. When my family told me that Christianity means faith in a loving, miracle-working God, I turned away and went looking for other religions—ones that respected the rational mind above all.

As I became a man, my belief in rationality helped me in my career. I became a salesman for the Bell System, and when I needed to formulate sales strategies and targets, logic unlocked a lot of doors on the way to success.

But other doors seemed to be closed. I felt dry, spiritually empty, and anxious. I tried meditation, ESP, and so on, but the emptiness increased to despair.

In utter defeat, I turned to God in prayer. His Spirit answered with, "I don't simply want belief that I exist. I want you, your will, your life, your dreams, your goals, your very being. And I want your faith, faith that I am sufficient for all your needs." My despair overcame my logic, and I yielded all to him. But just saying you have faith is not the same as having it. In my mind, I still had God in a box.

Maybe that's why I never thought to pray when my oldest son, Frank, came home from first grade one day and said he didn't feel well. What would God care about stomach flu?

A doctor whom my wife, Janice, and I consulted wasn't very alarmed about Frank's illness at first. "It's really not too serious," the doctor assured us. "Just a bad case of the flu complicated by a little acidosis. Give him this medicine and in a few days he'll be fine."

But Frank wasn't fine, not at all. The medicine worked for a day or so, but then his symptoms—the gagging, choking, and vomiting—came back more violently. His small, six-year-old frame was bathed in sweat and racked with convulsions. We checked him into the local hospital for further testing, but later in the evening, our doctor said the original diagnosis was correct. "He's just got a real bad case of it," we were told.

I went to work the next day fully expecting to take Frank and Janice home that night, but when I stopped at the hospital to pick them up, our doctor was there to meet me. "I'd like to have a word with you two," he said, showing Janice and me into a private room.

"A problem, Doctor?" I asked.

"Further testing has shown our previous diagnosis was incorrect. We think your son has acute nephritis. It's a terminal kidney disease." He paused, and I could feel the blood running from my face. "But we've found that in children there's a good chance of recovery. Your son has a 90 percent chance of being as good as new."

But by ten o'clock the next morning, the news was worse. Sometime during the night, Frank's kidneys had failed. Janice and I rushed to the hospital again.

"X-rays show Frank's kidneys are so badly infected that no fluid will pass through them," we were told. "The odds aren't in his favor anymore. If those kidneys don't start working within forty-eight hours, I'm afraid your son will die."

I looked at Janice, watching the tears well in her eyes as a huge lump formed in my throat. I took her hand in mine, and slowly we walked back to Frank's room. We were too shocked, too upset to even talk. All afternoon we sat at Frank's bedside, watching, stroking his matted blond hair, wiping his damp forehead. The stillness of the room was broken only by the beeps and blips of machines monitoring little Frank's condition. Specialists would occasionally come, adjust a few tubes, make some marks on Frank's chart, and then silently go. I searched their eyes for an answer, for some glimmer of hope, and got nothing. When our minister came to pray for our son, I could only cry in desperation.

Late that evening, after Frank was asleep, we went home. Friends were waiting with a hot meal, words of encouragement, and news of a vast prayer chain they had begun. And for a fleeting moment, I thought I saw in Janice's eyes the spark of hope that I had been looking for from the doctors all afternoon.

By the following morning, that spark of hope had ignited a flame of confidence in Janice. "I turned Frank's life over to God last night," she told me excitedly, before we were even out of bed. "I feel a real peace about what's going to happen, that God's will is going to be done."

"God's will?" I said angrily. "What kind of God makes little boys get sick? He doesn't care!" And I rolled over. Peace? God's will? No, little Frank would need more than that to get well.

But my anger didn't stop me from trying to reason with God. All that morning, while Janice kept a hospital vigil, I begged and pleaded and screamed at God, daring him to disprove my skepticism, trying to goad him into action.

"Who do you think you are?" I shouted once. "Why are you doing this to my son? He's only six! Everybody says you're such a loving God—why don't you show it?" I yelled until I was exhausted. Finally, convinced my arguments were falling on deaf ears, I took our other children to a neighbor and headed to the hospital, thinking this might be the last time I'd see my son alive.

I never arrived; at least a part of me didn't. In the car on the way, this Higher Being, this remote Power, this unjust God, spoke to me through his Spirit. I felt his presence soothing my still-hot anger. And I heard his voice, gentle, reassuring. He reminded me that I had made a commitment to him, that I had promised to trust him with my life, my all. And he had promised to take care of me, in all circumstances. "Take me out of the box you've put me in," he said, "and let me work." By the time I parked the car, my heart was beating wildly. I sat for a few moments longer and uttered but two words in reply to all that had happened: "Forgive me."

By the time I reached Frank's room, I knew what I needed to do as clearly as if someone had given me written instructions. There had been no change in Frank's condition, so I sent Janice home to get some rest. Then I walked over to Frank's bed. Placing shaking hands on where I thought his kidneys should be, I prayed as I never believed I would ever pray. "God, forgive me for my ego, for trying to make you what I want you to be. If you will, heal my son, and if you won't, that's all right too. I'll trust you. But, please, do either right now. I pray in Christ's name. Amen."

That was all. There were no lightning flashes, no glows, no surges of emotion like the rushing wind, only the blip-blip-blip of monitors. I calmly sat down in a chair, picked up a magazine, and began to wait for God's answer. There was only one difference. For the first time in my life, I knew I was going to get one.

Within moments, my eyes were drawn from the magazine to a catheter tube leading from Frank's frail-looking body. That tube was supposed to drain fluid from his kidneys, but for nearly two days, it had been perfectly dry, meaning Frank's kidneys weren't working at all. But when I looked closely at the top of the tube, I saw a small drop of clear fluid forming. Ever so slowly it expanded, like a drop of water forming on the head of a leaky faucet, until it became heavy enough to run down the tube and into the collecting jar.

This was the most wonderful thing I had ever seen—the hand of God working. I watched the tube, transfixed, fully expecting to see another drop of fluid form. In about two minutes, I did. Soon the drops were coming regularly, about a minute apart. With every drip, I could hear God saying to me, "I am, and I care."

When the nurse came in on her regular half-hour rounds, she could barely contain her excitement. "Do you see this? Do you see this?" she shouted, pointing to the collecting jar. "Do you know that this is more fluid than your son has excreted in the past forty-eight hours combined?" She grabbed the catheter and raised it, saying she wanted to get every drop, then rushed off.

Within minutes, she was back. Grabbing a chair, she sat down next to me, and, excitedly, we watched drops of fluid run down the tube. We were both awed at what was happening; for half an hour, we murmured only short sentences. "Isn't God good?" she asked me once, and I nodded. When she finally got up to call the doctor, I went to call Janice.

An hour and a half later, one of the specialists assigned to Frank's case arrived. Taking one look at the collector, he told us it was a false alarm, that the fluid was too clear. Anything coming from a kidney as infected as Frank's was would be rust-colored and filled with pus. No, he said, the fluid had to be coming from somewhere else. But I knew—Frank was well again.

By the next morning, more than five hundred milliliters of the clear fluid had passed into the collector, and it continued as the doctors ran tests and took X-rays to try to determine its origin. Finally, two days later, our doctor called us into his office.

"Joe, Janice, I think we've been privileged to witness an act of God. All the X-rays taken in the last two days not only show no kidney infection but also show no sign that there was ever an infection. Frank's blood pressure and blood-poison levels have also dropped suddenly. . . . It is a definite miracle."

And this time I wasn't about to argue. At last I fully believed in a God whose love knows no bounds—not the bounds of logic, not the hold of natural laws. Faith. That's what I now had—that and the knowledge that one's belief in God is essentially hollow if the belief isn't founded on faith.

A History of Violence

VIKKI BURKE

I don't know why I signed up to take that genealogy course. What I knew about my family I didn't like, and what I didn't know—a lot—only frightened me. But maybe I was looking for something redemptive in my poisoned family tree, one little twig of goodness: someone who prayed, something that might reassure me that cursed blood didn't run through our veins. I had always been haunted by that notion.

At the first class, the teacher gave some tips on how to search family histories online. But what really helped was pure analog.

"If you have an old family Bible with some information," she said, "names, birth dates, marginalia, you'll be way ahead of the game."

An old family Bible. I actually did have one. I'd hardly opened it since my grandmother had given it to me when I was twenty-one. Faint handwriting chronicled mysterious births and deaths and marriages. The pages were faded and brittle. They'd felt as if they would disintegrate in my hands if I wasn't careful. I'd thought it was better to leave the Good Book on the shelf. Maybe it was the only good thing about my family.

Yet that first class lit a kind of fire in me. I ran a dustcloth across the leather cover and the embossed words: Holy Bible. I could remember very clearly the day my grandmother, Mom's mom, had given it to me. She had a little apartment a couple of miles from our home in Southern California. I had dropped by to visit, and that day we were having lunch. She knew I was interested in developing my faith. She lifted the book from the mohair sofa and put it in my hands, saying, "This rightfully belongs to you."

I had long since moved out of my childhood home. My father was an alcoholic. He died of cancer when I was a teenager. I'd had enough of being told by my mom that I was stupid and worthless and would never amount to anything. Mom was still intoxicated by her own anger toward Dad, toward her life. I wondered sometimes why my grandmother never intervened, but back then I didn't know—and wouldn't know for years—how she too had suffered.

All I had was the Bible she had given me. I married a godly man, and the two of us went into ministry, preaching, teaching, bringing comfort to many. We moved a thousand miles away, and I managed to forgive my mom and maintain a civil long-distance relationship with her. But my questions about family were met by stony silence. The message was clear: you don't want to know.

Except now I did. I wanted to know everything. I turned the Bible's faded pages and studied the names. I copied them down and started doing some research.

What I discovered shocked me. A newspaper article from the 1920s revealed the terrible truth about my mother's family.

"Mom," I said, after getting her on the phone, "you never told me that your father had another family before you were born and what happened to them."

"I don't care about that," she snapped.

No wonder. Her father was a murderer. He had four children with his first wife, but when he discovered she was having an affair, he killed the other man. Tried and convicted, he served only a brief term, his sentence reduced because of his wife's infidelity. This was the 1920s, remember. He fled the state and married a younger woman, my grandmother, who found herself trapped in a marriage with a cruel, bitter man. So it wasn't surprising that their daughter, my mother, turned out the way she was. It didn't excuse her behavior, but it helped me understand her better.

I kept digging, asking questions and searching online. It just got worse. Mom's grandfather abused his wife so badly that she ran for her life. He wouldn't allow her to take the children and soon turned his rage on the ten of them, beating them bloody, including his son Ewing. Looking further back, I discovered that my four-times-great-grandfather owned seventy-three slaves—I think he was a slave trader. There were bootleggers, criminals, murderers. No matter which family line I researched, I found scenes of violence. Had they reverberated down through the generations to my childhood?

I regretted my research. What more evidence did I need that this was something in my blood, something inescapable, no matter how stable my life seemed now? I was ready to give up. Then I was talking to a cousin and heard about another relative to track down. My great-aunt Maybelle, who had been married to Ewing. Her name wasn't in the Bible. I looked her up. She was still alive at ninety. I packed my bags and went to visit her.

Maybelle was lovely, a pianist and a preacher. "Your uncle Ewing would have loved to meet you," she said. Ewing, she told me, had his own battle with rage. When he was sixteen, his father gave him a beating and left to go work in the fields. Ewing grabbed a rifle and chased after his father, determined to kill the man. *Yet one more tragic story*. But Maybelle went on: "When he stormed out, he heard a voice that said to him over and over, 'Don't. Don't do it.' He put the rifle back, left home for good, and gave his life to the Lord. He attended seminary and preached the gospel the rest of his life. He was the biggest-hearted man you would ever know. Love won out, not anger."

Maybelle pointed me to other good family members: circuit-riding preachers who took the gospel across the hard terrain of the Appalachians; relatives who gave up fortunes because they believed God's call for charity. That slave trader? His son, my great-great-great-grandfather, grew up to be an ardent abolitionist.

I studied the photos of my great-uncle Ewing in his prime. "I wish I'd known him when I was a kid," I said.

"Oh, but, Vikki, he knew you," Maybelle said. "He learned all about you from your grandmother. He prayed for you by name his whole life long. He never stopped."

Someone Else's Reunion

MARY CANTELL

Frankly, I was totally baffled. What on earth were we doing here, surrounded by at least a hundred strangers? And why hadn't I asked myself that question before? Not that my husband, Jeff, and I felt unwelcome. These were perfectly nice people milling around the campground pavilion. It's just that we didn't know a single one of them. Well, we knew one: Ken.

Ken was an old friend, Jeff's roommate before we got married, a big, warm, demonstrative guy known for his bear hugs. They could practically lift you off your feet. One Sunday after church, he charged right over to give us each a big squeeze. Jeff dodged— his back had been acting up again—and Ken understood. "I was hoping I'd see you two today," he said. "I wanted to invite you to my family reunion. It's at a campground in New Holland. There'll be food, games, good people. Lots of fun."

"Sure, why not?" I said, glancing at Jeff, who nodded.

"Fantastic!" said Ken. "Ginger's too busy to make it this year, and Abbie would rather spend time with her friends. So it'll be great having you two with me."

I don't know why the phrase "family reunion" didn't register. We always enjoyed getting together with Ken, his wife, Ginger, and his daughter, Abbie. Oddly, spending a day at the park sounded great—even without Ginger and Abbie.

"Let's remember to bring my ice pack," Jeff said. "If Ken's family hugs like him, I'll need it." In his teens, Jeff had injured his back lifting something heavy, and recently, he'd suffered a herniated disk doing yard work. He saw a chiropractor and did physical therapy, but most of the time he just grimaced through the pain.

Now standing in the camp's pavilion area, I felt so out of place being at some other family's reunion. Folks chatted at the picnic tables. Funky music poured out of a boom box. Kids chased each other around the grass. Stacks of soda and platters of hot dogs and beef patties were piled next to plastic containers full of homemade cakes and pies. Jeff and I had brought some food as well—cheese, crackers, olives, and fruit.

Ken came over with a couple of cousins. "These are my friends Jeff and Mary," he said.

The cousins were friendly. Nobody acted as if it was strange that Ken had brought us. "Even I don't know everybody here," Ken said. "We're a big clan."

A woman came up to us holding out her phone. "Say cheese!" We barely had time to smile before she took the picture. *Years from now, that shot will confuse her*, I thought. *Her grandkids will ask, "Who is that?" and she won't have any idea. She'll probably think we were freeloaders or something.* Well, maybe not. As she was leaving, she gave us each a major bear hug. Jeff winced.

"Your back?" I asked.

Jeff nodded.

"Want to go for a walk? Maybe it'll loosen up," I said.

We headed into a thick grove of trees. Squeals of laughter coming from a nearby pool drifted through the leaves. The scent of

71

lilacs hung in the air as Jeff and I ambled along a dirt path. It was nice to be away from "the family" for a while, from all the excitement we weren't really a part of.

I kept an eye on Jeff. *It must be so frustrating for him*, I thought. Sure enough, after we'd walked for a while, I noticed him slowing down. He put a hand to his back. "We'd better turn around," he said. "I'm going to need that ice pack."

We headed back to the pavilion. I spotted Ken next to a tall guy who was waving us over as if he wanted to meet us. "Sorry!" I called. "I have to get some ice."

The tall guy shook his head. "No ice," he said. "Just come over."

Jeff and I were so surprised we didn't question what he said. "This is my cousin Silas," Ken said as Silas pulled up a chair and gestured for Jeff to sit down.

"You're in pain, aren't you?" Silas said.

Jeff nodded.

"On a scale of one to ten, where's it at?"

"About a six right now."

"Take off your shoes."

Jeff removed his shoes while Ken explained that Silas worked in physical therapy. "I can spot people in pain a mile away," Silas said. "It's as if God alerts me." He examined Jeff gently but thoroughly, speaking of God the whole time. He talked naturally, as if he was just making conversation, but his voice rose and fell with passion. He quoted Scripture to illustrate a point. Others gathered around to listen and watch. I couldn't help feeling like this was a family reunion in *The Twilight Zone*. I certainly believed in God. I believed he could heal. But this was so strange and sudden.

Silas dropped to his knees to examine Jeff's feet. "God didn't make Jeff to be in this situation," he said. He took hold of Jeff's ankles. "See how his feet aren't lined up?" he asked. "God can fix that."

Silas passed his hands over Jeff's feet. He didn't touch them, just circled his palms above them and prayed. "How's the back pain now on a scale of one to ten?" he eventually asked.

Jeff stood up carefully. "One," he said, a note of disbelief in his voice. "No. Absolutely zero. There's no pain at all. How did you do that?"

Silas shook his head. "The Lord did it, not me. I don't have the power to heal anyone myself."

I was suspicious though. I thought Jeff was only being polite. Trying to fit in with Ken's family. Or maybe the pain had been dulled for a moment by something Silas had done that I hadn't seen. But it's been more than six years since that unusual family reunion, and Jeff hasn't felt the need to dodge one of Ken's bear hugs yet.

Reconnected

FRANCINE BALDWIN-BILLINGSLEA

Who was Mom speaking to? She sat next to me on the overstuffed couch in my sun-drenched living room, phone cradled at her ear, laughing and talking to whoever it was—her caramel skin setting off her big, bright smile. I'd never seen Mom look so happy. The sunlight seemed to get brighter and brighter.

"Who is it?" I asked.

Mom's smile grew wider, and she looked deep into my eyes. Without a word, she handed the phone to me. I put it to my ear. "Hello?" I said.

I woke up gasping, as if the wind had been knocked out of me. I hadn't heard the voice on the line, but it was obvious who it was. A voice I hadn't heard in nearly eight years.

The last communication of any kind that I'd had with my younger sister, Pam, was just before Thanksgiving. An instant message out of the blue. "What's going on?" she wrote.

"Not much," I answered quickly. That was all. Now it was nearly Christmas.

It never used to be that way with us. Mom always bragged about the bond Pam and I shared, even though we were almost eight years apart. I lived in Georgia, and Pam had settled in North Carolina, but we got together when we could and called each other all the time. "Girl, let me tell you . . ." Pam would say, and she'd launch into some story. I'd share another one right back. We'd talk and laugh our heads off for hours.

Everything changed after Mom suddenly passed away. She hadn't left a will. Soon Pam and I went from agreeing on how to split up her estate to clashing over everything. First, it was just a war of words. Then lawyers got involved. I blamed Pam for making things so complicated. She blamed me. We stopped getting together. We stopped speaking to each other.

That's when the dreams began.

Until now, they'd all been the same. Mom sat on the edge of my bed holding a portrait of Pam and me close to her heart. It was one we'd given to her the Christmas before she passed away. In it, Pam and I looked like the close, loving siblings we used to be. Mom, however, looked devastated, mournful even. That wasn't like her. In my heart, I knew why. *Mom, I'm so sorry*, I'd wake up thinking. *But I don't know what to do.*

This new dream made it seem so easy. I could just pick up the phone and dial the number I knew by heart. Apologize, forgive, forget.

In my head, I went over everything I'd say to Pam. But I was still too stubborn to make the call. Christmas came and went.

The first week of January I put out the tree for collection, then started packing up the decorations around the house. In my bedroom, the sight of a crystal-framed picture of Mom stopped me. She was smiling, the way I wanted to remember her, the way she had been smiling in that last dream. I picked up the frame and held it close to my heart, as she had. I cried softly. "Mom, I can't go through another year without talking to my sister. I just can't. I want this foolishness to stop. I want you to rest in peace knowing that all is well with us." I said a silent prayer, then put the picture back and collapsed onto the bed.

Not long after, the phone rang.

"Girl, we have so much to catch up on. Let me tell you . . ."

I burst into tears. Pam!

"I'm so sorry," I said.

"No, I'm sorry. This has been so silly, such a waste of time," Pam said. We jumped right into conversation, one story after another, as if there had never been eight years of silence. I could tell she was as thankful as I was that the ice was broken. We talked and laughed for hours.

That night I had no trouble drifting off. I didn't dream at all, sleeping more deeply than I had since before Mom had passed.

The next day Pam called again. "It may sound a little weird," she began. "I wanted to tell you yesterday. All these years we weren't talking . . . I often had dreams about Mom."

"Me too," I said.

"She was always sad, and you know that wasn't like her at all," Pam continued. "But recently, I had a different dream. Mom was talking on the phone, smiling, laughing, happier than I'd ever seen her. Then she handed the phone to me and smiled. I just knew it was you on the line. That's why I called. I couldn't ignore the dream any longer."

"Girl," I said, "let me tell you . . ."

The Cure

VIVIENNE L. GEORGE

Paco and I stared at each other through an invisible wall of mounting tension. "I'm not leaving," I said flatly. "I'm just too sick to travel."

Paco rolled his eyes upward, calling on his Guatemalan gods to witness the unreasonableness of the American tourist lady. "But señora," he protested for the fifteenth time, "the downriver boat isn't due until another two days. Perhaps by then . . ."

I closed my red-rimmed, watery eyes, hoping to close off the conversation. The cold in my head made it feel three sizes too big. My throat was on fire, and every shred of my body ached.

"Perhaps by then . . ." I was wallowing in self-pity. "Perhaps by then I may be dead!"

Immediately, I was sorry. After all, I was virtually an intruder in this small, little-known village in the far upper reaches of Guatemala. A week ago, I had traveled here, first by rickety, hedgehopping jungle airline, then by Jeep, and finally by boat, in order to photograph an obscure, old Mayan temple ruin.

From the village of 150 or so inhabitants, I had selected Paco's as the most promising of primitive guest facilities. He had been happy to receive me then, since I was his only customer. Shortly afterward, however, he had received word that a boatload of twelve students from a US university would be arriving to study the same site, on the very day I was scheduled to leave. Since they would be staying for six weeks, and he could rent his room to as many as three students, it was a windfall he and his family could ill-afford to lose.

I stifled my conscience telling me I was being selfish proposing to wait for the following boat—just long enough for all the students to get settled elsewhere. After all, I reminded myself, of all the bad colds I'd had, this one was undoubtedly the most painful and miserable. I couldn't afford to take chances by stirring about too soon.

But if I was desperate, so was Paco. He played his trump card. "There's only one thing left to do," he announced with finality. "I'll have to call on the *curadera*."

"Oh no!" I wheezed. "No lady witch doctors!" Then sympathizing with his situation, I softened. "You see, I am a Christian. Her magic wouldn't work on me." But we were both talking at once, neither listening to the other. *At least I owe him the courtesy of a hearing*, I told myself.

". . . and she is a very old woman," he was saying, "older than almost any of us. For most of our lives, she has kept sickness and bad luck from our village with the corn magic handed down from the ancient ones. But of late—since last spring—she has changed. Perhaps age has got the best of her. She no longer works the corn magic or burns the copal," a mixture of resins from tropical trees.

He glanced out the window and brightened. "What good fortune! There she is in the street outside. I will explain our plight. Perhaps just this one more time she will work the corn magic."

He dashed out, and I took advantage of the break to down two more aspirins from my dwindling supply. Then he was back, half dragging, half carrying a wizened little woman who was even more reluctant about our meeting than I.

Both were yelling, speaking far too fast for me to follow their Spanish, but their gestures told me what the argument was about. Paco was pointing in my direction and nodding vigorously. The *curadera* was pointing to me and shaking her head just as vehemently.

Whatever they might be saying, I approved of the woman's refusal to perform her magic on me. I made it a free-for-all, pointing at the *curadera* and nodding in my turn. "I'm with her."

Suddenly, the little woman broke off her yelling. The silence was more deafening than the clamor. Paco and I watched, both a little apprehensive, as she came across the room toward me. Then I saw she was not looking at me but at my Bible open on the nightstand.

Now she was pointing at a picture of Christ on the open page, groping visibly for her meager English. "You," she asked intensely, "you . . . Jesus?" I nodded, not fully comprehending.

Her smile washed over me like the breaking of floodgates. She placed both hands over her heart. "I . . . Jesus! I . . . Jesus!" she kept repeating, tears rippling across the wrinkles in her face. I took her hands. The moisture in my own eyes was not from the head cold. Paco turned on his heel and strode out, muttering in complete frustration.

The little woman groped in the tattered folds of her dress to bring out a crumpled tract, worn almost threadbare from repeated handling. "Read!" she implored. I was thankful now for my years of high-school Spanish that permitted me to come to at least a semblance of the correct pronunciation, even though I had to force the words past the burning in my throat.

My pronunciation didn't matter after all. She already knew every word of the tract by heart, and she mouthed each silently as I read, reveling in the hearing. The words were a simple telling about Christ and his way to salvation.

"Where did you get this tract?" I asked.

With Guatemalan courtesy, she turned back to the little English she knew. "Find," she gestured toward the boat dock. "Trash heap. American tourist, he read me." To these villagers, every "outsider" was a "tourist," even though few, if any, ever came here on vacation.

Suddenly, her countenance clouded, and she lapsed back into Spanish. "Forgive me! You are sick. I cannot work the corn magic any more. That is bad . . . evil. But I will pray. Jesus is good. He will take the sickness away."

She held my hand and prayed simply, with infinite trust, like a child asking Daddy to "fix."

"Thank you," I said when she finished praying. I was surprised to note my voice wasn't as husky as it had been. When I swallowed, the fire in my throat wasn't quite so painful. *Wow*, I thought, blindly, *the aspirins are finally beginning to work*. Instantly, I felt a nudge of rebuke. *She has more faith than you*, a gentle voice, not my own, said inside me.

In a flash of understanding, I knew why, during my last flurry of packing, I had impulsively substituted my Spanish-language New Testament for my favorite one. I opened it now and began to read to her about the Christ she knew only from the meager verses on the tract. She was like a starved child, drinking in every word and pleading for "more . . . more . . ."

I had been reading most of the afternoon before I realized that the hoarseness and hurt had been steadily draining from my throat. The ache was going rapidly too. As the fading light began to make reading difficult, I thrust the book into her hands. "Here, this is yours now. Jesus will always abide with you in his Word."

She burst into tears. "But you are leaving! Who will read to me?"

"Is there no one in your village who can read?" I asked.

"Oh, there is the schoolmaster and one or two more. But they will not read to me. They are angry because I no longer cure them with corn magic. They do not want to know Jesus. They do not even want me to know him."

I read one last verse to her, Acts 16:31: "Believe on the Lord Jesus Christ, and thou shalt be saved, and thy house" (KJV).

Explaining that in this case I was sure the word *house* meant "village," I urged her to go to the schoolmaster. "Ask him to read," I told her. "Then pray. The Lord will honor his Word."

I did not see her again until two days later when I boarded the boat—on schedule and without my cold. When I turned for a last look at the village, I saw two people standing hand in hand on the landing. They were the former village witch doctor and a young man who looked every inch a schoolteacher. The radiance on both their faces told me what I didn't need to ask.

"See," I called back as the boat nosed into the river, "already your witness is doubled. You must not rest until all the village knows him."

They both nodded eagerly and stood waving until the jungle underbrush closed in and blocked them from view. And all the way down the river my heart was singing in tune with the ripples. "Thank you, dear heavenly Father, thank you for the happiest, most miserable cold you ever permitted me to have."

The Rest of Her Life

Evan Miller

The world was a terrifying place for nine-year-old Beth Praed. She was afraid of everything. Worms, spiders, even little roly-poly bugs. Thunderstorms. A car driving slowly by her house in Indianapolis. You name it.

The dark scared her the most. She wouldn't go to bed unless her mother first checked the room, turning on the light in her closet and the one on her nightstand.

One night her mother tucked her in and kissed her good night, then switched off the light by the bed.

"Leave the closet light on," Beth pleaded.

"Yes, dear," her mother said and left the closet door open just a crack.

"A little bit more, Mom, a little bit more," Beth begged. Her hands trembled.

"Honey, you don't need to worry," her mother told her. "Jesus is always there watching over us."

Beth wasn't entirely sure what that meant. To her, it was one more unknown.

82

It wasn't that she didn't have fun. She and her two brothers played tag and rode their bikes with the other kids in the neighborhood. But even then there was a part of her that was anxious, afraid something awful would happen.

For Beth's tenth birthday, her mother invited all the neighborhood children to her party. It was a wonderful day, but that evening Beth began gasping for air. Her body felt like it was on fire. Her mother gave her a sponge bath with cool water, but the fever wouldn't break. Beth drifted in and out of consciousness. Her parents rushed her to the hospital.

The doctors were baffled. They ran test after test but couldn't determine a cause for her rapidly deteriorating condition. A week went by. Beth—weak, barely conscious, her skin ghostly white— drew closer to death. "There's nothing more we can do," a doctor told her parents. Their neighbors, friends at church, the kids at school were all praying for her. Her class sent handmade cards. But there was no improvement.

One night Beth was alone in her room. Deep in her being, she'd always believed something bad awaited her. Now she just wanted it all to be over.

I'm ready to die now, she prayed. *Please take me.* Her eyelids grew heavy. She could feel herself slipping away.

A sharp, stabbing pain ripped through her chest. Before she could scream, the pain was gone. A soft, golden aura filled the room. She could breathe again. Easily. Effortlessly. Slowly her room faded around her. In the distance, she saw a bright light, a pinprick that grew larger as it came closer. Her eyes fixed on it, and she realized it wasn't a light at all but a man walking—no, floating—toward her. He wore a brown robe and had brown hair and a beard. His eyes met hers and seemed to envelop her with warmth, a comfort she'd never known.

Are you ready to die? he asked. His lips never moved, but Beth heard him clearly.

No, she thought. *I'm just a little girl.* The man nodded and smiled as if he knew Beth better than she knew herself.

The question reverberated in her mind. Then, suddenly, as if she were watching a movie, she saw a woman with a son and two daughters. She saw her teaching music. Scenes of joy. And also sadness. She saw the woman struggling to walk, her face contorted in pain. She didn't understand everything she saw, but she knew it was a glimpse into time.

The man looked at her again as if to ask, *Do you want to live?*

She took a deep breath. *Yes,* she said. *I want to live.*

The man turned and left, just as he had arrived, until only the pinprick of light was left in the corner of her room. Beth looked down. Amazingly, she was standing in the middle of her bed. She tried to remember everything the man had shown her, but she could recall only the faintest of details.

A week later, she left the hospital, the doctors astounded by her recovery from what they were now calling a severe case of pneumonia. Back home that first night, her mother tucked her into bed and walked over to the closet to turn on the light. "It's okay, Mom," Beth said. "I don't need it."

It was months before she fully regained her strength. And not just physically. That summer Beth thought a lot about the man who had visited her and the questions he'd asked.

One day she told her mom about it. "I know who the man was," Beth said. "It was Jesus. He was there. Watching over me. Just like you said."

Beth's mother hugged her. Something had definitely happened to her daughter in the hospital. She was sure of that. Beth wasn't anxious anymore. She was practically fearless.

As the years went by, every detail the robed man had shown Beth came true. She grew up, got married, raised a son and two daughters, began a long career teaching music. There was always this feeling that she was journeying down a path she had seen before. It was so incredibly reassuring, the security of knowing she wasn't alone. She was sure there would be difficult times ahead, a terrible trauma, but she wasn't afraid. Every day—her entire life—felt like a gift.

Then it happened. In 1995, at the age of thirty-four, Beth began having difficulty seeing out of her right eye. Her legs and arms often felt numb. She had seizures. Some days she could barely get out of bed. Doctors eventually diagnosed her symptoms as multiple sclerosis, an inflammatory disorder of the brain and spinal cord for which there is no known cure. It wasn't a death sentence, but she could lose ten to fifteen years off her life. The attacks would get progressively worse with time. By the end, she'd lose the ability to walk.

A devastating outlook for anyone. Yet not for Beth. She yelled at God plenty of times. But she remembered the vision she'd had at ten years old, the man she'd seen and the words he'd said. They were as real as they'd been back then. She remained determined to live life to the fullest.

Today, though she uses a walker for long periods on her feet, Beth's MS has stabilized. For how long, she doesn't know. But she's far too busy to worry about that. She's gone back to school at Western Michigan University to pursue a master's degree in counseling psychology. She dreams of being a comfort to the dying. After all, she knows their fears and believes she knows the light that awaits them.

Healed

SAM VAUGHT

I was never going to get better. In fact, I was going to get worse. A vein attached to my retina had hemorrhaged. An occlusion, the doctor called it. The pressure from the blood slowly building up behind my right eye was nearly unbearable. Laser surgery would relieve the pain but not stem the loss of vision in my eye. In time, macular degeneration would cause my left eye to go blind as well. It was already starting. Darkness was taking over. Just when I thought a new life was beginning.

My wife, Shirley, and I had retired and were finishing up our dream house. I'd started my own bluegrass group, Uncle Sam & the Gospel Gang. These were supposed to be my golden years. Golden? Black was more like it. Blind. And the darkness ran deeper than my eyesight. It blotted my soul. I'd always been a faithful man, but if there was hope for me, I couldn't see it. All I heard was, "There's nothing more to be done, Mr. Vaught."

It was April, time for the town's annual ramp festival celebrating the wild onions that grow abundantly around these parts in the spring. Fry 'em up with potatoes and cheese and you've got yourself a delicious dish. People came from miles around for the feast. My wife and I joined the group cleaning the ramps, peeling away the outer layers, washing off the dirt, and cutting off the ends. It was hard work but fun with friends.

"I'm not going," I had told Shirley earlier. "I'd be lucky not to cut my fingers off."

"Sam, you can do this," she had said. "It'll be good to get out of the house."

I'd relented. Now I sat at the table by a mound of onions and started in. I held each stalk firmly against the table, carefully slicing through the end. Glancing to my left, I saw the pile Shirley had already gone through, while I'd cleaned less than a dozen. I focused what was left of the sight in my one good eye back on my work.

"You know what you get when you mix onions with baked beans?" I heard a woman across the table say. "Tear gas." Everyone laughed, even me. I looked over at her, a woman about my age. A man I took to be her husband sat beside her. I'd never seen them before. Must have been their first time. The look on her face was pure joy. Like this was the best day of her life. I marveled at how she sliced the ends off her ramps without even looking at them. *If only*, I thought.

There was something infectious about her. She kept the room in stitches. The day flew by. I looked at the heaping pile of roots I'd cut. I'd done better than I thought.

"It's been a pleasure," the woman said, standing up. "I just thank God for all his blessings. He hasn't failed me yet." She reached back a bit awkwardly and felt around for a long white cane leaning against the wall, then made her way out of the building, her husband gently holding her arm.

She's blind? She'd handled those ramps like a pro. Handled herself with such grace. Blessed—that's how she'd described herself. I felt a faint echo of hope reverberate through me.

I underwent the surgery to relieve the pressure in my eye. Like the doc said, the pain was gone, but my vision was no better. Still, something was different. I couldn't help thinking about how that woman *accepted* her blindness joyously, almost gratefully.

I started singing at churches and nursing homes. Heck, I could always play and sing with my eyes closed anyway. Evenings I'd sit on the deck with my wife, listening to the birds and breathing in the night air. I savored the sounds, the warmth of a touch, the sweetness of smell, a world as rich and full and beautiful as any I could see.

One evening at church, the preacher asked if anyone needed anointing. Not sure why, I raised my hand. The congregation surrounded me and placed their hands on me while the minister prayed. In each individual hand, I could feel love. An unmistakable feeling of comfort. The same feeling I'd had for months. Truth was, I'd already been healed that day cleaning ramps. I had been healed of the darkness that blotted my soul.

Two weeks later, Shirley and I were driving down the highway. Suddenly, the road, the cars, the trees on either side of us—all were crystal clear. I closed my left eye. The world was still there. "Shirley, I can see!" I shouted. "I can see everything!"

My doctor could hardly believe it, let alone explain it. But there I was in her office reading the eye chart like nothing had ever happened.

The Yellow Kite

BEVERLY NEWMAN

I stood at the window and watched the neighborhood children flying their kites on the hill behind our house. My four-year-old son, Michael, stood next to me with his face eagerly pressed against the glass. Then, looking up at me with pleading eyes, he again asked if he could have a kite like the other children. For days now, ever since he had first seen them congregate on the hill, Michael had been asking the same question and had been given the same answer: "Wait until you are a little older."

It was easier not to go into a long explanation, but Michael was too young to fly a kite all by himself, and that meant one of his parents would always have to go with him to help. Because of my health, I simply didn't have the strength or energy, and my husband was usually at work. Once again, Michael hid his face in my skirt, something he always did when he was going to cry and didn't want me to see.

As I turned from the window, I felt like crying myself. I looked around the room. The furniture was shabby and worn, and the walls were badly in need of paint. You could see the light places on them, the spots where previous tenants had hung their pictures.

Even though we had lived there for several months, I had not done very much to fix up the place. We had moved so many times, and each time it seemed the neighborhood was a little more run-down and the house was a little older, each one in need of repairs.

My husband, Bill, worked long, irregular hours at his job and earned a good salary. However, there was never enough money, and we kept going deeper in debt. I had lost three children through miscarriages, and the complications that followed had caused me to make several emergency trips to the hospital and to be constantly under a doctor's care. As a result, a tension had grown between us, and we found we could no longer get along with each other.

It all looked so hopeless; even God seemed to have forgotten us. I prayed so often about our problems, asking God for help, but things only seemed to get worse. I found myself thinking, *God doesn't care, and I guess I don't either.*

I walked over to the mirror and studied my reflection. It was almost like looking at a stranger. I looked pale and worn, much older than my years. I no longer bothered to fix my face or do anything with my hair. I stepped back and studied my whole image—the old dress I had worn all week was wrinkled and torn at the pocket, and there was a button missing at the neck.

As I stood there and stared at myself, a feeling of dread, almost panic, came over me, and it filled my whole body with fear. It was the realization that I was giving up on life. I had stopped caring about anything; I felt defeated. I could no longer rise above the depression that had taken hold of me.

In the last few months, my husband had grown rather quiet, and we did not talk much. I was aware of his eyes studying me when he thought I was preoccupied with something. I used to be so particular about everything. Bill had not said a word about the change that had come over me, but his actions said a lot. He made a special effort to get me interested in new things, but I did not respond to him in any way, and he did not know quite how to handle me anymore.

Michael was the one spark of life left for me. He could make me smile, and when he hugged me, I felt love. I clung to him much in the way one would cling to a life preserver. He needed me and I knew it—that kept me going.

As I tucked him into bed that evening, Michael said, "Mommy, may I pray to God to send me a yellow kite?" Then, fearing that I might again repeat what I had said, so many times before, he added, "Maybe he doesn't think I'm too young."

"Yes," I said. "We will leave it up to him to decide about it once and for all." I was tired of the whole thing and hoped that maybe this would make Michael stop talking about it.

Michael prayed his prayer and fell asleep with a smile on his face. As I stood there looking down at the beautiful child with the blond curls, so trusting in his faith that God would answer his little prayer, I found myself questioning God. Would he really answer such a small prayer when he had chosen not to hear any of my frantic pleas or send me any help to relieve my situation? "Oh, God," I prayed, "please help me! Show me the way out of this dark place."

The next morning as I raised the shade in the kitchen, I stared at the sight that met my eyes—a string hanging down in front of the window. Not quite able to believe the thoughts that were being put together in my mind, I found myself running out the back door and into the yard. There it was, a yellow kite, caught on the roof, with its string hanging down.

"Oh, thank you, God, thank you!" I repeated over and over again. I was thanking him for the yellow kite, and I was thanking him for the joy that was flooding into my soul. He had answered the prayer of a little boy, just a little prayer, but by answering that prayer, he had also answered my prayer for help.

Suddenly, I remembered Michael. I ran to his room, scooped him up in my arms, and carried him into the backyard. He was still half asleep and didn't quite know what to make of his mother, who was babbling about something on the roof and saying, "Wait until you see!"

He clapped his hands and bounced up and down in my arms when he saw the kite. "Mommy, Mommy, and it's even yellow!" he exclaimed.

I smiled at him and added, "It's a miracle too."

He hugged me and said, "I knew God would answer my prayer. I just knew he would."

I thought to myself, *This is why I have been so depressed. I lost my faith. I turned my back on God and then insisted that he had stopped caring.*

But the yellow kite was not the only miracle God sent to us that morning.

When Bill came home, we took the kite to the beach and flew it. It went so high that it was almost out of sight for a while. Bill said he had never seen a kite fly as high. We asked all over the neighborhood, but we never found a trace of the kite's former owner.

We moved several times in the years that followed, and the yellow kite always went with us. My depression left me, and as my health improved, so did my relationship with my husband.

At each new place, I hung the kite in some corner where I could see it as I went about my duties. It served as a reminder that, no matter how bad things might seem, we must never lose sight of the fact that God cares, that he hears our prayers. No request is too big or too small to bring before him.

Wide Awake

ROBERT E. LOHSTROH JR.

There is a photo on the wall in my house. A framed picture of a beautiful young woman with honey-blonde hair falling past her shoulders and a sweet, shy smile. She's not my wife, my sister, or my daughter. Not even a friend. I never knew her while she was alive. But she means everything to me.

Here's the sad fact of the matter: She lost her life at age twenty-eight, and I regained mine at age fifty-six. Even staring at those two numbers, I struggle to find God's justice in them, to see where his mercy lies. But it would be wrong of me to question his plan. Instead, I express gratitude for every day I have left, for every breath given to me.

A half dozen years ago, I was diagnosed with a deadly combination of emphysema and chronic bronchitis. My lungs were severely damaged, and I was placed on oxygen 24-7. Finally, the doctor said those words no patient ever wants to hear: "There is nothing more we can do for you." Nothing more than a double lung transplant, if I should survive long enough to get one.

When you become a candidate for a transplant—and I was considered a good risk because apart from my lungs I was healthy—you are put on a list. It's a bit like living on death row, waiting for a reprieve. Every day you wonder if you will be called. Every day that you aren't feels like another death sentence. Although you try not to think about it, it's a matter of odds. Where are you on the list? Are you close to the top? Who will die so that you can live?

I tried not to think about that but to simply trust in God. Trust in his plan. But that got a lot harder when I was moved from the list at the Cleveland Clinic to the one at the Methodist Hospital in Indianapolis. The former does more than five times the number of lung transplants than the latter each year.

By June, I was struggling to breathe even on eight liters of oxygen per day. The slightest task drained me. I knew I wouldn't live to see my birthday in August.

Then I got the call. July 20. They thought they had a set of lungs that would match my body size, blood, and tissue type. Was this the reprieve I'd hoped and prayed for? I was rushed to the hospital. They ran me through a barrage of tests and wheeled me into surgery.

Within twenty-four hours of the call, I was in the ICU, recovering. Awake. Lucid. I took a breath. And another. Cool air rushed into my chest. I kept drawing it in, filling my new lungs to capacity before exhaling. Never had something so basic to life seemed like such a divine gift. Never had a breath tasted sweeter.

I went from the ICU to a private room, gaining strength each day but sleeping fitfully. Someone had died to give me this miracle. That was always on my mind. I didn't want to think about what the donor's family was going through. That thought, more than the beeping monitors and the nurses coming in to check on me, kept me awake and restless.

On my fourth night in the hospital, I found myself staring at the clock, watching the minutes tick by. It was 2:00 a.m., and the room was lit only by a ribbon of light coming from the open door. I could hear the nurses talking at the nurses' station and then footsteps.

Someone appeared in the doorway, the light like an aura behind her. A young woman in a hospital gown.

She stepped into the room and took two paces toward me.

"Who are you?" I asked. "Are you my nurse just coming on duty?"

"I am your organ donor," she said. "I wanted to check on you and tell you that everything is going to be all right."

I couldn't respond. I just stared at her, this young woman illuminated by the hallway light, taking in every detail of her features. Her face was aglow.

Then she turned and walked back into the hallway, disappearing as quickly as she had come.

Mentally, I pinched myself. No, I wasn't dreaming. Yes, I knew what I'd experienced was impossible. My donor could not have appeared at my bedside. It had to be someone else. But who was she and why did her words give me such sudden relief and reassurance?

For very good reasons, you can never get in touch with your donor's family unless they reach out to you. Even then hospital protocol precludes any contact for months. But I wrote a letter to the donor's family expressing my gratitude and my sympathy and gave it to a hospital administrator. It was the least I could do.

To my surprise, I soon received a letter in return. It was from the mother of my donor. She asked me to give her a call.

She was warm and kind, all the things I hoped for, and was happy to meet with me. A kind of closure, perhaps, for both of us.

Her twenty-eight-year-old daughter, Priscilla, had died in a car accident. The family had been devastated by such a tragic loss. I hoped to show the mother that something good had come from it.

We met for lunch, and I told her about the blessing of her daughter's gift. How my daily death sentence had been lifted. I even told her about the strange visitor to my hospital room. My story seemed to give her some comfort.

"What about your daughter?" I asked. "She must have been really wonderful."

"She was," her mother said and poured out her heart.

When she was done, she reached into her purse and removed a photograph for me to see.

That was when I took my deepest breath yet. Long blonde hair, clear blue eyes, the shy, sweet smile.

It is the very same photo I keep on my wall today, the photo of the woman who came to my room that early morning in the hospital.

Miracle Baby

PAULA LENNEMAN

A football spirals deep down the field. A strong young man running like the wind reaches out his hands just in time to grab the pass for a completion, maybe even a touchdown.

That was the dream I had for the baby boy I was soon to have, my prayers for a healthy son. Now, though, everything was in doubt.

My eyes froze on the ghostly sonogram of my baby on the monitor, a pulsing inside his tiny body. His heartbeat was strong, the body fully formed, complete and perfect. Except for one small hole where a hole shouldn't be.

"This is where the stomach is pushing up inside the diaphragm every time the child breathes," the doctor said. "It shouldn't be doing that."

I squeezed my husband's hand. This was supposed to be a routine test. I could definitely see what the doctor was talking about. It was *all* I could see.

"We'll induce labor in the morning," the doctor said. "The baby will need surgery—immediately. But I'm afraid your child will never have the strength or energy of other children. There will always be a weakness in that spot near his heart and lungs."

"It's going to be okay," my husband, Russ, said on the drive home. But in his eyes, I could see he was as scared as I was.

We spent the evening calling family and friends, begging for prayers. "We'll put you on the prayer chain at church," people said.

It was like sending out a spiritual SOS. Finally, there was nothing to do but go to bed. Russ and I prayed together, hoping something had been amiss with the test or equipment. Something. *Lord, please make my baby all right.*

But there wasn't. Another ultrasound in the morning definitively confirmed the problem. "I'm sorry," the doctor said. "There is no doubt. We have to get this baby delivered and into surgery."

Only the baby wouldn't cooperate. My contractions grew more frequent and painful. The wait was excruciating. I thought of all the people praying for us. *Pray harder, please*, I thought. *I want my baby to be all right.*

The morning dragged on, past midday, then into evening. Russ stayed at my side. "Just relax," he said. "There are so many people praying for you. Just let it happen." I knew that. Why was God taking so long? All I could think about was the hole inside my son's chest.

Just after midnight, my son's head emerged. He was out. I'd scarcely heard his cries before the doctor cradled my son in his arms and rushed him away.

What if they can't fix the hole? I wondered. *What if something goes wrong? I never even got to hold him.*

"Try to get some sleep," someone said. "We'll let you know as soon as we hear from the surgeon."

I was groggy. Maybe it was just a few hours, maybe one. I lost track.

When we met with the doctor, he appeared in shock. "We didn't do the surgery," he said, his voice quiet.

My heart pounded. "Is our baby okay?" I asked. "What's wrong?"

"He's doing fine," the doctor said. "Just before the operation, the surgeon asked for an X-ray. And, well, I can't explain this, but the hole is gone. It's just not there anymore. Someone will be here to take you to him soon. Congratulations." Then he was off.

I could scarcely believe what I was hearing. The hole *was* there. I had seen it myself. So had Russ. I stared at him. Was this a mistake? It didn't make any sense.

Tears of relief, tears of joy, rolled down my cheeks. A nurse came in the room and asked if everything was okay.

"I'm just so happy about my baby," I said. "He was supposed to have surgery . . ."

"You're the mother of the miracle baby!" the nurse exclaimed. "We just had a staff meeting about you. The doctor showed us all the ultrasound images of your son. He asked us what we thought. We all said the same thing. 'The baby needs surgery.' Then he showed us the X-ray. We didn't believe him when he said no surgery had been performed. Everyone was just in awe."

Miracle baby. That's what everyone said. Friends from all over called when we got home. Prayers had gone out across the country, a network of praying people answering our spiritual SOS from California to Florida.

While I was in labor those fifteen hours, something happened, something no one, not even the doctors, could explain.

And today when I watch Michael take the field as wide receiver for his college football team, I remind myself that I am watching a miracle.

A Glimpse of Evil

Linda Stevens

A blinding light. Hands touching me. Terrible pain in my chest. My eyes adjusted. I was surrounded by doctors and nurses, a blur of activity. Every bone in my body screamed in agony, yet I couldn't move, my strength drained by the pain.

Then a voice: "This one's mine!" The voice was gravelly, distorted almost. Not a doctor—someone else in the corner of the room. There was a spooky gleefulness to his declaration, a sinister delight. I moved my eyes to the right, and that's when I saw him. A tall, shadowy figure leaning back, one leg propped against the wall, a black fedora pulled down over his eyes, gangster-style. No one else seemed to notice the knife in his hands, the casual way he used its gleaming blade to trim his nails. He was patiently waiting for the doctors to finish their work so he could begin his.

I knew who he was, why he was there. It was only a matter of time. People like me, we had debts to pay. The gangster was there to collect.

I'd already knocked back four or five cold ones at the bar earlier that evening, but that hadn't stopped me from pulling over at the convenience store on my way home for a six-pack of Bud. I'd had a tough day at work at my job as an electrician, and I needed a little something to take the edge off. I popped open a beer and pulled out of the parking lot.

My tiny Subaru Justy hugged the pavement. Rain was lightly falling on the windshield. It was a beautiful drive, narrow, hilly roads that wound back to my place deep in the woods.

Don't you think you've had enough? the voice of my son Michael whispered in my ear. Michael had been my conscience ever since he had died. Now, though, his voice tortured me. I took another sip. *Bad enough you want to kill yourself, but you want to put other lives at risk too?*

"One more won't hurt," I said. "I can make it home just fine."

I'd quit the drugs, tried to follow the Lord's path. To no avail. My ex-husband had written me off and driven a wedge between me and my two surviving sons. Could there really be a brighter future for me? I didn't believe it. Alcohol had become a crutch. I had no one to rely on in my life.

Up ahead I saw a curve. I hit the clutch. Downshifted. Suddenly, the headlights of an oncoming truck blinded me. I jerked the car hard to the right, hit something at the edge of the road, and went airborne. All I could see was a tree dead ahead. I closed my eyes. The Justy smashed into it head-on.

When I regained my senses, I was half in, half out of the car. I looked behind me, woozy. The Justy had flown over a ravine, the back tires hanging on the edge of the drop-off with barely an inch to spare. The force of the collision had jammed my legs nearly through the grille of the car. I couldn't move. Couldn't feel my legs. The entire weight of the engine, still running, still hot, pushed down on me.

I screamed for help. It felt like hours before I heard a man say, "I'm calling for help. Don't move!" Paramedics finally arrived. I was barely conscious when they lifted me into the ambulance.

"She's not going to make it," one of the EMTs said. "Don't crank up the oxygen. Best not waste it on her." I heard the scream of the sirens—there's no sound more terrifying when you know it's for you—and then everything went black.

Best not waste it on her. Those words echoed in the darkness, a cold, absolute void from which I couldn't escape. I knew immediately what the darkness was. Not merely death but a place meant for those who wasted the life they'd been given. *No, not here!* I prayed. *Lord, don't leave me here for all eternity.*

Then there was a flash of light. A loud, crashing sound. Like furniture being thrown around. I could feel myself spinning, being pulled and pushed by forces on either side of a furious battle. Suddenly, I was caught between two worlds, one of darkness and one of light and life. *God is fighting for me.* I could feel it. But why? Why was he fighting for me to live—someone not worth the oxygen?

I thought about Michael. My beautiful boy. My kids were the one thing I had gotten right in my mess of a life. Michael had been doing well, working construction, about to enter the Air Force. An artist. His paintings were beautiful. Such a sweet, peaceful kid. That's what finally broke me. When Michael was murdered. A senseless act of violence. It made me want to give up on life. Until now. *I can do better, Lord. Give me back my life, and I'll find a way to repay you.*

The roar of the fighting fell away. The darkness scattered. I was in the hospital, the doctors and nurses working frantically over me. Alive. God, it seemed, had won the battle. Or had he? The gangster was still slouched against the wall, sizing me up with an evil gaze. One by one the doctors and nurses filed out of the room, walking right past him. Why did no one kick him out? His presence filled the room. Like he owned the place. "Get out!" I wanted to scream but couldn't form the words.

A nurse returned to set up an IV. I reached for her hand. I spelled words in her palm, trying to warn her about the man in the corner. She looked around, bemused or confused, I couldn't tell which. "It's going to be okay," she said.

In the doorway, a silhouette of a man appeared. The nurse called to him. "I think our patient here needs you," she said, then turned back toward me. "This man is a priest. He'll pray with you."

The man approached my bedside. The gangster glared at me, his eyes threatening. The priest took my hand. "Last rites?" he asked.

"No!" I wrote in his palm.

He began to pray, his voice strong and confident. "Dear God," he said, "give this woman your mercy. Relieve her pain. Steer her course. Bring her closer to you and bless her with a long and healthy life. Keep fighting for her."

His words stirred something deep within me, some elemental spark of life. I'd drunk away the blessings God had given me. I believed my life was worthless. Yet God was fighting for me. He brought me back to life. He pushed back the darkness. He cared. He loved me. The expression on the gangster's face changed. He'd lost his cool—he was enraged now. I closed my eyes tight. *You don't own me*, I thought. *I'm not yours*. I'd made a new deal with God. From now on, I'd repay my debts to him alone. I joined the chaplain with my own silent prayer. *Lord, I will earn the life you returned to me.*

I took a deep breath and opened my eyes, turning toward the wall next to the doorway. The gangster was gone.

I endured years of physical therapy. The road back from my accident was brutal. But the battle was won. I dried out in the hospital. I devoted myself to my church and made amends with my sons. I've honored Michael by living the way he would have wanted me to. I'm paying off my life's debts, and the gangster hasn't threatened me since.

PART 3

The Writing on the Wall

In the same hour the fingers of a man's hand appeared and wrote opposite the lampstand on the plaster of the wall of the king's palace; and the king saw the part of the hand that wrote.

DANIEL 5:5

Mission Boulevard

DOROTHY FRISBY

I was living in Fremont, California, near San Francisco. My husband was out of town and my parents were visiting from Omaha, so I'd taken off from work. I had the whole day planned, from paddle-wheel boats at the park to lunch at one of my favorite spots overlooking Mission Peak. We'd just finished breakfast and were about to head out when I heard it. A quiet, insistent voice. No, more than a voice. A push from deep within. *Celeste. Find her. Now. She needs you.*

Find Celeste? My youngest daughter didn't want to be found. She'd made that clear. Last time I'd talked to her, more than a month before, she'd mentioned moving with her on-again, off-again boyfriend, Larry, to some hippie commune in the middle of nowhere.

"Chill out, Mom," she'd said, drawling in that hazy, distracted tone that told me she wasn't all there. "It's a nice place off Mission Boulevard. Nothing to lose your mind about."

That's all I did with Celeste. Lost my mind. She'd always been rebellious, even as a thirteen-year-old, sneaking out of her bedroom window at night. The more I laid down the law, the more she fought me. I told myself it was a phase she'd grow out of. Now, at twenty-two, she still hadn't found herself. Couldn't hold down a job. She drank. She smoked both legal and illegal substances. Jumped from one deadbeat guy to another. She'd already been married and divorced once—he was a real gem, as you can imagine. After all those years of bailing her out of trouble, seeing her hauled to juvie, helping with her bills, listening to her empty promises, and having my heart broken again and again, I'd given up. How could I help someone who didn't want to be helped?

And yet the voice persisted. *Celeste. Help Celeste!*

My parents didn't even ask about their granddaughter anymore. It was clear I wasn't comfortable talking about her, and what I did tell them they didn't want to know.

I stood at the kitchen counter, fighting the urge the way Celeste had always fought me, trying to push it away. It made no sense! I had no idea where she was. And yet . . .

"Hey, would you guys mind if we paid Celeste a visit before we go to the park?" I said, trying to keep my voice cheerful. It came out weird and tense. My parents glanced up from the kitchen table, bewildered.

"Of course, dear," my dad said. "Where is she?"

"Beats me," I said, shaking my head.

"How will we find her?" Dad asked, gently, like he was talking to a crazy person. "Maybe there are friends of hers you can call."

"We need to go now," I said. I grabbed my coat and pushed my parents out the door. "We'll find her."

Mission Boulevard was all I had to go on. About ten miles of busy highway along the base of the Hayward Hills. I zigzagged between lanes. Commuters blared their horns. I tried to ignore Dad's questioning gaze. I knew what he was thinking: she's gone nuts! Maybe I had. But the urge was even stronger now, pulling me like a powerful magnet. *You'll know the place when you see it*, I told myself. Really?

I scanned Mission Boulevard for some clue, some sign. I was desperate. All at once, I spotted a narrow gravel pathway shooting off from the highway, barely a road, headed up into the hills. "Hold on!" I turned sharply, the car bumping along on the uneven terrain. The trees grew thicker and closer together, blocking out the light. Dad clutched the sides of his seat, his knuckles white. In the rearview mirror, I could make out Mom, her eyes wide with fear.

Up ahead was a small wooden post with a bullet-ridden sign: Warning! Trespassers will be shot on sight! I should've turned right around. Instead, I tore past it.

"Dorothy, this is getting dangerous!" Dad said, lurching forward in his seat. "Where on earth are you taking us?"

"Over there!" I shouted. The trees cleared, and a huge, gray house came into view, a ghostly old Victorian, three stories high, with a dilapidated porch. Old cars were parked on the lawn. I pulled up behind the house. "Give me ten minutes," I told my parents, sprinting for the back door.

I stepped through a cloud of incense into an open kitchen. Three men were bent over the counter chopping vegetables, their faces obscured by their long hair. They barely acknowledged me. "Is Celeste here?" I asked. One of them nodded toward a winding staircase to the right. I raced up it two steps at a time.

I was gasping for air when I reached the top, but I had to keep moving. I came to a dark hallway, like something out of a horror movie. There were three doors on either side. One called out to me—the second door on the right. It was locked. I pounded my fist against it until a familiar mumble answered from inside.

"What the . . . who's there?"

"Larry, let me in! Is Celeste in there?"

Larry fumbled with the lock. The door creaked open. He poked his head out. "She's sleeping," he said, his words slurred, his eyes bloodshot.

"Larry, I need to see her," I pressed. "Now!"

"Well, I dunno," he said, scratching his beard. "I think something's wrong with her." He opened the door wider. In the center of the room was the bed. Two pale, skinny legs poked out unnaturally from beneath the dingy bedclothes. Celeste! I pushed past Larry and scooped my daughter into my arms. Her eyes were closed, her skin clammy. Her breath came in short, squeaky gasps.

"Larry, call 911!" I yelled. He bolted out of the room, suddenly alert and too stunned to argue.

I cradled Celeste's limp body and rocked her back and forth. All the arguments, all the drama between us—none of it mattered. I'd brought her into the world twenty-two years before, kicking, screaming, crying into life. It wasn't going to end in this evil place. I'd been brought here. It couldn't be too late! "Please, baby, don't leave me!" I cried.

She let out one final gasp and went rigid in my arms.

"Celeste, no!" I wailed. "Come back to me!"

I laid her back on the bed, pumped my hands against her chest, and tried to breathe life into her lungs—everything I remembered from a CPR class at work. I didn't stop until a pair of hands pulled me off her. The paramedics. They took over and strapped Celeste to a stretcher. I rode along in the ambulance, while my parents and Larry followed in my car. It wasn't until we reached the hospital that one of the paramedics cried out, "We've got a pulse!"

Celeste had tried to take her own life, swallowing a bottle of tranquilizers. I sat by her bed and held her hand, praying. Mom and Dad did too. "I've already seen one miracle today," Dad said.

The next day, when Celeste finally woke up, I was still there.

"Mom?" Her voice was still weak. "You came for me."

"Of course, I did," I said, smoothing her hair. "I'm right here. I always will be."

"You came for me," she repeated, groggy but determined. "Before I blacked out, I called out to you . . . and you came."

I later moved to Iowa. Celeste and Larry eventually made a good life for themselves in California and raised three kids. She calls me practically every day. We have a special bond, a closeness I never thought possible until the impossible happened.

Maternal Instincts?

ANN ELIZABETH ROBERTSON

I sat in the back row at church, my eyes glued on the clean-cut young man and attractive woman standing up in front. A guest preacher and his wife, they had invited all the young couples in the congregation to come forward after the service for personal prayers.

"Honey," my husband, Doug, whispered, tapping my knee. "Should we go up there too?"

I looked at the line of husbands and wives, hand in hand, forming a long procession from the front of the church all the way to where we sat. No doubt their needs were more pressing than our own. My life with Doug overflowed with blessings: eleven years of marriage and a beautiful, lively nine-year-old daughter, Ari. We belonged to a thriving church community. Doug and his brother had just started their own construction business, and I taught kindergarten at Ari's school, along with Sunday school and vacation Bible school. As a wife and mother, what more could I ask for?

Yet I was hoping for a miracle. Two years earlier, when I was twenty-seven, a cancer scare had turned my world upside down. Doctors discovered cysts and tumors in my uterus. I had a hysterectomy. I was grateful the tumors turned out to be benign, but Doug and I would never have another baby. We'd always wanted a big family. That was no longer possible. We had Ari. We had each other. That was God's plan, and it would have to be enough.

But everywhere I looked, in every facet of my life, I was surrounded by children—from the ones I taught to my friends' children to my own daughter and her little play pals. Every time I received an invitation to a baby shower or had nursery duty at church, I balked. Deep inside, I yearned to have another baby. I felt cheated, unfulfilled—and then guilty for having those feelings. Who was I to question God's plans?

One afternoon a friend asked if Doug and I would be open to adoption—her teenage niece was having a baby she knew she couldn't take care of. We said yes immediately. We hired an attorney and began working out the complicated legal details for the adoption. It was to be a baby boy. We picked out a name, Matthew, meaning "gift of God." But two hours before we left to meet our new baby for the first time, our attorney called. "I'm sorry," he said. "The mother just changed her mind. The adoption is off."

I cried all afternoon. We had known this outcome was a possibility. Over time, I accepted that the adoption wasn't meant to be, but I wasn't ready to give up. I looked into other options. Our state adoption agency had a seven-year waiting list. I didn't even bother. I prayed about our situation daily, but maybe my prayers weren't loud enough. Maybe God's answer was no. Could I accept that?

Now in church, while Ari played with her friends, Doug and I stood at the back of the line and waited our turn to join the couple for prayer. We'd waited for more than an hour by the time we reached the front. Finally, the young man and his wife greeted us. "Do you have any needs you would like us to pray for?" the man asked.

"We'd love to adopt a baby," I said.

The young preacher's face brightened. "We were just at a fundraiser last weekend for a new adoption agency in Oklahoma!" he said.

"I'll get you the number and address," his wife said.

What were the chances? I contacted the agency. I filled out piles of forms. Ken, the program's administrator, warned me the process could be lengthy. "It might be years," he said. "We won't know anything until after the baby is born and the birth mother has time to decide. Our council then prays for the right family before we finalize where the baby belongs."

I tried not to get my hopes up. Especially after what had happened before. But I couldn't help myself.

I continued praying. As the school year approached, I felt I shouldn't teach that fall. *What if I'm needed at home to care for a baby?*

To keep busy, I volunteered to direct a children's musical at my church. I spent months surrounded by kids and knee-deep in their fanciful animal costumes. Ari was in the show too.

One afternoon while I was driving to a friend's house to discuss details for the show, I was convinced I heard a voice say, *You will have a nine-pound, ten-ounce baby boy, twenty-one inches long.* It wasn't the radio, more like someone in the car with me. But I was all alone.

Nothing like that had ever happened to me before. Shocked, I told my friend what I'd heard. "The message was so clear, so emphatic. What does it mean?"

"I don't know," she said, "but let's hope for the birth mother's sake that's not the baby's weight. That's huge!"

I told Doug about the voice. This had to be it—Ken from the adoption agency would call any day now, I was sure. Convinced. Only the phone didn't ring. I focused my energy on the musical, which opened at the end of September. We got rave reviews. But when it was all over, I had to wonder, *Now what?*

I spent the week after the show catching up on laundry and paying bills. No call. That Friday I sat at the kitchen table, fresh out of ideas.

At that moment, I felt a lightning strike of pain in my belly, unlike any stomachache I'd ever had. I stooped over in the chair and winced. I staggered upstairs to my room and collapsed in bed. I called Doug at work. "I'm sick. Can you pick up Ari from school?" I stayed in bed all night and still felt weak on Saturday. On Sunday, I forced myself to go to church. And we'd promised to take Ari to our town's annual craft fair afterward. When we got there, Ari delighted in every hair bow and glitzy T-shirt she saw. "Mommy, look!" She pointed at a pair of sparkly earrings.

Again I felt pain in my abdomen. I tried to make my grimace look like a smile. "Pretty," I said, but Ari gave me a strange look. I grabbed Doug's arm.

"It's back," I gasped. "It feels like my insides are being ripped out." We left for home immediately.

"It's only two o'clock!" Ari protested.

"Mommy has a stomachache," Doug said.

A little before three o'clock, the pain subsided.

I lay in bed that night and wondered what was wrong with me. I hadn't felt pain like that since . . . well, since I had given birth to Ari. *How could I be having labor pains?* I felt crazy just thinking that. It had to be something else. Maybe I was exhausted from the show. I'd go to the doctor if the pain returned. A week passed and it didn't.

That Monday we got a call from Ken. "We'd like to speak to you," he said. "We've prayed, and we believe you are the right family for a newborn baby boy. Congratulations!"

I was overwhelmed with joy. Our baby! At last! "Is he healthy?" I asked. "Is he really ours?"

"I'm looking at his file right now," Ken said. "He was born nine pounds, three ounces, twenty-one inches. He had a checkup today, and he's doing great. As of this morning, his weight was up to nine pounds, ten ounces. That's a big baby!"

I almost dropped the phone. All I could do was shake my head in disbelief as tears flowed down my cheeks. Ken asked if I was still there. I managed to squeak out a plea for him to go on.

"He's just over a week old," Ken continued. "His mother experienced her first labor pains and checked into the hospital Friday afternoon a week ago. She was in labor over the weekend and had a C-section last Sunday . . . at two forty-five in the afternoon."

No wonder those pains had been so familiar. They were all too real.

Pray for Lisa

KIMBERLY WOOD

*L*isa. *Pray for Lisa.* It was the strangest thing, this urge that suddenly came over me. It was as if an actual voice had spoken, firm and commanding.

Pray for Lisa? I prayed for my six-year-old daughter every night, just as I did for her brother and sister. But why now?

We were on the road, headed to my parents' house for Christmas. Lisa was riding with my brother Bobby up ahead. I was following along in my car with my two other children. Bobby was holding the speed limit, just like I had asked him to. Lisa turned to wave at me through the back window. Everything seemed fine.

Pray for Lisa. Now. The voice again, even more emphatic. A chill ran through me. *Lord, please watch over Lisa. Keep her out of harm's way. Wrap your protecting arms tight around her.*

Up ahead, Bobby slowed. I could see a semitruck directly in front of him. Its trailer was weaving back and forth. Something was clearly wrong with it. The trailer bounced and then fishtailed. Bobby's brake lights flared.

Then to my horror, the trailer detached from the driver's cab. "Lord, keep Lisa safe!" I cried.

Bobby swerved, just enough to escape a collision with the runaway trailer.

Thank God, Lisa was safe. *Thank God for the voice*, I thought.

But I could only watch helplessly as the trailer slid into the other lane—smashing into an oncoming car. Bobby and I both pulled over and rushed to the demolished vehicle. The backseat behind the driver was completely crushed.

"Is everyone okay?" I gasped.

"I think so," the driver said. He, his wife, and their teenage daughter climbed out, shaky but unharmed.

The man stared at the backseat and let out a deep breath. "We just stopped a couple of minutes ago and my daughter switched places with the Christmas gifts," he told us. "If she had still been sitting there . . ." He didn't have to say more.

The man then introduced himself and his wife.

"And what's your name?" I asked their daughter.

"Lisa," the girl replied.

A Peaceful Presence

SUSAN FAWCETT

*G*reen. Everywhere. So intense it glows. I breathe in the sweet perfume of orchids and make my way through the lush vegetation. Up a winding dirt path. Waxy leaves on either side tickle my arms. The path grows narrower until it opens onto a grassy field. All at once I see her. She stands in the middle of the clearing. A petite woman with flowing dark hair. Her face tilted toward the sun. Lips moving soundlessly. She turns and greets me with a lopsided grin. A sense of calm enwraps me. Like a hug. She stretches her arms wide. We sit on the soft grass and talk, words I cannot hear. I only know one thing for sure: I'm at peace.

My eyes snapped open to a familiar sight. Beige walls. Fluorescent lights. Tangles of blue wires. The smell of disinfectant and mashed peas hanging in the air. The grim reality of my surroundings. To my right, my twenty-two-year-old daughter, Liz, was hooked up to a bank of monitors that blinked and beeped like some medical symphony. She was pale and emaciated. She squeezed my hand. I forced a smile.

119

"Mom, relax, I'll be fine."

I ran a hand through my hair and stretched out my legs. My back had assumed the contours of the armchair I'd slept in for the past two nights, ever since Liz had gotten sick.

It started with a fever. I came home from work and found her curled up in a ball on her bed, covered in sweat. She couldn't keep anything down. I rushed her to the urgent-care clinic, figuring it was a twenty-four-hour virus. If only.

The doctor ran blood work. Liz's blood-sugar levels were through the roof—above five hundred milligrams. The normal range is seventy to eighty. Her body wasn't producing any insulin. That meant only one thing—diabetes. Type 1. It ran in my family. But I'd thought my prayers had spared Liz.

What I wouldn't give for that peace from my dream! It had come to me for the first time three months earlier, before Liz had gotten sick. And I'd had it again four times after that. Always the same serene tropical surroundings, the same woman in the clearing. She was unlike anyone I knew. Speaking words I'd never heard that went straight to my heart. Only I couldn't remember anything she said. I'd had vivid dreams before, but never a recurring one, and never like this. I lived in the Missouri Ozarks. Travel to exotic locales wasn't exactly typical for me.

Instead, I was here at Liz's bedside, stiff and anxious. Insulin shots for the rest of her life. That's what the doctor had said. A nurse had just popped in to teach Liz how to administer them herself. My daughter had put on a brave face, but her eyes had filled with tears at the bee-sting pinch of the needle. Bee stings 365 days a year.

I wanted to pound on those beige walls, make it all go away. People kept telling me, "Everything's going to be okay." And "God has a plan." How did they know? I knew only too well how the disease could wreak havoc on the body.

My big sister, Shirley, had suffered her whole life. She was in and out of hospitals. A reaction to too much insulin or too little. I'd wake up in the middle of the night and find Mom forcing apple juice between Shirley's chattering teeth. I'd grown accustomed to the sound of my parents talking in hushed tones about her condition. Shirley was a trouper. She never complained. But her illness was her life. I didn't want that for Liz. Even though diabetes care had advanced quite a bit since Shirley and I were children, it was still a serious disease, a life-changer.

I closed my eyes, exhausted. In the background, I could make out the sound of squeaky footsteps on the linoleum floor. Great—the nurse was back with more needles?

Not a nurse. Was that . . . a nun? She stood in the doorway of Liz's room.

"Well!" she said. "I am just so happy to finally meet you. I'm Sister Elizabeth, the hospital chaplain."

She stepped inside and stretched out her arms as if she were hugging the air around us. She was a small woman, but she seemed to take up the entire room. Her hair was dark. I tried to compose myself. The nun hadn't taken her eyes off me since she had come in. My hands wouldn't stop shaking.

"Your name is Elizabeth?" I said after an eternity. "Same as my daughter, Liz."

She flashed a crooked grin. Then she reached for both our hands.

"I want you to know," she said, "that Liz is going to be okay. This isn't her whole story. Just a bend in the road."

I looked up. The nun's dark eyes were focused on mine. "He's watching out for you," she said.

She hugged Liz and handed me her business card. "If there's anything you need, just holler," she said.

Her words echoed in my mind as I heard her squeaking down the corridor. My shoulders relaxed. Just a bend in the road. Finally, words of encouragement I could believe in.

After all, this wasn't the first time Sister Elizabeth had known the right thing to say. She was the very same woman I'd met in my dreams, identical in every way.

Sunflower Promise

BARBARA JACKSON

I turned the corner onto our street and braced myself. I had to talk about rebuilding with our contractor, but just the thought of seeing that empty lot—where my family's house had burned to the ground seven months earlier—made me feel sick.

That night still haunted me. Waking up to the blaring of smoke alarms. Bolting out of bed with my husband, Keith, and grabbing our two young daughters from their rooms. Huddling outside in our pajamas, shivering, before seeking refuge with a neighbor. We lost everything but the clothes on our backs and a jumble of items a friend salvaged from the rubble. I knew I should be grateful my family had escaped unharmed. But I couldn't help wondering why God left us nothing to start over with but dirt.

Sunflowers? I stopped the car and rubbed my eyes in disbelief. Instead of a bare dirt lot, there was a field of cheerful yellow sunflowers—hundreds of them—growing exactly where our house once stood.

We'd never grown sunflowers. None of our neighbors did either. The contractor said they'd started springing up in our lot—and only ours—over the past few weeks. I stared at the vibrant flowers.

Surely they were a sign from God, a promise: life will blossom here again.

I snapped some photos and showed them to Keith.

"Sorry to burst your bubble," he said, "but there's a perfectly logical explanation. I had a bag of sunflower seeds in the garage. The bulldozer razing our house probably plowed them into the dirt."

So much for God's promise.

The contractor finished our new house, and we moved in. Our lives really did blossom again. Still, weeks passed before I could bring myself to sort through the box of things recovered by our friend.

Keith and I dragged the box over by the trash can and tossed out one charred item after another. I felt like crying. Then Keith gasped.

"Barb, look at this," he said. He held up the bag of sunflower seeds he'd kept in the garage—still tightly sealed, with all the seeds inside.

The Dream
That Wouldn't Go Away

George Hunt

<p>

Back when I was a young livestock rancher north of Roosevelt, Utah, I heard the news one cold November morning that a California doctor and his wife were missing on a flight from Custer, South Dakota, to Salt Lake City. As a student pilot, I had just completed my first cross-country flight with an instructor, though I had only twenty solo hours.

Paying close attention to all radio reports on the search, I was very disturbed two days later by a newscast saying that Dr. Robert Dykes and his wife, Margery, both in their late twenties and parents of two young children, were not likely to be found until spring—and maybe not even then. They had been missing four days, and the temperature had been below zero every night. There seemed little chance for their survival without food and proper clothing.

That night before I retired, I said a simple prayer for these two people I didn't know. "Dear God, if they're alive, send someone to them so they will be able to get back to their family."

After a while, I drifted off to sleep. In a dream, I saw a red plane on a snow-swept ridge and two people waving for help. I awoke with a start. *Was it the Dykeses? What color was their plane?* I didn't remember any of the news reports ever mentioning it.

I couldn't get back to sleep for some time. I kept reasoning that because I'd been thinking of the couple before falling asleep, it was natural for me to dream about them. When I finally did go to sleep, the dream came again. A red plane on a ridge—but now farther away. I could still see two people waving, but now I could also see some snow-covered mountain peaks in the background.

I got out of bed and spread out the only air chart I owned. It covered a remote area in Utah—the High Uintas region along the Wyoming-Utah border. The Dykeses' flight plan presumably had to pass over this range. I was familiar with the rugged terrain, for I had fished and hunted it as a boy. My eyes scanned the names on the chart—Burrow Peak, Painters Basin, Kings Peak, Gilbert Peak.

Again I went to bed. And again, incredibly, the dream returned. Now the plane was barely in sight. I could see a valley below. Then it came to me in a flash—Painters Basin and Gilbert Peak! I rose in a cold sweat. It was daylight.

Turning on the news, I found there had been no sign of the plane and the search had been called off. All that day, doing chores around the ranch, I could think of nothing but the Dykeses and my dream. I felt God had shown me where those people were and that they were alive. But who would believe me, and what could I do about it? I knew I wasn't really qualified to search for them myself. I knew, too, that if I tried to explain my dream to my flight instructor, a stern taskmaster named Joe Mower, I would be laughed out of the hangar.

I decided to go to our small, rural airport anyway. When I arrived, a teenage boy who was watching the place told me Joe had gone to town for the mail.

The force that had been nudging me all morning seemed to say, "Go!" I had the boy help me push out an Aeronca plane. When he asked where I was going, I said, "To look for the Dykeses." I gave the plane the throttle and was on my way.

Trimming out, I began a steady climb and headed for Uinta Canyon. I knew what I was doing was unwise, even dangerous, but the danger seemed a small thing compared to what I felt in my heart.

As I turned east near Painters Basin, I was beginning to lose faith in my dream; there was no sign of the missing plane. The high winds, downdrafts, and rough air were giving me trouble in the small, sixty-five-horsepower plane. Terribly disappointed as well as frightened, I was about to turn back when suddenly there it was! A red plane on Gilbert Peak, just as I had seen in my dream.

Coming closer, I could see two people waving. I was so happy I began to cry. "Thank you, God," I said over and over.

Opening the plane's window, I waved at the Dykeses and wig-wagged my wings to let them know I saw them. Then I said a prayer to God to help me get back to the airport safely.

Thirty minutes later, I was on the ground. After I taxied up and cut the motor, I gulped, for Joe Mower was there to greet me. "You're grounded," he hollered. "You had no permission to take that plane up."

"Joe," I said quickly, "I know I did wrong, but listen. I found the Dykeses, and they need help."

"You're crazy," Joe said, and he continued to yell at me. My finding the lost plane in an hour and a half when hundreds of planes had searched in vain for nearly a week was more than Joe could believe. Finally, I turned away from Joe, went straight for a telephone, and did what I should have done in the first place. I called the Civil Air Patrol (CAP) in Salt Lake City. When they answered, I asked if there had been any word on the Dykeses'

127

plane. They said there was no chance they were still alive and the search had ended.

"Well, I've found them," I said. "And they're both alive." Behind me, Joe stopped chewing me out, his eyes wide and his mouth open. "I'll round up food and supplies," I continued to the CAP, "and the people here will get it to them as soon as possible." The CAP gave me the go-ahead.

Everyone at the airport went into action. Within one hour, we were on our way. A local expert pilot, Hal Crumbo, would fly in the supplies. I would lead the way in another plane. I wasn't grounded for long!

Back in the air, we headed for the high peaks. Hal's plane was bigger and faster than the Aeronca I was in. He was flying out ahead of and above me. When I got to Painters Basin, at eleven thousand feet, I met the severe downdrafts again. I could see Hal circling above me and knew he was in sight of the downed plane and ready to drop the supplies. Since I couldn't go any higher, I turned around.

Back at the airport, I joined a three-man ground rescue party, which would attempt to reach the couple on horseback.

Another rescue party had already left from the Wyoming side of the mountains. For the next twenty-four hours, our party hiked through fierce winds and six-foot snowdrifts. At twelve thousand feet, on a ridge near Gilbert Peak, we stopped. In the distance, someone was yelling. Urging our freezing feet forward, we pressed on, tremendously excited. Suddenly, about a hundred yards in front of us, we saw the fuselage of a small red plane rammed into a snowbank. Nearby, two people flapped their arms wildly.

Charging ahead, we shouted with joy. At about the same time that we reached the Dykeses, the other rescue party came over the opposite ridge.

After much hugging and thanking, I learned what a miracle the Dykeses' survival was. They had had nothing to eat but a candy bar, and their clothing was scant—Mrs. Dykes had a fur coat, but her husband had only a topcoat. The altitude made starting a fire impossible, and at night, they huddled together in their downed plane, too afraid to go to sleep.

"We had all but given up, had even written notes as to who should look after the children," Mrs. Dykes said. Then turning to me, she said, "But when we saw your plane, it was the most wonderful thing. Our prayers were answered, a dream come true."

"Yes," I said, smiling, suddenly feeling as Solomon in the Bible must have felt after he received a visit from the Lord one night in a dream (1 Kings 3:5–14).

My dream, like Solomon's, occurred for a reason. In his own special way, God gave me that dream in order to help give life to two others. In the most mysterious of ways, he showed me he is always there, always listening. He heard my prayers and the Dykeses' prayers and answered all of us in his own infallible way.

A Sign

NITA TALBOT

I'm not an impulsive person. But three months after my husband, Lew, and I got married, I was struck by the strangest urge: to learn sign language. I couldn't understand it. We lived in Mammoth Lakes, California, a ski village in the Sierra Nevadas, where we planned to raise a family. We didn't know any deaf people. I ran a hair salon. Lew installed carpet. This was before the first deaf Miss America and movies like *Children of a Lesser God* made deafness and deaf culture more widely known.

I kept the urge to myself. It seemed so off-the-wall. Yet the harder I tried to push the idea out of my mind, the harder it pushed back. Finally, I went to a bookstore.

"We don't carry any books on that subject," the clerk said, "but we could order one."

In a catalog, I spotted *The Joy of Signing*, a book about American Sign Language. It sounded . . . happy. What could be joyous about living in a soundless world? Imagine never hearing music. Laughter. Or a warning, like a car horn or a fire alarm. How could someone learn to live like that? "I'll take that one," I said.

The book arrived, and I practiced signing in front of the bedroom mirror. It was more challenging than I thought. And confusing. My movements were awkward and slow. Lew came in and gawked at me. "What are you doing?" he asked.

"Practicing sign language," I said.

"Why?"

Without even thinking, I blurted, "Because I feel like we're going to have a deaf child!"

Lew and I stared at each other. Where had that come from? Never once had we talked about the possibility. I was way too young and inexperienced to handle a deaf child. What did I know about the challenges one would face and what to do? How could I make the right decisions to help him or her live a normal life? No, God wouldn't put that responsibility on us. This had to be newlywed jitters.

Apparently, Lew felt that way too. "Well, okay then," he muttered, giving me a bemused look.

We didn't talk about it again. The strange urge to learn sign language? It faded almost as quickly as it had arrived. Two years later, I gave birth to our first child, Crystal, two months premature. She stayed in the hospital for ten days—and came home completely healthy. Life became a blur of motherhood and work. *The Joy of Signing* was packed in a box and tucked away in a spare room.

Alaina, our second child, was born eighteen months after Crystal. Right on time, no complications. She was lovely, with sky-blue eyes and a mellow, happy disposition. She was always smiling. I leaned into her crib and smiled back. She laughed. I laughed back. Alaina giggled so hard that her cheeks puffed and her eyes watered.

I took Crystal and Alaina with me everywhere, even to work. Alaina lay in her portable car seat, fascinated by the scissors snip-snipping customers' hair, all the while babbling in her sweet voice.

Everyone was impressed by how well-behaved she was. She never cried, even with the loudest blow-dryer blasting away.

One afternoon I left Alaina in the bedroom while I ran downstairs to grab a load of laundry. I huffed back upstairs with the laundry basket and found Lew standing behind Alaina, talking to her. He'd just come home from work. He looked worried.

"I think we need to get Alaina's ears checked," he said.

I clutched the laundry basket. "Why?"

I didn't need to ask. I knew. Alaina's calmness was uncanny. Nothing startled her. At five months, she'd reached all the milestones that Crystal had. But a feeling had been building inside me, one I hadn't wanted to admit.

Lew pulled a jigsaw-puzzle box down from a shelf. He stepped back and let the box fall to the floor. Thwack! Alaina didn't flinch. I took Lew's hand. We walked in front of Alaina. She looked up, surprised to see us. Surprised.

There were no resources for deaf children in Mammoth Lakes, not even a full-service hospital. We took Alaina to a pediatrician, who referred us to a hearing institute in Los Angeles. The doctor there confirmed what we already knew in our hearts. Alaina had bilateral, prelingual, profound hearing loss. Completely deaf from birth. She'd never heard a single sound.

"Your most urgent job is to teach Alaina language," the doctor said. "It's crucial for her mental development. I assume neither of you knows sign language?"

I shook my head miserably, thinking of that book I'd stowed in the spare room.

"There are many ways for deaf children to learn language," the doctor said. "I can't recommend a particular one, because each family needs to decide which approach works best for them."

Lew and I researched our options. There was oral language only, basically lipreading; American Sign Language (ASL), the predominant form of nonverbal communication in the United States; and Signing Exact English, or SEE, which used signs similar to ASL's but more closely replicated English grammar and syntax. We had to start teaching Alaina soon, or she would struggle to adapt.

I dug out *The Joy of Signing*. I hadn't even been aware that there was more than one sign language when I'd bought it. ASL was popular, and I'd gotten a bit of a head start, but more and more schools were teaching SEE. Would that be best for Alaina? I felt totally inadequate to make such a decision. I couldn't help thinking I should have noticed Alaina's deafness sooner. Hadn't God tried to warn me? *God, you gave me a sign once,* I prayed. *Send me another.*

Lew and I agreed that SEE seemed to make the most sense. It would help Alaina sign out sentences in the same manner that she would later learn to read and write. Once she'd mastered the signs, she could pick up ASL as well. I brought home a new book called *Signing Exact English*, hoping we'd made the right decision.

One morning, at home with the girls, I was struck by another irresistible desire—for a spinach-and-mushroom omelet at the Swiss Cafe, our favorite breakfast place. While we waited for a table, I noticed a woman admiring the girls. "Your daughters are adorable," she said.

I thanked her but was relieved when the hostess seated us at a rear booth. I felt self-conscious signing to Alaina in public.

The food arrived, and I signed to Alaina, "Mommy's eating."

A loud whisper came from the next booth. "She's signing!"

I froze.

A woman peered around the booth. It was the lady from the waiting area, sitting with her husband and another couple. She smiled warmly. "Excuse me," she said. "I couldn't help noticing. Do you mind my asking how you're raising your deaf child?"

I said the first thing that came into my head. "We're teaching her how to sign out of a book you've probably never heard of. It's called *Signing Exact English*."

The woman's smile broadened. "My name's Esther Zawolkow," she said. "I'm coauthor of that book."

The whole restaurant seemed to quiet. I struggled to speak. "Can you . . . can you teach me how to sign 'I love you'?" I asked.

Esther showed me the signs. I formed the words for my daughter. Alaina just giggled.

I wasn't sure if she could understand me yet. As for me, I was beginning to understand everything.

"Forgive"

DORINDA AXNE

Where am I? I couldn't see anything, anyone. A sudden wind blew, fierce as a winter storm. I was swept into a great whirling tunnel of darkness. Far off in the distance, I heard someone talking. A voice I recognized—my neurosurgeon. *Relax*, I reminded myself. *You're still under. They said surgery could take as long as eight hours.*

An image bloomed before me as if I'd opened a giant pop-up picture book. A handsome red dun quarter horse neighed and pawed at the dirt outside his stable. Gunner. If it hadn't been for him . . .

"I'm getting close to the right optic nerve," I heard my surgeon say. I braced myself, but there was no pain. Only a cold sensation—a scalpel?—inside my skull.

I'd been having dizziness and mild leg tremors for weeks. Nothing serious, I thought. Then one day my gentle Gunner reared and nearly threw me from the saddle. The whiplash brought on suddenly worsening symptoms—severe headaches, my legs wouldn't hold me. A visit to the doctor revealed a tumor. Because of its size and location, the surgery to remove it would be complicated.

I felt the cold breath of the wind against my skin. It swept me deeper into the tunnel. Gunner disappeared. Now I was holding a phone to my ear. Another familiar voice was on the line, one that made each hair on the back of my neck bristle. Our conversation was stiff, stilted. Then it erupted. Accusations, yelling, fighting, again.

The wind carried the phone from my hand. Another voice, a friendly one, echoed in the darkness. My brother. "You have so much anger toward him, Dorinda," he said. "It's causing you so much pain. I keep praying something will happen so you can let it go."

Impossible. There's no forgiving what he did.

I reached out to stroke a russet mane. Gunner. I began brushing him, grooming him from head to hooves. Something I did after all those angry phone calls. I rested my cheek against his sleek coat, breathed in the scent of cut hay. He could soothe me like nothing else. I'd always wanted a horse, and when my husband had bought him for me, I couldn't have been happier.

I was surrounded by blessings. A loving husband, wonderful children, a devoted brother, a beautiful horse. And yet . . .

The air crackled. The surrounding darkness burst into red-orange flames. Fire pressed in on me from all sides, leaping up from nowhere and everywhere all at once. Heat pervaded my body.

A face flickered into view through the flames—my own. I was only nine years old, trying to make sense of what my father had told me. My mother was dead. She had been diagnosed with postpartum depression at age thirty-two and had been sent to a mental hospital. She'd undergone shock therapy but hadn't gotten better. She had committed suicide.

I felt something on my lower legs tightening, then releasing. The pneumatic compression stockings that the nurse had put on me before the operation. Air was being pumped into them to prevent blood clots. *You are still in surgery. None of this is real.*

But it was. The fire intensified, sending up plumes of ash and smoke. Through the haze, I saw another face, one that made me cringe. "Your new mother," Dad said. Less than a year after my mother had died. His second wife was cruel and controlling. When harsh words didn't keep my siblings and me in line, an occasional beating made up the difference. I finally escaped when I turned eighteen. But the damage was done. I could never forgive Dad for what he put us through. No matter how he tried to reach out. No matter what my brother said.

"I just don't want you trapped by your anger. You deserve to be free, Dorinda." My brother, his voice faint amid the roar of the fire. He had forgiven. I couldn't understand it. He'd suffered through the same trauma. He had been only a baby when Mom had died, so he'd never known a loving mother. How was he able to move on? How could I?

As quickly as it had combusted, the fire dissipated. The heat, the anger in me softened and cooled. The pressure on my legs. I felt it again. The air pumps working diligently. The anesthesia had to be the reason for all of this, yet how could it be so clear, so vivid? The reality of the operating room was still there, even as I felt outside my body, outside time and space itself.

The wind caught me once more, rushing against me, lifting me. My body went weightless. I heard something through the curtain of wind.

"Forgive him. He does not know what he does," said a deep male voice. Not a command, not advice. A voice of absolute love, absolute honesty. It wasn't the surgeon. Or my dad. Or my brother. I trusted it inherently, like a truth I'd always known.

All at once light flared from the nothingness around me, a star flowering into life. It was wondrous, shimmering brighter with each moment. The light pulsed in white-gold bursts toward me, then through me, suffusing me with an indescribable peace. All my anger and hatred were washed away. I could rest now.

When I opened my eyes, I was in the recovery room, my husband sitting beside my bed. "You're awake," he said, taking my hand. "How do you feel? Do you need anything?"

"I have to call Dad," I told him. "There's something I need to say."

Prompting in the Night

PATRICIA JOSEPH-LYLE

Call Karyn. Those words startled me from a sound sleep. I sat straight up, rubbed my eyes, and looked at the clock: just after three in the morning. My younger sister Karyn was a senior at Eastern Michigan University and was used to pulling long hours studying in her tiny on-campus apartment . . . but she had to be asleep by now.

My alarm wasn't set to go off for another two and a half hours. There was so much to do tomorrow. Get my two little girls to school, work a ten-hour day at the office, take the girls to violin and piano practice, cook dinner, check homework, and iron school uniforms. I needed every hour of rest I could get.

I'll call her in the morning, I thought. I lay back down and closed my eyes.

Call her, Pattie. A voice pierced the darkness. Was I going crazy? If I called her now, that's what she'd think. I turned over and buried my head beneath my comforter.

Call Karyn. Now.

Clearly, I wouldn't get any sleep until I called Karyn. I turned on my bedside lamp and dialed the phone. A few rings. I almost hung up. *This is nuts.* Then I heard my sister's voice.

"Hello?" she answered groggily.

Now what should I say? I chuckled sheepishly. "Hey! What ya doin', girl?"

There was a long pause. "Sleeping." Karyn sighed. "Why?"

"Oh. I, uh . . ."

I woke up my sister for what exactly? I wanted nothing more than to catch a few z's myself. So we chatted for a few minutes, then hung up. There. I talked to her. I could finally rest before I had to be superwoman in less than three hours.

Morning came too soon. I yawned as I made the girls breakfast. The phone rang. *Probably Karyn, calling to chew me out for waking her up last night.*

"Pattie? I'm just leaving the emergency room," she said. The emergency room?

Karyn said that after we hung up, her eyes were burning and it was hard to breathe. She went to the kitchen for a glass of water. "I turned on the light, and there was this strange mist in the air. I ran to a neighbor. The second she saw how pale I looked, she called 911. The doctor said it was a good thing I woke up. There was some kind of gas leak. It could have killed me."

A Poem for the Pain

LORI COHEN

I was in bed browsing Facebook and checking emails. My husband, Steve, was cooking dinner. The next thing I knew Steve was shaking my shoulder. "Wake up, honey!" he said. "Dinner's ready!"

Had I fallen asleep? I touched my cheek. Tears. I wiped them away and focused on my laptop. Facebook and my email had disappeared. A Microsoft Word document was open on my screen: a poem titled "How Can I Count My Blessings When I Am So Sad?" The cursor sat flashing on a section:

> Gone all our worries, cry no more,
> For he gave his life so we all could be more.
> And he cried along with us . . . but promised us this:
> I am
> I am
> I am.

Cry no more . . . My eyes were riveted on that phrase. Three months earlier I had lost my work-from-home sales job and with it any sense of hope that life was going to get better. A botched stomach surgery had left me virtually bedridden with complex regional pain syndrome (CRPS), a nerve disorder. That job was practically all Steve and I had to support us, since he stayed home to take care of me. My eyes fell on the words a few lines down:

> He wrapped me in his arms,
> He held me close through the storm.
> All fears, all doubts, all pain, I shout,
> There's no place for you here!

Oh, the pain! It was relentless. Just typing an email or a status update on Facebook could be uncomfortable. I skipped capital letters and punctuation to spare my fingers. CRPS caused burning sensations on my skin, swelling in my stomach and legs, stabbing pains in my arms and hands. My left knee was totally locked up. I dragged my leg, more deadweight than limb. I prayed every day, every night, for healing. My faith was strong, but sometimes my pain was nearly as strong. Whoever wrote this poem knew exactly what I felt. Knew it as intimately as I did. I read on:

> Enduring each moment that feels like a year,
> Not knowing what is to be next in our tears.

Yes! I hated not knowing! Especially now. I'd applied for disability, but it hadn't gone through yet. Would it ever? My work-from-home gig was the only way we'd been able to pay rent. Before I'd fallen asleep, questions had hammered at my mind: *What if we lose our apartment? Will this pain ever end? Where are you, God?* Yet here, seemingly, was an answer.

> I have his peace, I am loved.
> No more worries, no more fears.
> My blessings are so many, no room for tears!

The words seeped into me. A warmth fell over my body, went through every muscle, every place of pain, like some sort of healing energy. *My blessings are so many.* That was true. I had Steve and our twin daughters, who were grown now but always willing to come help. I had our cat. Friends and family near and far kept my spirits up.

Where had the poem come from? Not an email. Maybe I'd copied and pasted the poem from the web just before I had drifted off. That was the only explanation. I checked my browser history. Nothing there. I highlighted chunks of text and googled them, searching for the author. No results. *That's really strange,* I thought. Then I noticed a name at the top of the document. Lori Cohen.

Me? Lori, who didn't know anything about poetry, whose emails and posts were always riddled with typos and contained no capital letters or punctuation? There was even a copyright symbol next to my name—I had no clue how to make one of those using Word!

What would I say to Steve? "This was written on my computer, but I didn't write it"? Even to me that sounded pretty far-out! Steve brought dinner to me in bed. I decided not to say anything to him.

In the morning, though, I had a powerful urge to tell some friends of mine about the mysterious poem. "It had to be the Holy Spirit working through you," one said. "That poem was meant to be shared." So I posted it on Facebook. For once, not an update on my condition or my hardships. I'd never had so many "likes" for a post!

That night I told Steve. "I know it sounds really weird . . ."

"If it comforts you and others, that's all that matters," he said. So whenever I felt down, I read it and reread it.

Over the next few months, I found more blessings. We qualified for some medical-bill assistance that I had no idea was even available. Our daughters were able to help out financially, along with a church food bank. My disability benefits finally came through. I started saying affirmations several times a week for healing in Jesus's name. Soon I could move my left leg more than before. Slowly I was improving.

Never far from my heart was that Word document, the poem that held me close through the storm.

The Picture
in Aunt Lana's Mind

Pacific Beach, Washington, where Grandma and Aunt Lana
lived for many years, is a very small town in a very bleak
part of the world. Forlorn, one could call it. Not many people
want to live there, or go there, for it rains incessantly, the people
are poor, and the Pacific's waves are much too rough for surfing
or swimming. Still, I loved my visits there, and never more than
during the summer of 1973, when Aunt Lana included me in one
of her spiritual "adventures." It was an adventure in blind trust.

Aunt Lana and Grandma went to live in Pacific Beach because
that's the only place where Aunt Lana could find employment.
She's a teacher. She is also disabled. In 1949, she was struck down
by polio, and this robust, six-foot-two woman has been in a wheelchair ever since. Aunt Lana is a triumphant woman, however, with
a hard, practical hold on life and a bold grip on the life of the
Spirit. I think she's especially attuned to spiritual things because
she's disabled and not running around wastefully the way most
of us are.

On the last day of my summer visit in 1973, when I was four-teen, I realized that something was troubling Aunt Lana. The sun was dancing across the surf when I went down to the kitchen that lovely morning. But as we breakfasted on apricots, toast, and hard-boiled eggs, Aunt Lana was silent. Not so Grandma. "The sun always shines a day in Pacific Beach," she said cheerily. "But for the rest of the days, you'd better keep your coat on."

Grandma and I cleared the table, and just as I was about to go back upstairs, I saw Aunt Lana sitting in her room, just staring.

"Anything I can do?" I said, concerned. She shook her head. Then as I was about to leave, she changed her mind.

"Well, maybe there is something you can do. I'm stymied."

She told me a strange story about a picture that had come into her mind a few days before. She hadn't paid much attention to it at first, for it was simply a scene that had flashed into her consciousness—some sand and some rocks and a body of water, that's all. But the scene kept coming back, persistently intruding on her prayers and thoughts.

"I have a feeling that the picture comes from the Lord, that he's trying to tell me something," Aunt Lana said. "But what?"

To me, this was pretty deep spiritual stuff. I felt a little timid about presuming to advise Aunt Lana in this special area of hers, but I was soon involved—and fascinated. We talked for a while, and then, remembering that Aunt Lana loved stories, I said, "What do you think one of your detectives would do?" That started Aunt Lana taking the picture apart piece by piece, as though each held a clue.

"All right," she said, closing her eyes and summoning the pic-ture into view. "The sun is shining. There's water on the left, sand on the right, a bluff of rock hovering over that—so that must be north. And if that's so, then this is very likely a beach on the West Coast."

"Maybe one here in Washington?"

"Yes, it looks like our shoreline," Aunt Lana replied, "but there's nothing to distinguish it, no man-made thing." She was silent now, her eyes still closed. "But the water," she said so suddenly that I jumped. "Look at the water! It's smooth, no ripples. That could mean a cove of some sort." Then she said a little sadly, "But not on this wild coast of ours."

Aunt Lana and I wrestled with these meager facts for a little while, and then we had to admit that we could make nothing of them. Still, Aunt Lana couldn't shake the conviction that the picture had some special meaning for her.

At noon, we were just getting ready to dry the luncheon dishes and Aunt Lana was reaching for the dish towel when her hand stopped midair. "Bobby," she said, "there's some quiet water up north of here, up in the Indian reservation. I feel sure I've seen some."

"Let's try to find it," I said, and with a flurry of excitement, we made plans for the search. We were about ready to leave when Grandma suggested that as long as we were heading up near the Quinault Reservation, we might drop off some old clothes she'd been saving to give away. Aunt Lana thought that was a good idea. One of her students lived up in Taholah with an aged grandmother. Maybe they'd have some use for them.

With Aunt Lana at the wheel of her white Impala—with the hand brake she'd designed herself and had someone weld—we headed north. The road paralleled the ocean, winding over hills and through creek canyons. We passed storm-sculpted rocks where sea birds took shelter from the turbulent breakers. Bizarre pillars of stone dotted the beaches like human forms in windblown garments. "The Indians say these pillars are women waiting for the men to return from the sea," Aunt Lana said, filling me with wonderful facts about the Quinault Indians who once had earned their livelihood from whaling.

We traveled on. The road narrowed and threatened to become gravel, though it never quite did. Soon we crossed into the Quinault Reservation. About a mile or so deeper in, she stopped the car. "Point Grenville!" she shouted. "Quick, Bob, over there! Run to the beach. See what's there." I was out of the car lickety-split and in a few minutes came panting back.

"It's there!" I called. I described the cove with the ocean on the left and the beach with the looming rocks on the right and the sun's rays glistening on the water's quiet ripples.

Aunt Lana threw up her arms in a wild expression of joy. She reached over and hugged me and kissed me on the forehead. Then she became serious. "Now tell me what else you saw."

"I didn't see anything else, Aunt Lana."

"Nobody was there?"

"Nobody."

"You didn't see anything odd?" I shook my head. Aunt Lana's face darkened. She put her head down on the steering wheel; I knew she was praying.

"Well," she said finally, "I don't know what it means. Stymied again."

It seemed a shame to give up now. We discussed the possibility of just staying there and waiting for something to happen, and for a while, that's what we did. As time passed, I guess we both felt disillusioned. At one point, I looked into the backseat and saw the boxes of clothes Grandma had given us; I suggested that we bring them to the Native American family.

"What clothes?" Aunt Lana said. She'd forgotten about them. My idea prevailed, however, and we started up again and drove toward the little town huddled in a small valley by a river. In Taholah, Aunt Lana drove up to the fish cannery and sent me in with instructions to buy a fish for dinner. I bought a small salmon, wrapped it in three layers of the *Aberdeen World*, and put it in the trunk. Fishing meant

148

jobs, and the noble salmon provided for the needs of many of the town's families, most of whom were desperately poor.

After that we drove to Second Street and turned down it. The houses we passed were blank-walled—the Native Americans thought that a house facing the street would be haunted and bring bad luck. We drove to the house on the corner, the only one that was painted—a bright canary yellow with a blue stripe around the middle. Aunt Lana honked the horn, and presently a small child toddled out, squinted at us, and ran back inside.

"The grandmother is very old," Aunt Lana explained to me. "I am told she has eighteen children of her own, and who knows how many grandchildren."

Soon the old grandmother appeared. By the time she shuffled up to Aunt Lana's door, I was out of the car and waiting with a box of clothes. The old Indian reached out to touch Aunt Lana's outstretched hand. "You've come," she said. "I've been expecting you."

Aunt Lana and I looked at each other. Then we both looked at the grandmother. Perhaps we hadn't heard her correctly.

"You were expecting us?"

"Yes, yes," she said, and gradually, in stops and starts, fumbling for words, she told us about the trouble in the family, the people out of work, someone in jail, the hunger, the lack of warm clothing, the ever-pervasive need. Then one day, she continued, when her feeling of helplessness was at its worst, she had wandered down to the beach.

As the old woman mentioned the word *beach*, I saw a glimmer come into Aunt Lana's eyes. "And then?" Aunt Lana said.

"I walk along the edge of the water. A long time." As she talked, I pictured her moving aimlessly among the rocks, while the great waves thundered and splashed. "Then I come to a place where the ocean is more quiet and the wind is very kind . . ."

149

A cove, I wanted to say. *You came to a cove.*

". . . and there I talk to God. 'Please, God,' I say, 'tell someone to bring help. Not for me, God—for the little ones.'"

It was almost unnecessary to ask her when she had prayed in the quiet cove. I knew, Aunt Lana knew, that the old woman had been talking to her God three days before, the very day, the very hour when the picture had first come into Aunt Lana's mind. And so it proved to be.

I carried the boxes of clothes into the house, while Aunt Lana sat in the car making arrangements for help. Then we left. The old grandmother, surrounded now by a crowd of children, waved good-bye. "God is taking care," I heard her say. "God is taking care."

At the end of the day, just before leaving Aunt Lana's home for my own, I took a last walk on the beach. I wore a coat to shield me from the windblown rain. The beginning of a storm from the southwest brought waves that washed my rubber boots. It had been a day like no other, a day in which Aunt Lana had helped me learn what she had known for a long time: that God has countless ways of letting us know he is there, taking care.

What's in a Name?

KATHA BARDEL

The name is Katha. Not Kathy. Or Kat. Or Kathleen. It's Katha. Why, oh, why did my parents have to give me such a strange name? Growing up in Toledo, Ohio, I wished I could've been a Jane. Or a Sandy. Or even a Belinda! Anything but Katha. No matter how many times Mom insisted that the name was divinely inspired, I wasn't buying it.

She claimed that it came to her one afternoon during her eighth month of pregnancy. She'd spent most of the day with a massive baby book, browsing for the perfect name for her daughter-to-be. Nothing seemed to stand out, especially when paired with our ordinary last name, Brown. Exasperated, she pushed the book aside and drifted off to sleep. She awoke with one word on her lips. A name. She repeated it a few times to make sense of it. It didn't even sound like a name for a person. When she whispered it to her belly, though, it just felt right. And so, two weeks later, she named me Katha.

Mom repeated that story every time some stranger inquired about my "interesting" name or a classmate's birthday invitation arrived in the mail addressed to a Miss Katherine Brown.

"Katha came in a dream from God," Mom would say. "Don't you forget it."

I had my own dream—to become a dancer. Mom liked to joke that I'd come out of the womb dancing. At the age of four, I begged her to put me in ballet classes. She didn't know where the idea came from. No one else in our family had much rhythm, certainly not my older brothers. But from that first plié, I was hooked. There was something about the costumes, the music, and the steps. When I steadied myself at the ballet barre, I wasn't Katha. I was a storyteller. I could tell a great romance or a heart-breaking tragedy through my movements. I could convey a feeling with just one pirouette.

I went on to study at the School of American Ballet in New York City and danced as a principal and soloist with companies in New Mexico, Arizona, and Oklahoma. Eventually, I settled down in Oklahoma City with my family and opened my own studio. I called it Katha's School of Ballet, though I taught jazz and tap as well. It made me proud to see my quirky name in pink script on the sign out front. But the confusion over my name only continued.

"What exactly does Katha mean?" curious dance moms would ask. "Is it an ethnic name?"

I took on more students every year, choreographed countless shows, and eventually expanded to a new space outfitted with nine studios. My seventeen-year-old twin daughters, Mindi and Mandy, wanted to take Katha's School of Ballet in a new direction though. They had studied dance all their lives and had just returned home from touring with a Christian dance troupe.

"Mom, we have this amazing idea," Mindi said, her eyes all dreamy. "Why don't we start up a spiritual dance company? We can praise God through dance!"

"We can tell stories from the Bible through the choreography," Mandy added.

"I'll think about it," I told the girls. I'd never considered combining my faith and my passion before. I had to admit the idea appealed to me. Something about it just felt right.

Two weeks later, Mom called me at the dance studio. "I know what it means!" she said.

"What are you talking about?" I asked.

"Your name . . . it really was a gift from God."

Not another story . . .

Mom continued excitedly. Her old college roommate had just sent her a letter. Inside the envelope was a program for a performance by a dance company from India that was touring the States. "They specialize in an ancient Indian dance form," Mom said, "dramatic storytelling that praises God through movement and music."

I hadn't told Mom yet about her granddaughters' idea. She hadn't given me the chance. "What does this have to do with my name?" I asked.

"Get this—the dance is called Kathakali, from the Sanskrit word for storytelling, *katha*," Mom said. "Seems to describe someone I know, doesn't it?"

Yes, it did. A dance company that glorified God through its storytelling? The project had my name written all over it from the very beginning. I should have known.

If You Can't Be in Vancouver . . .

SHARON WALLACE

The dream was so weird it made me laugh. I was in a room with colleagues from a former job, bent over some maps. "Shouldn't you check on your child outside?" someone asked. I went out and found a little girl sitting in my car. Not my daughter, Meaghan, but in the dream, I thought she was mine. It was freezing out, and the little girl's face was blue. I scooped her up and carried her inside. Everyone called the girl by name—a relief, since I didn't know it. Suddenly, my father's voice boomed out, "If you can't be in Vancouver, you might as well be in Belarus!"

It was a strange way to start that January morning. My sister-in-law lived near Vancouver, but Belarus? Where did that come from?

I padded into the kitchen and found my husband, William, making coffee in the dark. I told him about the dream. "Weird," he said.

I flipped through the newspaper. There was a photo of one of my former colleagues, the one from my dream! He was involved in an organization called Canadian Friends of Chernobyl's Children,

154

which sponsored summer homestays in Canada for kids suffering the effects of the Chernobyl nuclear disaster. Though it had been more than twenty years since the Soviet power plant had exploded, spewing radioactive fallout over most of Europe, areas directly downwind continued to suffer contamination—especially the impoverished nation of Belarus. The article gave the date of an upcoming information session for people interested in hosting a child.

I got an eerie feeling. For the past few days, I'd been praying for direction from God. I felt torn between work, church, and parenting Meaghan, who was five. This seemed like a sign. But of what? William and I had our hands full already. I decided to attend the event anyway.

A few weeks later, I sat and listened to a presentation about Chernobyl and the heart-wrenching stories of kids affected by it. While I was touched, I knew as I left that I wouldn't be attending the follow-up meeting a few weeks later. This wasn't for me or my family.

In the car, I turned on the radio. Chernobyl was the first word I heard. It was a documentary. "The amount of radioactive material released was four hundred times greater than in the atomic bombing of Hiroshima," the narrator said. "Belarusians, especially children, continue to suffer health effects from the disaster." *Okay, God*, I thought. *I'll go to the next meeting.*

The meeting was in a church basement. "Most of the kids don't speak English and may be intimidated by your big house and grocery stores," the speaker said. What would I do with a frightened, non-English-speaking child all summer?

Near the end of the meeting, the speaker mentioned that the group needed another board member. "What about this lady in the pink sweater?" the speaker said, pointing at me. "Would you be interested?" My face grew hot. Before I knew it, I was nodding.

As the meeting broke up, another board member handed me a stack of forms for hosting a child.

I couldn't just hand them back. It was all happening so fast. Like I'd climbed aboard a runaway train.

Back home I told William what had happened. "We don't have to apply," I said. Yet one day not long after, I caught myself imagining Meaghan and her new Belarusian friend climbing trees in our big backyard.

"Maybe we should just fill out the forms," I said to William. "It will look terrible if I don't offer to host a child. We can always change our minds."

We were matched with a seven-year-old girl named Nastya from a tiny village. That's all we knew. We didn't even get a photo. Seeing her name threw me into a panic. Meaghan was excited to meet her "summer sister." But how would we bridge the language divide, the culture shock?

William came home from work a few days later shaking his head in disbelief. "I just found out one of my business partners speaks Russian."

"I was talking to the neighbors," I said. "They speak Russian too."

I called the day camp where we'd enrolled Meaghan. Yes, they had room for Nastya. And, of course, one of the counselors spoke Russian.

On a warm July night, I drove to the pickup spot. William stayed home with Meaghan. I was so nervous I arrived an hour early. At last the bus pulled in from the airport. I stood with other host families watching twenty-four tired, apprehensive children step out.

My eyes gravitated to the youngest-looking child, a thin girl with blonde hair and blue eyes. She looked more anxious than the other children. I barely restrained myself from scooping her up in my arms.

"This is Nastya," one of the organizers said. I knelt and introduced myself. Nastya burst into tears.

"She lost her duffel bag at the airport in Belarus," an interpreter explained. "She had gifts for you."

"It's all right, sweetheart," I said. "Meeting you is enough of a gift."

Actually, it was a dream come true. Nastya was shy at first but soon warmed up. Meaghan taught her to ride a bike. They developed a secret lingo of their own, giggling at mysterious jokes and playing elaborate games with Meaghan's dolls. They climbed trees almost every day. Nastya ate bowls and bowls of Cheerios, her favorite food.

The lost duffel bag arrived eventually, with the gifts Nastya had brought. One was a set of Russian nesting dolls, the kind that open up to reveal smaller and more precious dolls inside. Just like Nastya herself, our own precious summer gift.

PART 4

Right Place, Right Time

And we know that all things work together
for good to those who love God, to those who
are the called according to His purpose.

ROMANS 8:28

How Booth Saved Lincoln

RICK HAMLIN

History is full of mysteries, the fates of nations pivoting on an unexpected and seemingly random turn of events. One extraordinary moment in American history happened on a train platform in Jersey City, New Jersey, in the darkest days of the Civil War. Abraham Lincoln's oldest son, Robert, a twenty-year-old Harvard student, was waiting for a train when a rowdy crowd put him in mortal danger.

"There was a narrow space between the platform and the train car," Robert later recalled. "There was some crowding, and I happened to be pressed by it. The train began to move and I was twisted off my feet, and dropped, with feet downward, into the open space, and was personally helpless."

President Lincoln and his wife, Mary, had already endured much tragedy. They had lost their son Eddie when Honest Abe was still a rising Springfield lawyer, and Willie, a much-doted-upon eleven-year-old, had recently died of typhoid fever, throwing the president and the first lady into a deep depression. Their youngest son, Tad, was often sickly (he'd end up surviving his father by only six years). Is it any wonder that Mary was so protective of her eldest, Robert? She protested against his enlisting, much to his dismay. But that evening in Jersey City, it seemed Robert was destined to become another tragic death in the saga of the Lincoln family.

The train lurched, coming close to crushing Robert, when he felt someone tug his coat—"vigorously seized" it, as he later wrote—jerking him back up onto the platform and out of harm's way. Robert's rescuer had no idea whose life he'd just saved, how important a role he'd play in the course of both a family and a nation. But Robert never forgot that man. How could he?

Robert went on to have a distinguished career. He managed to enter the Union Army late in the war, serving as a captain under Ulysses S. Grant, and was an eyewitness to Robert E. Lee's surrender. On April 14, 1865, he was in Washington, DC, but decided not to join his parents at *Our American Cousin* at Ford's Theatre that terrible night when John Wilkes Booth emerged from the shadows and took President Lincoln's life. Robert later served as secretary of war in one administration and minister to England in another. He was often recommended as a presidential candidate. The sole heir to the Lincoln name, he corresponded with his father's biographers, providing tremendous insight into the Lincoln presidency. He died at the age of eighty-two.

Robert was forever grateful to his rescuer. While the man hadn't recognized him, Robert had known exactly who the man was: one of the greatest Shakespearean actors of his day. An adamant Unionist who had proudly voted for Lincoln, the actor was devastated when the news of the president's assassination reached him. For a time, he retired from the stage, refusing to perform, until a letter from a friend, who'd heard the story from Robert, told him the identity of the young man he'd rescued. The truth helped inspire the actor's return to the stage.

While John Wilkes Booth would forever be known as a notorious assassin, his brother Edwin Booth is remembered today
for defining Shakespearean characters for American audiences,
founding his own theater, donating his home as a club for actors
and artists . . . and saving Abraham Lincoln's only surviving son.

The Earthmover

LES BROWN

"Child choking! . . . Handle code three!" Dreaded words. I responded immediately, flipping on red lights and siren as the dispatcher gave the address and directions. *Just my luck*, I thought as I sped past parked cars and passed drivers who did not pull over on the highway.

I had just begun my working day. Actually, it was my day off, and I had been called in to cover for another officer who was ill. I knew next to nothing about this particular beat in Los Angeles and had intended to drive around it to familiarize myself with the area. Now my first call was a life-and-death emergency several miles away.

I had been a patrol officer for some time, but no matter how many life-and-death situations an officer faces, when a child is involved, the heart beats a little faster, the foot is a little heavier on the accelerator, the urgency is greater.

I decided to take the unfinished freeway; it was next to impossible to get through the traffic on Highway 101. Just ahead was the street that would take me to my destination. Then anguish swept through me. There was no off-ramp. Between me and that road was a deep, wide ditch and a steep embankment.

Tires screeched as I stopped, red lights still flashing. I got out and looked down at the busy road so far below me.

God, help me! I cried out silently. *What am I going to do? If I go around, I'll be too late.*

"What's the matter, Officer?"

I looked up and saw a man sitting on top of the biggest earth-moving vehicle I had ever seen. He must have been sitting two stories high.

"Child choking to death . . . I have to get down there." I gestured blindly. "But there's no road. If I go around, I'll never make it."

Years of discipline had taught me to control my emotions, but I was in an agony of frustration.

"Follow me, Officer—I'll make you a road!"

I jumped in my car and took off after him, amazed at what the mammoth machine could do. The huge buckets on the side of it were full of dirt. He dumped them into the ditch.

The clock had become my enemy.

Hurry! Hurry! Hurry!

The earthmover started down the long, sloping embankment, scattering dirt. Huge clouds of dust enveloped us. It seemed like hours, but in reality, it was a short time before the earthmover lumbered down on the highway, blocking traffic in both directions.

Hurry!

I raced, siren screaming, the few short blocks to the street I had been given and frantically searched for the correct address. Almost at once I found it.

As I burst through the doorway, a terrified young mother handed me her tiny baby boy. I could see she was going to be no help. The baby was already blue. Was I too late?

God . . . help.

All I remember about the next few seconds was turning the baby upside down and smacking his back. The deadly object flew from his throat onto the floor. It was a button that had let a tiny bit of air through but not enough.

I was aware of another siren.

A fireman rushed into the room.

Precious oxygen.

The child screamed, turned red, flailed his tiny fists. He was angry but very much alive.

Back in my car, I logged the incident, reported in by radio, and drove down the street shaken but elated.

I glanced up at the sky. *Thank you.*

This, then, was what it was all about. Lately, I had found myself wondering if this kind of life was really worthwhile. The hostile, the criminals, the dregs of society. The petty little things that took time and energy to deal with. A thankless job. Was this the life I wanted?

Yet with God's help, we had just saved a baby's life. And in this act, my own life had suddenly come into perspective. That little mite in distress had taught me that I had important work to do and that I would be helped in this work by a loving, caring God who would hear a prayer and help a troubled cop get his car over a ditch.

Another call came, then another, and so on through the day.

The next day I was determined to learn the patrol area before anything else happened. I never wanted to get caught like that again. As I drove along, I approached the place where I had stood in desperation twenty-four hours before. I slowed as I again saw the gigantic earthmover. I wanted to thank the driver. He waved and yelled.

As he ran toward me, I could see he was deeply moved. He stammered, "The . . . the baby . . ." He stopped, unable to speak.

Surprised at his deep emotion, I tried to reassure him, "The baby is all right. Thanks to you—you helped save his life. I never would have made it in time. Man, that was teamwork."

He gulped, "I . . . I know . . . but what I didn't know when . . . when I helped you was . . ." He bit his lip hard, then added in a whisper, "That was my son."

The Baby in the Backseat

DANIEL KESSEL

Life is made up of moments that lodge in our minds like scenes from a movie. Strung together, they tell a story of where we've come from, who we are, what we want to be. It's no fluke that when we play back the video of our lives, the scenes we remember most vividly are those when our story overlaps with another's, however briefly. These shared scenes change each of us in powerful ways. For better or worse.

Such a convergence occurred one day in March 1988, a scene Shelley Cumley wanted to forget. The twenty-five-year-old from Seattle was driving south to Lake Tahoe for a week of skiing with her friends. She rolled down her car window and stuck her hand out to catch the breeze. Nothing but green hills stretched out on either side of Interstate 5, California's Cascade Wonderland Highway.

She looked in her side-view mirror. A red sports car was coming up fast. Too fast. It swerved over the double yellow lines and zoomed ahead, barely missing Shelley. She glimpsed the driver's face. Wild eyes. He seemed intoxicated. He vanished around the next curve.

Farther down Interstate 5, traveling north, Roanna Farley glanced in the rearview mirror at her seven-month-old baby, Nicole, fast asleep in the back. Was the car seat secure? Nicole was her first child; Roanna could never be cautious enough. She turned her attention back to the road—just in time to see a flash of red cross into her lane.

The instant Shelley rounded the curve, she saw a trail of debris on the road. Broken glass and twisted steel littered the asphalt. A head-on collision between the drunk driver and another vehicle. Shelley pulled over, jumped out of her car, and ran toward the smoldering wreckage.

Roanna opened her eyes. The smell of gasoline and burning rubber hung in the air. She couldn't move, but that wasn't her concern. "My baby," she cried weakly. "Where's my baby?"

Shelley approached the crumpled sedan. She peered inside. A woman was trapped between the front seat and the dash, fading into unconsciousness. In the back, a tiny, redheaded baby was in a car seat, crying.

I have to get her out, Shelley thought. The leaking gas, the smoke. This car could blow up at any minute. Shelley wasn't a mother, but a maternal instinct took over. The child's safety came above all else. She opened the door and lifted the baby out of the car seat.

Roanna looked up in a daze. Nicole . . . a stranger was holding her—it was the last thing she saw before she lost consciousness completely.

Shelley rode in the ambulance with the baby all the way to the hospital. She learned the girl's name in the emergency room: Nicole Farley. A triage doctor gave the baby an initial examination and told Shelley that Nicole was not in immediate danger. The mom was critical. Shelley stayed at the hospital, praying for the woman's life until Nicole's father arrived.

Roanna opened her eyes in a hospital bed. She vaguely recalled riding in a helicopter. A kind EMT. White lights. Doctors and nurses crowding around her. After a week in intensive care, she was finally lucid. Her foot had been impaled by the car's seat adjuster, her left eye and nasal cavity were caved in, her pelvis broken. But she didn't care about her own injuries. "Where is Nicole?" she asked. "Is my baby okay?" All she remembered was a stranger holding her.

In Lake Tahoe, Shelley sat in a ski lift and stared at the mountains in the distance. She kept thinking about the accident. Was Nicole's mother going to be okay? Driving back home to Seattle at the end of the week, she made a detour. She stopped at the hospital to check in on the Farleys.

"Roanna is still in serious condition," the nurse told her, "but she's going to pull through. Baby Nicole is in the pediatric wing."

Shelley gave the nurse a puzzled look. "Why?" she asked. "The doctor told me the baby was fine."

"I'm sorry, but we discovered Nicole suffered a spinal cord injury. She's paralyzed from the chest down."

The room spun. Shelley couldn't breathe. Was it her fault? Had she hurt the baby when she had pulled her from the car seat? She left the hospital quickly. She needed to get away. Away from the little girl whose life she'd ruined.

It was almost a month before Roanna could leave the hospital. She and her husband assessed the situation with Nicole. They would need nurses, physical therapists, all the help they could get. But they were determined to help Nicole adapt to her injury and grow up to be independent.

"Always push a little harder"—that was the physical therapists' advice to the Farleys. In Nicole's toddler years, they encouraged her to do things for herself, like take out her own toys and put them away again. As she grew, she learned to propel her wheelchair on her own. As soon as Nicole was old enough to understand, Roanna told her about the accident and the mysterious stranger who had come upon the scene.

Whenever Shelley thought of the Farleys, she was consumed by guilt. She pushed the memory of that week in 1988 deep within her. She joined a church in Seattle. Pursued a career as a dental assistant. Married and started a family of her own. Once, when she took her kids to Disneyland, her mind went straight to Nicole. *She lives in California. Maybe she's here.* Shelley scanned the crowds, looking for a redheaded girl in a wheelchair. She yearned to see her yet at the same time dreaded that moment. What if the Farleys held her responsible for the injury?

After twenty-five years, Shelley had decided she was better off not knowing the answer. *Nicole would be twenty-five now. The same age I was then.* Yet Nicole would never ski at Lake Tahoe with friends. Shelley couldn't bear to hear the sad story of what had happened to the little girl.

In the Farley home, Nicole sat with her mom, sifting through photos of her life, beginning with that fateful day on Interstate 5. Pictures from the accident scene. Articles that ran in the paper. Shots of her and her mom in the hospital. One by one she put them in order, a timeline of the tragedy and of what came after. She typed a script to go along with the photos, a message she wanted to share. A tech-savvy friend would take the images and Nicole's words and produce a video she could upload to YouTube to share with friends.

The idea to tell her story had popped into her head out of the blue, though she hadn't known if she was up to the task. But "always push a little harder" had become her mantra. "If this video can stop one drunk driver or encourage one person with a disability, then this is all worth it," Nicole said. The only thing left to do was choose the soundtrack.

Not long after, in Seattle, Shelley sat down with her lunch in front of her computer and checked her email. One new message—the daily e-newsletter from GodVine. She opened it and scrolled through the day's inspirational videos. There were five, each with a thumbnail image. One showed a baby girl smiling. Shelley clicked. Dark, dramatic music began to play.

"A stranger's irresponsible decision changed my life forever . . ."

A newspaper photo of a 1988 car accident filled the screen. A crushed sedan. Debris. All hauntingly familiar. A name flashed on the screen: Nicole Farley. The little girl who had lost her chance at a normal life. Shelley's breath caught.

Then the music changed. "Nothing is impossible for me," a woman sang in a sweet, powerful voice. "You can do more than just survive," the text on the video read. "You can overcome." In frame after frame, the redheaded girl was living. Reeling in the catch of the day on a fishing trip with her family. Swimming with dolphins. Traveling abroad with friends. Winning bake-offs. Even skiing! She was extraordinarily bright and had graduated from high school a year early. Now she lived on her own and ran a day care out of her home. From her toddler years to her early teens, all the way up to adulthood, Nicole had been independent. She was thriving. "My story isn't just about the pain; it's about faith, hope, love, and trust in the face of tragedy," the text read.

At the end, the captions revealed that the girl singing, with the beautiful voice, was Nicole.

Tears welled in Shelley's eyes. Nicole had grown up to have a full, happy life. According to the video, Roanna had made a full recovery. Shelley played it back a dozen times, unable to get through it without crying. One frame in the video jumped out at her. Nicole's email address.

That night Nicole checked her video on YouTube. Over ten thousand views! Friends had shared it with other friends on

Facebook, and GodVine had picked it up. *So this is what it's like to go viral*, Nicole thought. Her in-box was flooded with emails from people who had been inspired. One was from a woman named Shelley Cumley.

"Dear sweet Nicole," it began. "Your video took my breath away the second I saw your name. . . . You see, I am the person who pulled you out of the car that day. . . . I have struggled over the years second-guessing myself and wondering if I made your injuries worse. . . . I am so overwhelmed that your video literally was delivered to my in-box. . . . You are truly an inspiration. . . . Please know that if you ever wanted to talk to me, I am here. . . . Much love, Shelley."

How was this possible? Hearing from the mysterious stranger who had arrived on the scene that day twenty-five years before?

She had to reach out.

"Dear Shelley," she wrote. "My family has nothing but gratitude for you. As my doctors have always told me, my spinal cord injury occurred on impact. Your actions saved my mother and me. We hope to meet you face-to-face someday soon. With love, Nicole."

In February, Shelley, Nicole, and Roanna reunited in Portland, Oregon, sharing a scene once more—one they all want to remember.

A Husband at My Door

BONDA OWENS

Lonely? Sure, sometimes. But that was my cross to bear. After all, I'd asked God not to bring another man into my life. Not unless that man would stick with me for the rest of my days. I wasn't about to put my heart out there only to get hurt. "If God wants me to get married again," I said, "he'll have to drop the guy at my doorstep."

I remembered the moment I decided. After sixteen years of marriage, my husband told me he loved another woman. That night everything fell apart; it felt like the walls of my bedroom were closing in. I tossed and turned, kicking at the sheets and pounding the mattress. I couldn't get his words out of my head: "Bonda, it's over."

I was thirty-five, with two kids and minus a husband. I buried my head in my pillow, smothering my tears. I had just one request for God. *I'm begging you*, I prayed. *Don't even let another man ask me out unless you plan for me to marry him. This hurts too much.*

God sure kept up his end of the bargain. For eleven years, not a single man asked me out. Not even for a cup of coffee. I put all my energy into raising my son and daughter and focused on my job as a secretary. That kept me busy, at least until the kids went off to college.

There weren't many single people in my small town in South Carolina, so I was used to playing the third wheel. Weekends were the worst though. All my friends had husbands. I spent my free time playing the piano or doing chores like organizing the linen closet. Until I met Brenda and her husband, Charles, at a Bible study.

Brenda was the instructor, and we became instant friends. She was so kind, so down-to-earth. But a real firecracker too. The life of the party. She looked out for me, made me feel like family.

On Friday nights, Brenda and Charles would show up at my door armed with plans to get me out of the house. We'd laugh all through dinner, poking fun at Charles's bright red suspenders.

Charles was a good ol' boy, the kind of man who mounted deer antlers on his walls and loved a good juicy steak. But he was a gentleman too. He pulled out chairs for Brenda, opened doors, hung on every word she said. They made no secret of their devotion.

While Charles was off hunting on Saturdays, Brenda and I would check out flea markets, watch movies, cook together—she even showed me how to debone a chicken. "Not that I'll do this often when I'm cooking for one," I told her. Her daughter, Charmaine, would join us too. We talked about everything. Brenda knew the Bible backward and forward. No matter how serious our discussions got, though, we always ended up in a fit of giggles. *Maybe I don't have a husband*, I thought, *but at least I've found a soul sister.*

One day I met Brenda for lunch. She wasn't her usual self. Hardly touched her food. She was very pale. A few days later, she called me. "Bonda, I've been diagnosed with leukemia," she said.

The bottom fell out of my world. How could I go on without my soul sister? Brenda's condition worsened quickly. Soon she could barely speak because of the pain. I sat by her hospital bed and held her hand. It was all I could do. Charles consulted every specialist, researched new treatments. "You think this is worth a try?" he'd ask me, desperation in his voice. It was hopeless. We all knew that. Still, nothing could've prepared me for when Charmaine called me at three thirty one morning from the hospital. My friend was gone, just twenty-six days after her diagnosis, like a candle that had been snuffed out in an instant. She was only forty-eight.

The weeks that followed were some of the darkest of my life. I could only imagine what they were like for Charles. I helped him go through Brenda's things and mail out thank-you notes. I thought it might be awkward for us. Instead, it was comforting to share my grief. Charmaine told me Brenda had worried about how Charles would fare without her. "She'd be happy to know you're here through this," she said. "She was counting on you."

I struggled to get back to my routine. It was hard. A huge hole had opened in my life, as bad as when I had gotten divorced. One day I decided to go home on my lunch break to fix a sandwich and be alone with my thoughts. I hadn't been home long when the doorbell rang. Who even knew I was there?

"Charles?" I said, opening the front screen door.

"I saw your car in the driveway," he said. "Got worried you were sick."

"I'm okay," I said. "Just stopped home for lunch."

He stood there and fiddled with his keys, flustered. I stared back.

"I'm so tired of eating TV dinners," he blurted. "Would you maybe want to grab a pizza with me tomorrow evening?"

I was about to make an excuse. Frankly, I didn't much care for pizza. Then it hit me. There he was, a man standing on my doorstep, the first man to ask me out in eleven years, since I'd made my deal with God.

My cheeks burned. Why did it have to be Charles? Of all people! He was Brenda's husband! I'd never thought about him like that. It was just plain wrong. But he looked so lonely, like a lost little boy. This wouldn't be a date. We would just be two lonely people eating pizza together. Old friends. "Sure I will," I said after what seemed like an eternity.

So Charles and I just kept on being lonely together. Dinners. Movies. We sat together in church, did some of the activities we'd once done with Brenda. Charmaine didn't object to our relationship. In fact, she seemed to encourage it, sometimes inviting the two of us over for dinner. One day she told me why.

"The night she died Mom made one last request, something I never told Dad," she said. "She said she wanted Dad to get married again. He needed a wife, I needed a mother. And she told me who she wanted that woman to be."

Charles and I have been happily married for twenty-five years now. Not a day goes by that I don't say a prayer of thanks for Brenda. And for the man who landed on my doorstep.

Long Lost

Diana Aydin

Mary Frank sat at the desk at St. Bridget's in Mesa, Arizona, addressing invitations for the church's annual pancake breakfast. She crossed names off a list as she made her way through the stack. Stuff, seal, inscribe, stamp, repeat. Volunteering kept Mary busy. No reason to slow down now, even at age seventy-six.

She added another envelope to the growing pile and moved on to the next name. Ethel McLaughlin. Mary's neat production line came to a halt. She adjusted her glasses and read the name again. A common Irish surname, but one that had haunted her all her life. McLaughlin. The last name she had been born with. The family she never knew.

As much as she tried to fight it, Mary felt that familiar ache, the one that had never really gone away, even after she had married and had her own family, the longing to connect with roots she knew were out there somewhere.

The name McLaughlin was one of the only clues Mary had about her past, which was cloaked in mystery and confusion.

When Mary had turned eighteen, the caseworker who'd placed her with her last foster family had handed her a faded birth certificate with an apologetic smile. "We tried contacting your mother," she said, "but it may not be the best time right now."

"I don't understand," Mary said. "You told me that when I turned eighteen . . ."

"The family doesn't want to connect. Perhaps in the future. I'm sorry, Mary."

Everything about Mary's origin was shrouded in secrecy. She'd pieced together a vague narrative over the years based on the whisperings of her foster parents and social workers. All she knew was that her mother's name, like her own, was Mary McLaughlin and that she was from Ashland, Wisconsin. The line for "father" on the birth certificate was blank.

There'd been a scandal surrounding her birth—that much Mary knew. She was born in 1932 at a hospital for unwed mothers in Green Bay, four hours from Ashland. Her early years were spent in an orphanage in Sparta, Wisconsin, with an imposing wrought-iron gate and white beds lined up in two neat rows. As a little girl, Mary was delighted when the caseworker informed her she was going to live with a foster family, the Gaffneys. Finally, she'd have a family all her own. Mr. Gaffney, whom she called Grandpa Tony, was a kind, gentle man, the only father figure she'd ever known. She stayed on the Gaffneys' farm for five years. But when she was eight, Grandpa Tony took her for a walk, stopping on a hill overlooking the farm's windmills. There he explained that the family couldn't take care of her anymore. His wife was ill. Mary ran into the house and hid in a cupboard. But it was no use. She was sent off to another foster home.

Mary spent the rest of her school years shuttling from one family to the next, working as a farmhand or helping to raise other people's children. By the time of her eighteenth birthday, in 1950, she had lived in eight homes.

The promise that she'd someday be reunited with her mother, or at least find out the circumstances of her birth, had helped keep hope alive in Mary. That and her faith. At night, she prayed, pleading with God to be reunited with her family. But her biological family, for whatever reason, didn't want to be found.

Mary never gave up the quest, even after she got to know Val Frank, a former World War II pilot with an irresistible smile. They met at a dance in Sauk City, Wisconsin, and were married in 1953. They had four children and spent their married life building up the Frank family grocery and sausage-making business. Whenever she and Val traveled to a grocers' conference in another state, Mary would pore through phone books for the name McLaughlin, making calls, writing letters. She thought about all the seats at her wedding that should've been occupied by her next of kin.

In 1967, one of Mary's friends wrote to relatives in Ashland— maybe they had heard of the McLaughlins? They had! Mary discovered that her mother and her mother's sister had moved together to Chicago. Mary found their address and sent a letter. The response that came back crushed her hopes. A neatly creased letter from a great-aunt. "Your mother would be so proud to see the fine woman you've become," it said. "But we've decided now isn't the best time for you to meet her."

Some urged Mary to drive to Chicago, to knock on her mother's door, to force the issue. But she wouldn't force a relationship that wasn't wanted.

Now, in the office of St. Bridget's, Mary felt a pang of regret. Her mother had to be long gone. She stared at the name. Ethel McLaughlin. Mary and Val had retired to Arizona almost ten years before. They were active in the community. She'd never heard of an Ethel McLaughlin in the area. She would have taken note.

She asked the priest and found out that Ethel was an eighty-nine-year-old retiree—from Wisconsin. One of those "snowbirds" who wintered in Arizona. Someone in the office had Ethel's number. Mary dialed the phone. Waiting for Ethel to answer, she couldn't shake the feeling—maybe, just maybe. . . . She could always say she was just calling about the pancake breakfast if she lost her nerve.

"Hello?" a woman answered.

Mary couldn't speak. "Hello? Is anyone there?" the woman repeated.

"Yes, hello. My name is Mary Frank," Mary said. "My maiden name is Mary McLaughlin. I . . . I was given up for adoption, and I've been searching for years to find a connection to my family. I'm wondering if you knew another Mary McLaughlin."

"My dear! You sound just like one of my cousins," Ethel answered. "She had a sister named Mary, who died several years ago."

The next day Val and Mary drove to Ethel's apartment complex. The women embraced. "You look like a McLaughlin," Ethel said. "I know you belong to us!"

Over lunch, Mary discovered that Ethel was a cousin by marriage. It took a while to finally piece the whole story together though. How her mother and her mother's sister were sent to live with relatives in Ashland after the death of their own mother in 1916. How the unwed Mary became pregnant, gave the baby up for adoption, and eventually moved to Chicago. Her sister was fiercely protective. She'd feared that Mary's attempts to reconnect would reopen painful wounds. Few in the family were told anything about the baby; as far as they knew, the elder Mary never married, never had children.

On a sunny day, one year after the pancake breakfast, Mary met the entire McLaughlin clan at Ethel's home in Wisconsin. Brats and burgers sizzled on the grill, and a big white cake on the picnic table was emblazoned, Welcome to the Family!

To think it all began with invitations to a church pancake breakfast. Mary's lifelong prayer had at last been answered.

Danger in the Night

IRMA DEWATERS

I can't explain why I was saved. Why another girl wasn't. I've thought about it for fifty years. All I know is that evil tried to take me that night and how close I was to being a killer's next victim.

It was early August 1965. Almost midnight. The Laundromat on the outskirts of town was deserted, my brown-and-white Buick the only car in the lot. Inside, rows of machines were dormant, their round, glass doors flipped open. No Herman's Hermits or Four Tops on the radio. Not at this hour. Just the sloshing of the washer I'd started. I leaned against a table and thumbed through a magazine. Fifteen minutes to go . . .

I washed my baby's cloth diapers at that Laundromat every few nights, stopping in after my shift as a long-distance operator for Ma Bell. It was several miles from the place my husband and I had moved into the year before. "Irma, you be careful there so late at night," warned Toby, a cabdriver who had become a good friend of ours. "It's the back of beyond. Even I never drive out that far."

"I'll be careful," I promised. Actually, I liked that the Laundromat was so isolated. The quiet helped me unwind. A break from the bustle of work and a new baby. Plus, it saved me from scrubbing the baby's diapers on the washboard at home.

I was almost finished with my magazine when car headlights in the parking lot caught my eye. I glanced back at the timer on the washer. Ten minutes . . .

That's when he walked in. A man I'd never seen before. Tall, with dark, shaggy hair, wearing jeans and a black shirt. No laundry or laundry basket. Strange. He took a seat by the door and sat for a while. Maybe he was just waiting for someone. Yet something had come into that Laundromat with him. A feeling. A bad feeling.

I started to hum "You'll Never Walk Alone," my go-to song in times of stress. In between verses, I peeked behind me to get a better look at the man. Sunken eyes, pale skin. His expression chilled me.

Bzzzz!

I nearly jumped out of my shoes. But it was only my wash. I quickly transferred the diapers to a dryer far away from the strange man. I stared at the timer, willing it to tick down faster. In a soft, quivering voice, I sang, "When you walk through a storm hold your head up high and don't be afraid of the dark."

A shadow fell over me. Two ice-cold hands slid down my chest inside the front of my shirt. I screamed and wrenched away. The man lunged at me. I ran to the front door. He was right behind me.

I flew out into the cool midnight air and sprinted across the parking lot to my car. I grabbed the door handle, fumbled with my keys. My hands were shaking so badly.

"Got ya!" the man snarled and grabbed my left arm. He was a foot taller than me, at least. I was no match for him. I gripped the door handle tightly with my right hand. One by one he started prying my fingers loose. I tried to scream, "Let me go! I won't tell anyone," but the words didn't come out. My hand cramped, just two fingers clinging to the handle.

Then a bright light appeared in the distance. Headlights!

The man let go of my fingers and thrust his body against mine, pinning me against the car door. From the road, no one would be able to see me. I squirmed to get free, but his weight was crushing me. The car zoomed past. "You're mine now," he said, breathing heavily.

The sound of tires crunching on the gravel road faded. It could be hours before another car came by.

The man stepped back. I gasped and clutched the door handle again just as he wrapped his arms around me. He tried to pick me up and drag me away, but I hung on. My palms were sweaty, my fingers were slipping. I couldn't last any longer. *Lord, watch over my baby boy and keep him in your hands.*

Screeeech!

A car slammed on its brakes. There was the roar of tires kicking up gravel. A cloud of dust rose over the parking lot, clouding my vision. Blinding headlights spotlighted the stranger and me.

The driver jumped out, the silhouette of a baseball bat visible in his hands. He charged at my attacker, waving his weapon over his head like a samurai warrior. "Let her go! Get away from her!" he shouted.

I knew that voice. Toby?

The stranger cursed and shoved me against the car. Then he bolted, vanishing behind the Laundromat.

I collapsed in Toby's arms. He took off his windbreaker and put it around my shoulders. "I've already radioed the police," he said. "You're safe now."

"I thought you never came out here," I said, trying to hold back my sobs.

"I don't," Toby said. "Business was slow, so I decided to drive around while I waited for a call to pick up a fare. I can't explain how I ended up here, but when I saw that man standing by

185

your Buick, I knew something wasn't right. That's when I turned around."

The officers arrived shortly to take a statement. They didn't seem to find much to go on. Over the next week, I had nightmares—I couldn't get the man's face out of my mind.

Then one morning I picked up the paper. And I saw him. On the front page. Definitely him. The sunken, empty eyes, the pallor of his skin.

My hands trembled. The paper shook as I read. He'd been charged with the murder of a woman months earlier and the kidnapping and attempted murder of a second woman . . . only a few days after he'd attacked me. She'd survived, the article said, thanks to the hem of her dress catching in the trunk latch of her car, preventing it from closing. Her escape had led to the man's arrest.

The murdered woman had last been seen alive at a Laundromat on the outskirts of town.

Family Ties

MEG BELVISO

What's your big family secret? The story whispered beyond earshot of the kids, the question nobody asks Grandma? Will it stay buried? Some secrets should. Others, though, yearn to see the light. Nothing can stop them from coming out.

Raymond Gooch was a young man who was missing a piece of his past, a piece he never expected to find. A twenty-three-year-old partner in a leather-goods store, he traveled from town to town taking orders from fashion retailers for custom, handcrafted belts. On a sunny summer day in 1980, Raymond climbed out of his car on the south side of Knoxville, Tennessee, ready to sell. He was optimistic about his prospects. But as he started his rounds, he felt a strange urging: *Go to the north side of town.*

The north side? His potential customers were here on the south side. Raymond puzzled over the strange feeling and decided to compromise. *If I don't sell anything at my first stop, I'll know I'm supposed to be on the north side.*

Raymond strode confidently into the first business he saw and launched into his pitch, but the manager cut him off without even glancing at his samples. "We're not interested," he snapped.

North side it is.

He got back on Interstate 75 and drove north to the first exit: Merchant's Drive. That sounded promising. As his dad, Buddy, would say, "Go with your gut, son." He parked at a shopping center. Clothing store, shoe store—great places to sell—but the urge took hold of him again. The Baldwin Piano Company—that's where Raymond had to go, even if he didn't have a clue why.

Pamella Parker had no idea either. The twenty-seven-year-old piano saleswoman had worked at the Baldwin Piano Company for about a year, since moving to Knoxville. She'd dealt with plenty of people selling used instruments or wanting to leave flyers advertising piano lessons. So she just didn't know what to make of the young man selling . . . belts. She wasn't surprised when her manager politely sent the man on his way.

"You have a good day now, Mr. Gooch," Pam overheard the manager say. She saw Raymond headed for the door.

Pam called out to him, "It's nice to hear a familiar name! My maiden name is Gooch."

Raymond turned, a bit stunned. He'd never met anyone outside his family with his last name. "Maybe we're distant cousins," he said, half joking.

The two salespeople got to talking. Pam had grown up in Orlando, but she'd moved to Knoxville after a divorce. "I came to work here because I love to play music."

"Me too," Raymond said. "I've been playing piano since I was six."

"I got the music gene from my late father," said Pam. "He played piano and saxophone—he could play anything he put his mind to, really."

"My grandfather was a fantastic musician," Raymond said. "He met my grandma playing piano and sax with a jazz band. At least that's what Grandma Irene told me. Dad . . . well, he never knew his father . . ." Raymond trailed off. There was more to the story, he'd always felt. His dad and grandma never talked much about it. But in his heart, he knew.

"My father was Elmer Gooch," Pam said. "Maybe your grandma would know who . . ."

"Elmer?" Raymond interrupted, his eyes widening. "That was my grandfather's name!"

Later that day, Buddy listened to Raymond's excited phone call. "I don't believe it," Buddy said and hung up. Five minutes later, he called back. "Tell me this again," he said. "I have a half sister? Twenty-two years younger? You actually met her?"

Weeks later, Pam, Raymond, and Buddy paid a visit to Irene Gooch. Pam brought a photo of her dad. "That's him," Grandma Irene said. "Buddy's father. We were married for three months. He left me in Ohio to look for work in Florida. Soon after, I discovered I was pregnant. I waited for him to send for me, but he never did. All these years, we wondered . . ."

"I knew he'd been married before," Pam said, "but I never suspected the truth. He took it to his grave." And it had stayed there. Until a young belt salesman followed an urge he didn't understand and found an aunt he never knew. And a family secret was finally revealed.

PART 5

Sure and Steadfast

This hope we have as an anchor of the
soul, both sure and steadfast.

HEBREWS 6:19

RTD-17

JACKIE CLEMENTS-MARENDA

It's not the prettiest picture in the world, I know. It's no rainbow. The nondescript industrial building, the patchy lawn, the gray sky. When I look at it, though, I remember a time when I'd lost all hope—and I see something wonderful.

The trouble began with a loud crash. I shouted to my husband, Tom, from the family room, but he didn't answer. I ran to the kitchen to find the chairs toppled and Tom slumped over, gasping, clutching his chest. A heart attack? I don't even remember our neighbor driving us to the hospital.

Not once in our forty years of marriage had Tom been sick. He had a stomach of steel and a monster immune system. None of that mattered now. I stood in the emergency room, focused on the machine that displayed his vital signs. His pulse and blood pressure were plummeting. The doctors placed metal paddles on his chest, trying to shock his heart back into rhythm. Tom was dying.

Not yet. The doctors got Tom's heart working again. "It's the seventeenth," Tom said weakly. "My lucky number, remember? No way was I going to die today."

Nice try, I thought. He wasn't out of the woods.

"Your husband has atrial fibrillation, an arrhythmia," the doctor explained. Tom had two more attacks after that and needed to be shocked both times. Within a few months, however, his condition stabilized—according to the medical staff, at least. Easy for them to say.

How could I be certain? I feared another attack. I hounded Tom about his health and discouraged him from leaving the house. I even checked his pulse at random, a habit he hated.

"Stop that, Jackie. I'm fine," he said, swatting my hand away from his wrist. "You can relax. Let's get out. I'm going stir-crazy."

Not even prayer gave me peace. *If only my three aunts were here*, I thought. Mom's sisters had brought me through times like this before. I had been only eleven when my dad had died. My older brother Thomas had died as a young adult. My aunts had become my lifeline. Dolly knew how to handle any situation, Rita was a fountain of acceptance and generosity, and Theda could always make me laugh. They had never married and had poured their love into the rest of our clan. They were such a solid team that my family had rarely referred to them by their individual names, just by their initials—our own family trinity. After they died, I imagined them beside me when I spoke to God. That felt silly now. Did anyone hear me in the pandemonium of prayers God must be subjected to?

One day Tom suggested we visit a furniture store in New Jersey to buy a cabinet. I shuddered. The store was twenty-five miles away. Were hospitals nearby? How fast could an EMT get there? I resolved to get the trip over with as quickly as possible.

Does he look pale? I wondered once we arrived. *Is his breathing strained?* We made our selection, then sat in the office while the salesman did the paperwork. I tried to resist checking Tom's pulse. Couldn't. My hand had a mind of its own.

"Would you quit that?" Tom grumbled. "You're driving me nuts."

I wished I could. I wished I could stop feeling and acting like this. Driving Tom nuts? I was driving myself nuts. I stood up and walked to the window. Not much of a view—just a string of gray buildings. I glanced at the one across the street.

The letters over the door caught my attention. RTD. Exactly what my family had called my three aunts, Rita, Theda, and Dolly! RTD. Always in that order. "RTD to the rescue," they'd say.

Then I saw the address—17. Tom's lucky number. His birthday was May 17. We met on November 17. He grew up in a house at 17 St. John's Place. Then there was the date of his first attack, February 17, when I'd been sure he wouldn't make it. And yet he had. He was still here. I could almost hear my aunts. *Time to enjoy your blessing and stop being afraid.*

That's when I took that photo. RTD-17. Not as pretty as a rainbow but just as powerful a promise. We'd made it through the storm.

Those Fish!

PEGGY WOOD STEWART

If you come to our house these days, you'll find a fish mobile dangling over our kitchen table. Those fish swinging in the air always remind me of the real fish that insisted on entering our lives. And I never fail to remember the dreary night that I reluctantly took that first batch of fish from the freezer.

"This is the last straw," I muttered angrily as I slapped at the hot grease that had just spattered my arm. The pungent odor of fish frying permeated my kitchen, and I had been battling waves of nausea already.

Those fish had been in the freezer for a month, the meager results of the last fishing trip the boys had taken with their father. The four weeks since then had been the worst of my life. Now, looking at those fish I was about to serve, I thought grimly, *I'm not that hungry*.

Well, I was that hungry, for with the exception of a pound of ground meat, designated for Sunday's dinner, we had nothing else to eat. Monday was payday, so we had survived the month, but no one in his right mind would call this victorious living. What about God's promises to meet our needs? Philippians 4:19, for instance? "My God shall supply all your need according to His riches in glory by Christ Jesus." *Probably another fairy story, like living happily ever after*, I thought bitterly. I was fool enough to believe that one too.

Fred and I had had such high ideals and dreams when we married, but his habit of taking a "social drink" gradually developed into a real drinking problem, and we finally lost everything we owned. I'd taught school before our three sons were born, and when our youngest entered kindergarten, I returned to teaching to provide a stable income. But Fred's drinking became even more intense, culminating in full-scale alcoholism that tore our family apart. Reluctantly, I filed for divorce. And one month ago, my marriage of thirteen years was declared null and void.

Now my sons and I were left with the choice between these unappetizing fish—or nothing at all. Worse, it seemed indicative of a future that didn't promise anything better. So the boys came in, and eat those fish we did.

After dinner, I was left alone with my worries, staring at the months ahead. Almost unconsciously, my thoughts turned into a grumbled prayer: *Lord, if you don't help us, there's no way we're going to make it.*

Suddenly, I was aware of an unearthly stillness that filled the kitchen. The presence of Jesus was very real, and I seemed to hear clearly the command, *Make a list of all the things you're so worried about.*

"That's easy," I replied. I grabbed a pencil and paper and wrote house payment, new glasses for Grady, gym shoes for Woody, jeans for David, groceries . . .

Then the same presence brought to mind the verses from Matthew: "Do not worry about your life, what you will eat or what you will drink; nor about your body, what you will put on. . . .

But seek first the kingdom of God and His righteousness, and all these things shall be added to you" (6:25, 33).

I looked at the list. Every item fell neatly into one of those categories.

"Lord, that's easy to believe when things are going all right," I protested. "But I'm alone now, scratching to make ends meet. Like tonight. We had nothing left to eat."

And then I thought, *We did have those fish.*

A few months later, soft autumn sunlight warmed the church pew where I sat, insides churning, palms sweaty. The choir was singing heartily, but I couldn't concentrate on the music or the words. I could only concentrate on that offering plate coming closer and closer. We were broke. Although Fred was legally responsible for child support, he never contributed any money at all, which left my sons and me a monthly income of five hundred dollars. After the bills, we were left with exactly one hundred. And if I gave my tithe of fifty dollars . . . that would leave me the choice of getting shoes that two of the boys desperately needed—or buying food. I held the check in my hand as the plate got closer and closer. How could God want me to have to make this choice?

Do not worry about your life, came the whisper again.

"But my boys," I protested.

Do not worry . . .

The usher handed me the plate. I dropped in the check.

I didn't feel relieved or virtuous. In fact, when we got home, I was a portrait of self-pity. I stopped again in the kitchen, staring at a can of tomatoes, wondering how to turn it into a meal, when there was a knock on the door. There stood my friend Betty Jean, and in her hands was a pan of fish. "Carolyn and I cooked fish together and had these left over. I can't refreeze them. Can you and the boys use them?"

Those fish. We had a wonderful meal. More than we could eat.

That year, for the first time in my life, I dreaded Christmas. Every carol, every holiday symbol brought bittersweet memories of happier times. Of course, our budget was stretched to the limit, but we'd get by. Then, without warning, I had a blowout on the old station wagon. I got the car home and put on the spare.

Dejected already, I couldn't bear to stay in the house just then, surrounded by ghosts of Christmases past. I absentmindedly got in the car and drove to the supermarket. I got a cart and walked the aisles without purpose. I thought it would help to be surrounded by piped-in carols and bustle and people, but it just made me feel more alone. So alone.

I felt a touch on my shoulder and heard a friendly voice behind me.

"Why, Peggy, it's so good to see you! How in the world are you and those boys? By the way, do they like fish? Ed just came home with another catch, and I have no more room in my freezer. I was just wondering what to do with them."

Those fish. I had to smile. I knew the spare would be okay until I could afford a new tire. I also realized that, regardless of what I felt, I was *not* alone.

For over two years, we got along all right, just barely, but we got along. My frustration and self-pity abated a little at a time. And then—whop! I got the worst case of mumps on record. Never had I been so sick! I would see the boys off to school, then collapse on the sofa for the rest of the day. My fellow teachers took turns bringing in our supper, but my convalescence seemed to go on forever. Discouragement enveloped me again. And then my coworker Mary put a pot of chili on the stove and came out to the den where I was resting miserably.

"Peggy," she said, "I know this sounds awful right now, but if you tell me where your freezer is, I'd like to leave a catch of fish that you can cook up when you're feeling better."

Those fish!

I'm sure she thought I was delirious as I began to laugh joyfully. Now I couldn't help but remember the many times Jesus used fish to minister to the needs of people as he walked this earth. He fed the multitude of five thousand with five loaves and two fish, and again the four thousand with seven loaves and a few fish. After his resurrection, to reassure his faithful followers, he asked for some fish and ate with them. Later, at the Sea of Galilee, he cooked fish for his disciples and called Peter back into service. And he'd never forgotten us in our time of need.

I looked at Mary where she still stood, amazed. "Thanks a lot for the fish," I told her. "As a matter of fact, I'm feeling better already." And do you know, I really *was* feeling better.

Fish in the freezer. This was exactly where I'd started, grumbling, those years before, so alone and bitter. Again the freezer was stocked. We'd come full circle. But how much I'd changed.

I wasn't the only one. Soon after, three years following our divorce, I received a letter from Fred. God had taken care of him too. He told how he had spent the past fifteen months at the Anchorage, a Christian rehabilitation center for alcoholics. While there, he'd come to rely on God, and his life had been changed. He asked for our forgiveness and sent us some money. From that day on, he began to help with our financial needs.

Eventually, Fred and I were remarried in the little chapel at the Anchorage. I had prayed that the Lord would be faithful and save our marriage. Instead, he was faithful to save us and made a new marriage with new people. The hopeless end for us was God's beginning.

Indeed, if you come to see us these days, you'll find that fish mobile over our kitchen table, a reminder that if we seek God first, everything else really will be provided. And when visitors like you notice it, as they usually do, I have a wonderful chance to tell them how God once again used fish to minister to the needs of his people.

Comfort in the Drive-Through

PEGGY FREZON

Traffic was pretty bad on I-95, but my husband, Mike, tapped his fingers on the steering wheel cheerfully. Our two kids were in the backseat, excitedly talking over which rides they wanted to go on once we got there. We were driving from our home in upstate New York to Disney World. Our first big family vacation. Who wouldn't be excited?

Well . . . me. I suffer from extreme anxiety when I travel. An unfamiliar place can give me a full-blown panic attack. I'd managed okay for the first part of the drive, but now worries flooded my mind. Had I packed Andy's ear medication? Kate's teddy bear? Why was there so much traffic? What if the car broke down?

Mike glanced over and saw the stress all over my face. "Let's take a break," he said. "There's a McDonald's at the rest area up ahead."

I just nodded. My mouth was so dry I couldn't talk. Maybe a cool drink would help.

Mike pulled our minivan into the drive-through behind a long line of cars. "Can I have French fries?" Andy asked.

"Where's my teddy?" Kate said.

My heart hammered. Every muscle in my body tensed. *Relax*, I tried to tell myself. *That's what vacation is for*. But I just wished I was back home, where I felt safe.

Another sound reached my ears. Music. I rolled down my window. Voices rose together in perfect harmony. "In times of trouble, he will shelter me. . . . He will keep me safe." Where was it coming from?

We inched forward in line. The singing got louder. A grassy island between the drive-through and the parking lot came into view. There, in two neat rows, wearing long burgundy robes, stood a dozen members of a church choir. Their jubilant voices floated into the minivan, their song of praise stirring something deep inside me. "He will shelter me . . ." My heart rate slowed. The stress left my body. Calm settled over me.

"What a strange place for a concert," Mike remarked.

No, I wanted to say, *not really*. Instead, I closed my eyes and drank in the music.

A Calendar for Courage

MARGARET HILLIS

The gatekeeper at our mission compound limped into the kitchen doorway, bowed crookedly, and announced, "*Hsieh si-mu* [pastor's wife], here is His Excellency the Colonel."

I held my breath. The colonel commanded the troops currently protecting this city of Shenkiu in central China. It was January 1941; the invading Japanese were only a few miles to the east.

The colonel entered briskly and made his announcement: "The enemy is advancing into Henan Province. We have orders not to defend this city. You should find refuge in one of the villages outside."

I crossed my hands over the sleeves of my wadded *e-shang* and bowed politely, thanking him for his gracious concern for a "miserable" woman. As the colonel left the room, the icy January blast swept through the doorway. My baby cried. Suddenly, the enormity of our danger overwhelmed me.

Our Margaret Ann was scarcely two months old, Johnny just over a year. Yesterday my husband, urgently needing medical care, had been taken by rickshaw to the hospital 115 miles away. I looked at the little daily Scripture calendar on the wall: January 15. Not until early February would he be back. How would I manage without him? How would I make the myriad decisions that now crowded upon me?

You see, I had not yet experienced the full wonder of God's power to guide us when all other guides fail. Nor did I guess that as his instrument he would use anything as prosaic as a calendar on a kitchen wall.

By midafternoon, the army garrison in our little city was empty. The departure of the soldiers created panic. Families packed their goods and fled.

The elders of the church called on me before they left. "Come with us," they pleaded. "We will care for you while Pastor Hillis is away."

I looked at the concern in their eyes, and I thought of the country homes to which they were headed. My husband and I loved those village homes because we loved the people in them. But they held death for Western babies, as too many little graves in our mission compounds showed.

How could I explain to these friends—without offending them—that I could not take my children into their homes, un-heated, mud-floored huts in which three and four generations crowded together amid vermin and filth? Just a few weeks ago, the six-month-old son of the nearest American family had died of dreaded dysentery. No, my babies were chained to this kitchen where I could boil dishes, milk, and water.

But these were not things I could say to Chinese friends. I bowed, I thanked them, I spoke of waiting for my husband's return, of watching the mission property—and I went to bed that night shaking with terror. When Johnny woke up whimpering in the cold, I took him into bed with me and lay awake a long time, listening to the wind rattle the waxed-paper windowpanes and praying that my little boy would live to see his daddy again.

The next morning I was in the kitchen early to start the water boiling for Margaret Anne's bottle. Automatically, I reached up to the wall calendar and tore off yesterday's date. The Scripture verse for the new day gleamed like sunlight. "What time I am afraid, I will trust in thee" (Ps. 56:3 KJV).

Well, I was certainly afraid. I fulfilled that part of it. Now, indeed, was the time to trust God. Somehow the verse sustained me all through the tense day.

The city was being evacuated rapidly. Other church members came to invite me to their family huts. But the Scripture held me. I was not to *panic* but to *trust*.

By midmorning the next day, the city was nearly deserted. Then the gatekeeper came to me, eyes blurred with fear. He had to leave, he said, and begged me to find refuge with him in his village beyond the city.

Should I? What could I do without our gatekeeper? The deserted city would be an open invitation to bandits and looters. But the risk to my babies outside was certain; here I still faced only fears. I declined the gatekeeper's offer and watched him as he sorrowfully took leave.

It was noon before I remembered to pull the page off the little daily calendar on the wall. The tenth verse of the ninth psalm read, "And they that know thy name will put their trust in thee: for thou, LORD, hast not forsaken them that seek thee" (KJV).

As I bowed my head over my noonday meal, my heart poured out its gratitude to God for those particular words at that moment.

My main concern now was food. All the shops in the town were boarded shut. Meat and produce no longer came in daily from farms. I still had the goats for the babies' milk, but the man who milked them had left for his village. Tomorrow I would have to try to milk them myself. I wondered if I could ever make the balky little beasts hold still.

I slept uneasily that night, wondering how I would feed my children and sure of very little except that we should stay in the city and, somehow, trust God. The sound of distant gunfire woke me.

Before facing the goats, I fixed myself a bowl of rice gruel. Then I tore the old page from the calendar and read the new day's message: "I will nourish you, and your little ones" (Gen. 50:21 KJV).

The timeliness of the daily verses was becoming almost uncanny. With some curiosity, I examined the back of the calendar pad. It had been put together in England the year before, but God in his all-knowing had provided the very words I needed a year later, here on the other side of the world.

I was still eating the gruel when a woman stepped into the kitchen. She was carrying a pail of steaming goats' milk. "May I stay and help you?" she asked. "See, I have milked your goats."

Mrs. Lee had been our neighbor for years, but that morning I stared at her as though she had dropped from heaven. She had no family living, she explained, and wished to show her gratitude to the mission.

Late in the day, a loud rapping at the gate set our hearts pounding. Braver, Mrs. Lee was the one who went to open it. Her face beaming, she returned leading our caller.

"*Gee-tze! Gee-dan!*" she cried triumphantly. "Chicken! Eggs!"

A frail, black-robed country woman came in with a live chicken and a basket of eggs. "Peace, peace," she gave the customary Christian greeting as she bobbed to us shyly. The noise of the cannons had not kept her away when she remembered that the missionaries would be hungry.

The calendar promise had come true! God *would* see to it that our little ones were nourished! That night my heart was full of hope. To the sound of shells bursting in the sky, I prayed that somehow God would spare this city and these gentle people we loved.

The next morning I rushed down to the little square of paper hanging on its nail and tore off the page. "When I cry unto thee, then shall mine enemies turn back: this I know; for God is for me," the Scripture declared (Ps. 56:9 KJV).

But this time it was too much to believe! Surely it couldn't be right to take literally a verse chosen just by chance for an English calendar?

As the gunfire drew closer, Mrs. Lee and I began to prepare the house for invasion. Any papers that might possibly be construed to have military or political significance had to be hidden or destroyed. We searched my husband's desk and the church buildings. By nightfall, the gunfire sounded from both sides of the city. We went to bed dressed, prepared at any moment to meet the Japanese invaders.

I awoke abruptly in the early dawn and strained my ears for the crunch of military boots on gravel. But only a deep stillness surrounded me. There were no tramping feet, no shrieking shells or pounding guns, only the waking murmur of little Johnny in his crib.

Misgivings warred with excitement as I woke Mrs. Lee and we went to the gatehouse, each carrying a child. She was the first to stick out a cautious head. "There is no one in the street," she told me. "Shall we go out?"

We stepped through the gate and watched as the streets began to fill not with Japanese soldiers but with townspeople returning from their country hiding places. Had the Chinese won?

As if in answer to our question, we met the colonel. "Pastor's wife!" he greeted me with relief. "I have been concerned about you!"

Then he told us that the Japanese had withdrawn. No, they had not been defeated, nor could anyone arrive at a reasonable conjecture concerning their retreat. The enemy had simply turned back.

I stepped into my kitchen, eyes fixed on a little block of paper pinned to the wall. Oh, you could say it was just a calendar. You could say strangers had chosen those verses without any thought of China or of the war that would be raging when those dates fell due. But to me, it was more than a calendar, and no stranger had picked those lines. To me, it was the handwriting of God.

Luke 1:37

It was the day before Christmas and all through the house, not a creature was stirring—except for me and my cat, Mittens. It was just the two of us this year. I wasn't sure what was worse—having a broken heart or becoming a lonely, old cat lady.

My soon-to-be ex-husband had just picked up our nine- and twelve-year-old sons, Patrick and Michael, to spend Christmas Eve at his new condo, as we had agreed.

"Mom, seriously, what're you gonna do?" Michael had asked as his father beeped the car horn from the driveway. "You gonna be okay?"

"Who, me?" I asked, forcing a grin. "I have the whole day planned, kiddo!"

A big fat lie. My plan was to eat a pint of rocky road and stay in bed all day.

I flopped onto the couch and pored over last year's Christmas photos. I was so blissfully unaware back then. How could I have predicted what was coming? The past six months felt like a tabloid news story. My husband of fourteen years casually asking for a divorce one morning at breakfast. Me begging him to stay. Trying to understand how a forty-eight-year-old homemaker from Minnesota, who thought she'd built a white-picket-fence life, could end up in such a mess.

A cry from Mittens interrupted my pity party. I found her rolled up on the kitchen floor trying to get at something stuck to the back of her paw. It was a small card that'd fallen from its spot on the basement door, where I'd taped all the Christmas cards. I pulled it loose and turned it over.

"Merry Christmas, Margaret. My gift to you is Luke 1:37. Love, Ruth."

I rolled my eyes at my pastor's latest attempt to get me to crack open the Bible. She'd snuck a copy into my mailbox that summer with a sticky note that said, "Read me fifteen minutes a day." I'd started attending her church not because I was much of a believer but because it seemed like a good idea when your world was falling apart. Ruth was persistent, I had to give her that. But I didn't know what Luke 1:37 was, and no way was I making this day even worse by puzzling over an ancient book that couldn't possibly apply to me.

I put the card back up, right next to a photo of my married neighbors looking gorgeously happy in their matching sweaters. I peered down at my own outfit. Two p.m. and I was still in flannel pj's. Michael's sweet question from earlier brought tears to my eyes. What was I going to do?

It was too much. I wanted to run away from that empty house and all the unknowns ahead of me. I threw on some clothes and escaped into the bracing cold outside. Fifteen minutes into my walk, I was freezing. Finding myself on a boutique-lined street, I ducked inside the only store that seemed to be open.

It looked like a Christmas explosion inside. No corner had been spared. Tinsel, mistletoe, ornaments. A saleslady emerged from a labyrinth of porcelain vases and ornate end tables. She wore a white wool pantsuit, red pumps, and matching lipstick. *A young, hip Mrs. Claus*, I thought. She handed me a glass of cider. "Welcome to my shop," she said. "What kinds of antiques do you like?"

"I guess anything with a good story," I said.

"Oh, then you'll love this." She reached down behind the register and pulled out a framed painting. "Just got it in this morning. Considered keeping it for myself!"

She went on about the artist. I wasn't listening. Not a word. I was totally lost in the scene the painting depicted. Three boats dead in the water. No wind to carry them to shore. Stuck, just like me. Hopeless. But six words emblazoned in four-inch Gothic-style letters across the top of the painting made my heart skip a beat: With God Nothing Shall Be Impossible.

"It's from the Bible," the saleslady said. "Do you know it? From Luke. Chapter one, verse thirty-seven."

The painting came home with me. I dug out Ruth's Bible, which I'd stashed in my closet months earlier, and Mittens curled up next to me on the couch as I opened it up to Luke 1:37. I began to read, letting the message sink in. I remembered my son's question: Mom, are you going to be okay? Yes. Yes, I was.

A Soldier's Story

The Canadian soldiers found him crossing the border from Germany into the Netherlands. A twenty-five-year-old Dutch ex-prisoner of war named Henk. He'd walked all the way from a Nazi labor camp in Hamburg. Covered in flea bites. A skeleton in rags, like most of the freed prisoners roaming the countryside in the last days of the war. Lost, dazed, not sure he had a home to return to. They took him to a cottage in the recently liberated city of Enschede. It was empty save for a lanky soldier writing letters at a desk. At the sight of Henk, he dropped his pen, ran to the kitchen, and soon returned with a steaming plate of food. Henk's eyes widened. Bully beef and potatoes. In the camp, he'd survived on boiled grass.

"You best cook ever," Henk said between forkfuls. The soldier laughed, said he was just an army truck driver. Henk cleaned the last bit of potato from his plate and struggled to get up. His hometown, Driebergen, was still far away, nearly one hundred miles on foot. It was unlikely he'd make it, he thought, but at least he'd die a free man. He stretched out his hand to thank his

213

chef. The Canadian hesitated, then pulled something from his uniform pocket.

"When you're tired and don't know if you'll make it, eat these," he said. "A little at a time to get yourself home."

Henk inspected the gift with trembling hands. Two chocolate bars in plain wrappers.

That's how my dad always told the story, ending with the two chocolate bars the Canadian soldier gave him. My five siblings and I heard it many times while growing up in Ontario. Dad never talked much about his life in the Netherlands. But he made sure we knew we were here because of the soldier he'd met in May 1945, two days before the war ended. Canada was where Dad wanted to live and raise a family because of the kindness he associated with its countrymen.

In 2013, at the age of ninety-three, Dad was stuck in a different kind of prison, his mind ravaged by Alzheimer's, the same disease that had taken Mom eight years earlier. It was only a matter of time, his doctor said. All I could do was pray that Dad would leave this world at peace.

The furniture store I worked at was in the middle of a big promotion, with sales on everything from dining room tables to ottomans. I sorted through a stack of brochures in preparation for another busy day. But I couldn't concentrate. I'd just visited Dad at the care facility. Now I couldn't get the image of him slumped in a wheelchair out of my mind. The light was gone from his eyes. He didn't acknowledge anyone. It had been weeks since he had last spoken to me.

The sound of customers broke me out of my trance. An elderly couple testing out leather recliners.

"Do you ship to Port Perry?" they wanted to know. The town where my husband and I lived. I walked over and introduced myself. George and Joyce Emmerson were looking for a new chair.

Joyce went back to examining different models. George was more interested in conversation.

"You know, I'm ninety-one years old," he said with a twinkle in his eye. "Still healthy as a horse, working in insurance!"

I couldn't help smiling. He had charm to spare, even at ninety-one. He said he'd lived in Port Perry all his life.

"You must know my husband Gordie's family, the Carnegies," I said.

"Gordie? His father's my cousin!" George said. "That makes us family."

How strange. We'd never crossed paths before. I would have remembered George. He wanted to know all about me. Where my family came from. When I told him that I was born in the Netherlands, his eyes lit up. He'd been stationed there and all over Europe during World War II.

"My father was a prisoner of war in Germany for most of the war," I said. "He practically starved to death, had to boil grass . . ."

George nodded. He'd seen droves of laborers and ex-prisoners wandering the roads at the end of the war, most of them just skin and bones.

"My buddy once brought a prisoner to the house where we were stationed," George said. "I'd never seen a man in such bad shape! I made him some bully beef and potatoes. I didn't know if he'd even make it out the door, poor fella. Before he left, I gave him some chocolate to take with him on the road."

"Chocolate?"

"Two chocolate bars. I remember it like yesterday. My parents had sent some from Ontario the week before."

I grabbed the back of a sofa for support, my head spinning. The Canadian soldier?

"George, that man . . . I think that man was my father."

The next time I paid Dad a visit, a kind veteran with twinkly eyes was waiting for us at a table in the cafeteria.

"Hi, Henk. Remember me?" he said.

Dad stared at George, not saying a word. I'd warned George not to get his hopes up. But he wasn't deterred. He held Dad's hand tight, reminisced about the war. Afterward, I brought Dad back to his room, kissed his cheek, and turned to leave. Maybe this reunion had come too late.

"Where did that man go?"

It was the voice I thought I'd never hear again. For a moment, the blank look on Dad's face was gone. There was a spark of something behind his eyes. A glimmer of recognition.

In the months before Dad died, he was unresponsive, didn't want to eat. Except, that is, when George would stop by to visit. George never showed up empty-handed. He always brought a treat Dad couldn't resist. Two chocolate bars.

Crash Landing

BARBARA WALKER

The door creaked, and my eyes snapped open. I sat bolt upright in bed. An old woman in a floor-length, white nightgown with lace trim hovered in the doorway, her wispy gray hair piled on top of her head in a bun, her pale blue eyes full of life. *Granny?*

My favorite grandmother. The one who lulled me to sleep when I was young with tales of her childhood in Ireland, told in her soft brogue. Back then Ireland was a far-off, magical land to me, a girl who hadn't seen much more than rural Pennsylvania. I never dreamed I'd find myself married to a military man, living halfway across the world on a US Army base in Bad Kreuznach, Germany. What was Granny doing here in my bedroom at two o'clock in the morning? She'd died fifteen years earlier.

I shook my head. Rubbed my eyes. Next to me, my husband, Frank, was out like a light. *It must be a dream.* I'd tossed and turned all night. Frank and I had moved to Germany three days after we were married. A year later, I had given birth to our son, Christopher. Now Frank's three-year assignment was nearing its end, and in a few hours, I'd be on a plane back home to the States. Frank was to follow us in six months. The thought of flying alone, just me and the baby, made me a nervous wreck. Now I was seeing things!

Granny tiptoed toward the foot of my bed. I clutched my blankets tighter.

"Everything's going to be all right, dear," she said. Her brogue made the words sound musical, like a lullaby. "Everything's going to be all right."

The next thing I knew it was morning. Only two hours to get Christopher ready and head to the airport in Frankfurt. I pushed the strange experience out of my mind.

The plane was a small, four-engine model, carrying military dependents only. Nine hours on a plane full of army wives and crying kids. That would be interesting. But I was so tired from lack of sleep that I laid Christopher across my lap on a pillow and dozed off.

The cabin was dark when I opened my eyes. Everyone was either sleeping or playing cards. Christopher snuggled in my lap. Such a good boy. I looked out the window. All at once an orange flash jumped from the right-side engine, the one closest to me.

That's not right. I glanced across the aisle at the other window. Another flash! What was going on?

A flight attendant passed by with an empty tray. I tugged on the sleeve of her uniform. "I think the engines are on fire," I whispered.

I pointed out the windows on either side. Her eyes widened. She put a finger to her lips. "Shhhh!"

She raced to the front of the plane. I could see flames now on both sides. Finally, a voice came over the PA.

"Attention all passengers, this is your captain speaking. We are experiencing some mechanical difficulties. Please stay seated and put your heads between your legs. If your child is on your lap, place your body over them."

The plane dipped. My stomach lurched. My seatmate made the sign of the cross. I held on to Christopher and did what the captain instructed. We were descending. Fast. I could feel the velocity.

"We will be making an emergency water landing," the captain announced. "Please remain calm."

Remain calm? What were the chances we'd even survive?

Then I heard it. The familiar Irish brogue spoken to me in those early morning hours. *Everything's going to be all right.* I relaxed. Closed my eyes. Took a deep breath. I believed those words. Believed God had sent them in a vision of my Irish granny.

The plane landed with a violent jolt. It bounced and skidded across the water and came to a stop. The flight attendant ushered us out of our seats to the emergency exit, where an inflatable slide and raft were waiting. I took off my shoes and slid down with Christopher securely in my lap. The cold ocean air hit me full force. I couldn't see a thing. All I could hear was the sound of choppy waves thrashing against the raft and the downed plane.

The passengers huddled together. Nobody talked. I should've been terrified. Instead, I was calm. Those words still played in my mind. *Everything's going to be all right.*

Finally, a ship appeared to take us to shore. "Thank you for your patience," the ship's captain said when we were all safely aboard. "A plane will be coming tomorrow from London to get you back to the States. In the meantime, we'll put you up in a hotel."

"Where are we, sir?" the woman next to me asked.

"Just off the coast of Ireland, near Shannon Airport."

Shannon, Ireland. The very place where Granny had been born.

Mrs. Joseph's Angel

CHARLOTTE HALE ALLEN

W hen everything's going wrong, sister," Mama used to advise me, "just stop what you're doing and scrub the kitchen or turn out a big washing. With that kind of job, you see results. It gets you going again."

That's why I'd hastily stripped the beds and gathered up damp towels that warm and gusty morning and headed very early toward the apartment complex laundry room. I hoped I'd see no one. I didn't feel like engaging in neighborly chitchat.

For days, it seemed, things had gone maddeningly wrong. My work, usually so satisfying, exasperated me. My closest friend seemed almost spoiling for a spat. The apartment needed cleaning, but I had little time. And now my throat felt scratchy.

Worst of all, my prayers seemed to bounce off the ceiling. I'd lost my joy, seemed headed into depression, and didn't know why. *No wonder God doesn't listen*, I thought. *My problems are so tacky they bore him. I wouldn't listen to me either!*

My self-pity lifted, however, when I discovered Mrs. Joseph, my downstairs neighbor and one of my favorite people in the world, already stuffing rose-colored tablecloths and flowered napkins into a machine. "Whatever did we do before permanent press!" she exclaimed by way of greeting.

Mrs. Joseph always delighted me. I loved everything about her—her flowered dresses, her exquisite shoes, the music that drifted out of her windows. Her apartment was exactly like mine but much more modern with white carpets, glass tables, and accents of hyacinth blue and chrome yellow. She was seventy-nine and independent and refused to live with any of her four middle-aged daughters.

Of course, she loved to go shopping with "the girls," take them to Bible study or to an art show. But live with one of them? Nonsense!

"I had twenty-four ladies from my church circle to tea," Mrs. Joseph explained. "My apartment is too small for that. Since old ladies like to sit down, I set up card tables. Had six tables and put a bud vase with a fresh rose on each one. It looked real pretty!"

"You're the hostess with the mostest," I smiled, my spirits rising.

"Honey, there are so many lonely people! You get to my age and everybody you know is widowed—or divorced—and they mope around to beat the band. Keep moving is the secret, keep moving. Every day find something worthwhile to do." She shook a tea towel vigorously and pitched it into the drier.

"You do get around," I said. "I hardly ever see you anymore. What are you doing these days, Mrs. Joseph?"

"Mostly I try to help Imogene. You did hear my daughter Imogene went blind last fall?"

"No!" I simply stared at her, horrified. Shock waves hit me, and I couldn't think of what to say.

"Thank God she's well taken care of," Mrs. Joseph answered slowly, her brown eyes filling with tears. "My girls inherited eye problems, you know. Two of them, Imogene and Rosemary, learned nearly three years ago that they might go blind."

My mind whirled as I considered the tragedy, wondering what I could offer my friend in the way of comfort. At last I asked tentatively, "Mrs. Joseph, do you believe God heals?"

"Honey, I *know* God heals," she answered firmly. "I never questioned that. These past three years he has answered our prayers in miraculous ways. The girls got right busy and learned Braille, learned to clean house from memory, studied the Bible, did everything they could in case they lost their sight. He helped them with all of it.

"You should see Imogene get around. She's a miracle in herself, her faith and cheerfulness. Yes, God heals!" She gazed at me for a moment, seeming to decide something. "When we first got the news," she confided, "the day we all had to accept that my two girls might go blind, I thought it would kill me.

"I cried most all night, then woke up the next day feeling so bitter. I felt cold, cold like after Mr. Joseph died. It didn't make a piece of sense to me! I said, 'Lord, I've had a lovely, lovely life, and now I'm old. Why couldn't it be me, Lord? Why Imogene? Why Rosemary?'

"That day I asked him just to take me on home. I cried real tears all morning, and it seemed like he didn't answer. Ah, it was a bitter time. I hurt till I thought it would kill me."

"How did you stand it?" I asked, deeply ashamed of my own paltry grumblings. "However did you stand it?"

She searched my face again, then replied with a question. "Do you believe in angels?"

"Yes, I do."

"Maybe you won't believe this, but that morning, so brokenhearted, I said, 'God, I can't even pray. You must help me with this.' You ever get where you just can't pray?" I nodded. "Well, he sent help. Honey, I heard an angel sing. It was 'Amazing Grace,' all the verses, sung over and over. It had to be an angel, 'cause there was nobody there, and it came from all over the apartment—verse after verse.

"When I heard that music, I knew we'd all stand it, no matter what. I knew God would bring us through. Now I'm old, but I'm not crazy. Do you believe I heard an angel?"

I knew exactly what she'd heard, but I couldn't say a word. I simply cried and hugged her and helped her gather her load of neatly folded linens. At the laundry room door, she paused and called back to me, "Honey, God won't do those things we can do for ourselves, but when we can't do another thing, he always sends help. Call on him and he'll answer you. Read Jeremiah 33:3!"

What was it she had heard? As I folded sheets and towels, I relived that day nearly three years earlier when Mrs. Joseph had anguished alone. I didn't know her then, of course, for it was the Saturday morning before I was to move into the apartment above hers. I'd been depressed that day too. The empty rooms echoed with loneliness. I'd brought shelf paper and cleaning supplies to busy myself as I waited for the telephone installer, but as the hours lengthened, I ran out of jobs to do. Outside, a misty rain had turned into a chilly drizzle. I sat on the floor of my newly carpeted dining room, fighting off the loneliness and near-despair.

What's the point of all this? I thought. *Why bother about moving, about cleaning this stupid apartment, about anything? Who cares?* At last I prayed—an honest, unadorned prayer. "God, I'm so tired of struggling. I'm so lonely. My life lacks meaning; it really doesn't matter to anyone. Help me. Please speak to me."

He spoke immediately with force and authority. "Get to your feet. Stand up. Walk through this apartment and claim it for me. Walk through every room and praise me for your health and strength and every good and perfect gift I have given you. Ask a blessing on every person who walks through these doors, who eats here, sleeps here, visits here." The impression, tremendously strong, could not be disobeyed. I did exactly as I was told. "Now do one more thing. Lift your voice to praise me in song in every room of this house."

Why not? Feeling bold and a little crazy, yet filled with joy, I walked through one room after another singing verse after verse of my favorite hymn, "Amazing Grace." Who cared, after all? There was no one else around to hear me. For fifteen or twenty minutes, I sang with all my strength.

Soon after, the phones were installed and I could leave. God had spoken to me in a very real way, and I had responded. Now I could depart in peace. The episode seemed finished.

Now I wondered, *Should I have told Mrs. Joseph the truth about the singing? And if so, what is the truth? Surely I'm no angel, and I certainly didn't sing like one. Or did I? What is the truth, God?*

At once Mrs. Joseph's words returned to my mind. "God always sends help when you need it. Don't ask him to do what you can do for yourself. Call on him . . . he will answer you."

The laundry basket, piled high, felt featherlight as I hurried upstairs, eager to walk again through my apartment. In the dining room, just thinking of the kind of God who'd use me as an angel, I laughed out loud.

I wondered if Mrs. Joseph could hear me laugh. I knew God did.

A Survivor's Song

DANIELLE ELISKA LYLE

T he French army had collapsed. The German Reich of Adolf
Hitler took over the north of the country, and the government
in the south was free in name only. In the town of Montluçon,
the factories were put to work for the German war machine. At
one of them, Ernest Armand Huss, Armand to his friends, kept
his head down and quietly performed his duties in the tool shop,
working on sonar devices for aircraft. Under Nazi occupation, it
was best to go unnoticed, especially for someone like him.

Born in 1922 in the Ivory Coast to an Ivorian mother and a
French father, Armand had left Africa for Paris at the age of
eight. His skin color wasn't an issue in French society. He went
to boarding school and then had a year of engineering courses.
After an apprenticeship at a car manufacturer, he was hired as
a toolmaker by the SAGEM factory in Montluçon, which had
shifted its resources to the war effort as the Nazis exerted control.

One night Armand and another young man worked late. Armand saw the other man planting unfamiliar devices around
the tool shop. He suspected the man was part of the French
Resistance, but he could do nothing to stop him. He wasn't

sure he wanted to. As the two men left for the night, the worker shook Armand's hand and with a meaningful look suggested that he not go to work the next day. Two hours later, the factory exploded.

Gestapo agents rounded up Armand and twelve others and took them to their headquarters for interrogation. Beaten and exhausted, the men were transferred to the prison La Mal Coiffée and locked together in a tiny, wretched cell. It was in those dark times that Armand's life purpose was revealed.

Fear and the anguished cries of other prisoners kept Armand awake at night. Every morning the Gestapo would enter the cell block and grab victims for torture—or the firing squad. As footsteps neared their cell, Armand and the others would hold their breath—afraid they'd be chosen next. Only when the heavy boots moved down the corridor did they exhale in relief.

One morning it was Armand's turn. The Germans hadn't forgotten that he had been one of the last to leave the factory the night the bombs went off. To them, a black man was barely human. They spared him nothing, brought their full sadistic arsenal to bear upon his weakened body. Yet he refused to give up the young man he'd shaken hands with that night.

For three weeks, Armand and his comrades were rotated from the cell to the torture chambers and back. The men were unsure they would make it another day, let alone see freedom again. Late one night, one of the prisoners, Pierre, spoke up. "We should each sing a song to break this silence that has us by the guts."

One man after another sang melodies they knew by heart. Armand hesitated. He'd never sung before, save for hymns he'd incanted at church as a child. He'd heard the story of Paul and Silas in Philippi. Savagely beaten and thrown into prison, they prayed and sang hymns to God. "Suddenly there was a great earthquake, so that the foundations of the prison were shaken," according to

Acts 16:26. The prison doors flew open and everyone's shackles were broken. If only such a miracle could happen now.

Armand wasn't sure what voice would emerge, but he looked at the weary faces of the men in the cell and sang "The Volga Boatmen," a popular Russian folk song about endless toil. He stumbled over the first few bars, but with each note, his deep voice filled the dank space with a melody that stirred the men's souls. When he finished, there was complete silence. His fellow prisoners stared at him in awe, then applauded.

Pierre rested his hand on Armand's shoulder. "I predict a great singing career for you, my friend!" That night a seed of desire was planted inside Armand—the hope of one day being set free and living another life.

Armand was sent to Neuengamme, a notorious concentration camp. He was one of a dozen or so black men grouped separately from the other prisoners in equally inhumane conditions. Starving inmates were forced to work twelve hours a day. But Armand's voice pierced the hopelessness and became a balm to him and countless others.

After the war, Armand began a new life. No longer a toolmaker. No longer even Armand. He adopted the name John William and won fame as a singer in France and around the world. For the twenty-fifth anniversary of his freedom, he was invited to sing at a televised mass. Overwhelmed by the experience, he devoted the rest of his career to singing spirituals. "These songs touch what is most sensitive in us," he wrote later. "No one can resist them. They are like a universal language. . . . I had discovered my true path."

PART 6

Divine Consolation

Jesus said to her, "I am the resurrection and
the life. He who believes in Me, though he may
die, he shall live. And whoever lives and believes
in Me shall never die. Do you believe this?"

JOHN 11:25–26

The Smile

LORRAINE STANDISH

That smile. If only I could see that smile again . . .

The colorless walls of the hospital waiting room closed in on me as I watched the minute hand creep around the clock. Three hours down. Two more to go. *Oh, Lord, this is torture*, I thought.

I leaned forward on the stiff couch in the corner of the room and leafed through the dog-eared, coffee-stained magazines that littered a table. Desperate for a distraction. Anything to take my mind off my husband, Myles, undergoing his third heart surgery in less than two years. But it wasn't just Myles. Another loved one haunted my thoughts. I flashed back to the day six years ago when the life of our daughter, Linda, came to a tragic, inevitable end.

I had been in a hospital just like this one. Those same suffocating beige walls closing in on me. The soulless beeping of the heart monitors in the ICU. And Linda lying there helpless, a swelling the size of a tennis ball on the back of her head. Clumps of dried blood still clinging to her scalp. The official cause of death was head trauma, but Myles and I knew the truth. She had passed out and fallen down the stairs, drunk before breakfast.

If I closed my eyes, if I pushed my memory, I could still see Linda as a happy girl. She had a smile that could make the grumpiest person smile too, like the sun bursting through the clouds. It was hard to pinpoint exactly when that smile began to disappear.

Linda started drinking in high school, maybe to fit in, maybe out of boredom or insecurity, maybe because of me and my history. I'd never know. She dropped out of college and went to rehab. One year later, she was carrying a thermos of vodka to work, "just in case." No recovery program—not even some time in prison—was enough to divert her from that dark, descending path she was on.

If anyone could understand where that path led, it was me. I knew those depths all too well. I'd been sober since Linda was a baby, but I'd never hidden my alcoholism from her. I told her what it was like and how I'd struggled until she was born. She'd even gone to AA meetings with me. But my salvation was not hers. The program just didn't take. By the time she was forty, Linda's liver was failing, and I'd stopped keeping count of the number of blood transfusions she'd had, the number of detoxes and rehabs.

"Mama, I'm going to get clean," Linda promised me a year before she died. "You wait and see. I'm going to be happy again."

I hugged her tight. "Okay, baby girl," I whispered, wishing I could believe her, wishing I could give her the desire to stop drinking.

The call I'd long dreaded finally came. Linda was in a coma. "There's too much alcohol in her system," the doctor said. "We couldn't operate even if it would help."

My beautiful, troubled daughter. Gone forever at age forty-five.

I stood up from the waiting room couch and began pacing, as if I could walk away from my memories. I twisted my hands together, wringing them. Out of the corner of my eye, I noticed a smaller room connected to the waiting area. I wandered toward it and found myself in a cramped, stuffy nook with even more magazines. One stood out. It practically shone—a bright yellow cover featuring lemon pie, my favorite dessert. "Spring Is Coming," the headline proclaimed, though sunny days were months away. I took a closer look. An issue of *Southern Living* magazine from five years before. But it looked brand-new! No creases, no stains, no wear at all, apparently.

It was so strangely well preserved that I couldn't resist flipping through it, pausing now and again to peruse a recipe. I found an article about Foley, Alabama, a city close to where Linda once lived.

All at once time stopped; the waiting room walls receded. It was just me and the magazine in my hands. I stared at an unmistakable image. There, on page thirty-two, in one of the photos from around town, was a young woman beaming as if lit from within. That smile. Those eyes, so full of life. Of love. Linda. She looked happy. Joyous. Free from the pain that clouded her life. I held the magazine to my chest, dazed yet comforted.

Myles got through his surgery just fine. I contacted *Southern Living*. They had never gotten Linda's name. They weren't sure when the photo was taken or what the circumstances were. They couldn't explain how a mint copy would show up after six years in a hospital waiting room. They did, however, send me a copy of the photograph. Every time I look at it, I take it as a reminder of the healing that awaits us all.

Pat's Cards

PEGGY HARTMAN

My best friend, Pat, made the most wonderful cards. Layers of colorful, textured paper, hand-drawn flowers, graphic cutouts, glittering rhinestones, and beautiful calligraphy. She never forgot an occasion. Not just my birthday and anniversary but also my children's and then my grandchildren's milestones. For me, the best part of any celebration was opening an envelope and seeing what wonder Pat had created this time.

Last year, Pat passed away after a long illness. Most of her card supplies were sold in a craft sale at our church in Nelsonville. I bought some items but didn't have time to do anything with them. *It's just as well*, I told myself. *It's not as if anyone else could ever make cards like Pat's.*

Not long afterward, my granddaughter Emma had her eighth birthday party at the Ohio Valley Museum of Discovery. She and her friends had fun making jewelry, playing games, and watching a puppet show.

I kept glancing at the stack of cards on the table by the presents and thinking about the one card that wouldn't be there. If only Pat could have been part of this. It just didn't seem like a celebration without her.

After Emma opened the presents, I was helping my daughter-in-law and some of the staff with the cleanup, gathering up the crumpled wrapping paper, when I spotted an unopened envelope still on the table. "Emma, dear," I said, "you missed a card."

Emma took the overlooked envelope and tore it open. The card was so much like one of Pat's! Handmade and beautifully decorated—right down to the rhinestones and calligraphy! But it was signed by someone named Tiffany.

Who?

My daughter-in-law introduced us. Tiffany was part of the museum staff. "Do you always make cards for the kids?" I asked her.

Tiffany smiled. "Not at all," she said, a note of surprise in her voice. "But I happened to buy all these amazing card-making supplies at a church craft sale in Nelsonville—glitter, glossy cutouts, textured paper. Somehow I just couldn't resist making a special card for Emma."

The Shepherd's Touch

ANGELICA SPRAKER VAN WIE

D o you believe that God still sends extraordinary signs to ordinary people—as he did so often in biblical times?

I do, and so do my family members and the neighbors who saw, with me, a tender—and extraordinary—expression of his love.

It came the spring after my mother's death. At seventy-six, she had been a peaceful great-grandmother, the calm, strong center of our big family network. Like my father two decades earlier, she died praising God, her faded blue eyes focused on wonderful things we couldn't see, murmuring, "Oh, it's beautiful, so beautiful."

As her oldest daughter, I had been "assistant mother" for the younger children, and that made Mother and me especially close. I grieved. But the faith that she had relied on—and nurtured in us—seemed to sustain me.

At least it did until we began, in April, to dismantle her old riverside homestead. The house had been closed for the winter, and my sister Catherine and I had set aside a few days to get organized before the appraisers came to evaluate the furnishings.

That first morning in Mother's house, an aching sorrow gripped me, the kind that's a long time coming and a long time going away.

As I moved through the familiar rooms with my dust cloth, mop, and broom, I felt as if I were saying good-bye over and over again. Everything I saw evoked memories. Here was the butler's pantry with cupboards big enough to hide a playful little girl. Here was the west parlor with the stern-faced portraits of our ancestors that had intimidated me as a child. Here was the front hallway with the burnished, curving banister that my fingers had traced as I'd come down the staircase as Charlie's nineteen-year-old bride.

Finally, I sat down on the steps, harshly shaken, as if I'd blundered into a closed door during the night. I'd expected to feel a warm closeness to Mother in this house where I'd grown up in her care. But instead, I felt cold, diminished, shorn.

So much about me—the way I raised my children and kept house, the way I made ginger cookies, husked corn, crossed my legs at the ankles—came from her. Mother's presence in my life affirming those similarities had been a kind of security blanket. Now that was gone.

The next few days working in the house with Catherine were agony. She noticed my low spirits, of course, and so did Charlie. Both tried, and failed, to comfort me.

On the afternoon we finished our chores, Catherine made a pot of tea, and we sat down together at the big, round table in the kitchen. I brooded there, chin in hand, filled with a dull, penetrating chill. *Dear Lord*, I wondered, *will I ever have those good, warm feelings again?*

Catherine leaned across the table and patted my cheek. "You look so miserable, and I don't know how to comfort you."

I shook my head and glanced around the room to avoid her sympathetic, questioning eyes. In a corner sat boxes and baskets filled with pictures, utensils, and bric-a-brac to be discarded. My eyes lighted on a dingy shape. And then a very odd command marched into my head: *Go and get it.*

For a moment, I stared and hesitated. What was this all about? I felt as if I were being pulled. Slowly I went over and picked up the object. It was a little statue of a lamb and a mother sheep curled up together, shoulder to shoulder—the mama with her head raised high in a proud, protective way and her baby cuddled close, looking safe and loved. I brought it back to the table and sat down to study it. The bare plaster form was dull with grime.

Catherine had been watching me with puzzlement. "What's so interesting about that?"

I did not have the faintest idea. My voice said, "Are we throwing it out?"

"Why, yes, I thought we would. It's just an old knickknack that's been in the spare room ever since I can remember."

I turned it over. It was hollow and had no identifying mark inside.

Take it home and care for it, came the urging.

"I guess I'll keep it," I muttered, realizing how foolish it must have seemed.

That night, using a soft brush, I gently scrubbed the little animal mold in a pan of warm water and soapsuds and rinsed it carefully. The curlicues of plaster fleece were too ingrained with dust for me to get them completely white, but the sheep and lamb figures looked much brighter. Feeling a strange stirring in my spirit, I put the statue on the dining room table and went to bed.

About six the next morning, Charlie and I went downstairs together. He opened the front door to go out on the porch for the newspaper. With a vague sense of anticipation, I went on toward the kitchen, noticing the just-awakened stillness of the new day, the fragile sunlight filtering through my lace curtains, the mellow chime of the mantel clock. As I passed through the dining room, I glanced at the statue on the table. I blinked and stood stock still.

The lamb and the ewe were covered with snowy fleece.

Dimly, I was aware that Charlie had paused beside me. "What's the matter?"

Silently, I pointed.

I heard him draw a breath. I felt his fingers close around mine. At last we touched the fluff-covered animals. Their covering felt exactly like wool. It was perfectly contoured around the heads, muzzles, bodies, and bobtails.

I'm not sure how long we stood there staring at the soft, implausible mantle of whiteness that had transformed the sheep. But I do remember the understanding that came, haltingly, into my mind. Now, just as before my mother had died, I was wrapped in God's miraculous, enfolding love. *That* was the continuing presence in my life, as it had been in hers . . . as it would be throughout the lives of my children. No death could deprive me of *his* comfort and protection.

"The Lord is my shepherd," I whispered. I felt the welcome warmth of tears on my cheeks.

During the next few days, many people saw the little statue— our children, our neighbors, some of our close relatives. Then the fleece crumbled into dust and vanished.

In the years that followed, my sons and daughters blessed me with six grandchildren, and recently, a great-grandson arrived. Sometimes one or another of them will remember the story of the little statue and ask, "Do you think it was a chemical reaction, Mother?" or "Did someone play a trick on you, Nannie?"

I just smile. For I know that the Shepherd tends his sheep in wonderful, extraordinary ways.

Grandma Anita

DEBBIE BADANO

Noah!" I yelled. Could my five-year-old son even hear me over the crashing waves and the noisy buzz of the Labor Day crowds on Oxnard Beach? "Noah!"

I ran across the sand, my heart racing, weaving through a forest of beach umbrellas and sunbathers. Every few feet I stopped to ask, "Has anyone seen my little boy? He's got dark hair and blue eyes. He's three feet tall and wearing camo trunks." No one had. I looked up toward the road at the bike riders and skaters zooming by.

What if Noah had wandered off the beach and somebody had lured him into a car? He could be miles away by now.

Normally, I wouldn't have let my son out of my sight. Today, though, we were with our extended family. It was our first big outing together since my husband's mother, Noah's beloved grandma Anita, had passed away two months earlier. With all the extra eyes around to keep watch, my husband and I had felt secure in running back to the car for some beach toys Noah had forgotten. We had returned to find our twenty-three-year-old daughter, Tawny, near hysterics. Her husband, Jeff, was trying to calm her.

"He was right there playing in the sand," Tawny said with a sob. "I turned around for only a second, and then, when I turned back, he was gone!"

We called the police and split up to comb the beach and the surrounding neighborhoods. At first I told myself not to worry. Noah ran like the wind, but he never went far. *Maybe he's scared and hiding*, I thought. *He'll come out if he just hears a familiar voice.* I'd taught Noah never to talk to strangers and to approach only a police officer or someone he knew and trusted if he got lost.

Five minutes turned into ten. Then twenty. I was growing frantic. *Lord, please protect Noah.*

I heard my cell phone ring. It was Tawny.

"Noah's all right," she said. "Jeff found him on the street walking back to the beach with two elderly ladies."

I almost fainted with relief. I found our family gathered around Noah, but the two good Samaritans had just left.

"They told us they knew somebody had to be searching for him," Jeff said, "but he wouldn't say a peep. Until one of them introduced herself. She told him he could call her Grandma Anita."

Number 75

RIKI LAMBRIGHT

A blur of purple-and-white jerseys surrounded the coach on the middle school football field. The Granger Lions. I sat in my car in the parking lot waiting for my twelve-year-old son, Joseph, to finish practice. It was his first year on the team, and I couldn't have been more proud. Joseph was tall and confident, with wavy brown hair just like his father's. He was going to be a linebacker. *If only his father could see this*, I thought.

Two years earlier, my husband, Kelly, had died suddenly. He'd been a linebacker himself on the high school football team. We hadn't gone to the same school. He'd lived more than two hundred miles away, but we'd met on a camping trip the summer before our sophomore year, and soon those two hundred miles meant nothing.

I got to see him play only once, when I visited his town. I sat in the bleachers with his parents and cheered him on like crazy. Even after all these years, I could still picture how strong and handsome he looked when he took off that helmet, his jersey mud-streaked and grass-stained from sacking the quarterback

242

or tackling a runner behind the line. It was so dirty you could barely read his number.

Kelly had taught Joseph how to throw and catch a football. He'd encouraged our son to go out for the team when he got old enough. Soon Joseph would play his first real game. Without Kelly. Without his dad. Without my husband. I could only pray that his young heart would feel a moment of relief from the deep pain.

Practice ended. The boys ran to the locker room to change out of their pads and into street clothes. Five minutes later, Joseph came out and hopped into the car.

"How was it?" I asked, forcing a smile. I pulled out of the parking lot and turned toward home.

"Good. We got our practice jerseys today," Joseph said. "Coach gave me a number I really like. I hope I get it for my game jersey too."

"What number is that?" I asked.

"Number seventy-five."

I nearly stopped the car. "Joseph, do you know whose number that was?"

My son had no idea. The coach hadn't known either. But when Joseph ran onto the field for his first game as linebacker for the Lions, his official game jersey was blessed with his father's number, seventy-five.

The Image on the Mirror

JANIS HEAPHY DURHAM

My husband, Max, died at 12:44 p.m. on a sunny Saturday in May surrounded by friends and family in the living room of our Sacramento home. His last breaths were labored. He lay on a narrow hospital bed, his emaciated body propped up to face the patio doors so he could feel the warmth of the sun. I held his hand gently—gently because it felt like all bone, not the hand that had held mine with such strength for the past five years—and read from the twenty-third psalm. "He makes me to lie down in green pastures; He leads me beside the still waters."

A lovely melody suffused the room, tones so resonant and deep they could have been coming from one of Max's classical CDs. I turned and saw the heavy wind chimes over the patio swaying. But the air was still. Not a breath of wind at all. There was no breath from Max either. His hand fell from mine. He was gone.

In late November, Max had received the diagnosis: esophageal cancer, late stage. He didn't want to die in a hospital. We'd made him as comfortable as we could at home.

We'd sit overlooking our yard and talk. About Tanner, my son from my first marriage, whom Max treated as his own. About music, good food and wine, philosophy—his passions. About the trips we'd taken, like the one to Auberge du Soleil, a resort in Napa Valley where he'd first told me he loved me. These things were easier to talk about than the future. I was fifty-three. I'd thought we'd grow old together. Now? "It's easier for me," Max said one day. "It will be harder for you because you are being left behind."

"I don't know what I'll do," I said.

"I will still be here," he insisted. "My love will never die. It's immutable."

What did Max mean? He'd never talked like that. I was the daughter of a Presbyterian minister, but Max was an agnostic. The twenty-third psalm was music to him, not Scripture. The idea that anything but a memory of someone could survive death didn't appeal to his sense of reason. I couldn't fault him for it. His intellectual rigor was one thing that had attracted me to him.

I'd met Max in 1999, a year and a half after I'd moved to Sacramento to become the publisher of the *Sacramento Bee*, one of California's largest and most respected newspapers. I was divorced and had a nine-year-old son. I didn't have time for love. Then Max invited me to a meet and greet event held by the political consulting firm he worked for. I declined—obvious conflict of interest for the newspaper—but agreed to a friendly lunch.

He was a true Renaissance man: an Air Force vet, a mathematician, an accomplished chef, a former college weight lifter. He played trumpet and piano and had even written his own symphony. He read at least a book a week. He astonished me.

Eight months later, we were married. Max, Tanner, and I built a home together, a life. Two weeks before our fourth wedding anniversary, we discovered that that life was nearing an end.

In his final months, Max spent a great deal of time with our friend and his caretaker, Helen. He'd insisted that I continue working, so Helen was there when I couldn't be. One day she revealed the strangest thing. The two of them were in the kitchen when there was a brief sun shower. "We both stopped and looked," Helen said. "I told him, 'I know you don't believe in God, but this is something God created for us today. If you can find a way, let us know there's something out there, that it doesn't just end.'"

"I will," Max said. "But it will be up to you two to see it."

Max said that? I believed in heaven, as my father had understood it, a faraway place filled with love. Max never did. But the nearer death drew, the more cautiously open he became to the notion that there could be more, as if a force stronger than his reason was reaching through to him. He spoke with less certainty about the end. The day before he died, weak and fading, he asked for directions. "Where, Max?" I asked, confused.

"To the place I'm going," he explained.

The afternoon Max died some friends took Tanner. I waited for the funeral home staff. I retreated to the master bathroom to try to compose myself. I flipped on the light, but the bulb above the sink had burned out. "I thought these things were supposed to last forever," I grumbled.

We held Max's funeral at a church in downtown Sacramento. A friend conducted the service, and people filled the pews. Tanner and the other pallbearers carried Max's coffin to the front of the sanctuary. I was set to follow behind with my brother and sister-in-law. *Will I make it through this?* I wondered. *Will I fall apart?*

Suddenly, a sound boomed through the sanctuary. A heavy door to an anteroom had slammed shut. No one was near it. It shocked me out of the downward spiral I was in.

Only back home did I think about the music of the chimes on that windless afternoon. The burned-out bulb. The slamming door. What was going on? The newspaperwoman in me said, "Nothing at all." A flying bird could have brushed the chimes. We hadn't changed the bathroom bulb since we'd moved in. A draft in the church could have slammed the heavy door. Max had been logical to a fault. He would have guffawed at "signs" like these.

It was grief that made me notice more little things. Lights flickering when it wasn't even stormy. Noises coming from the guest bedroom, where Max had slept for most of the last month. One morning I returned home after taking our yellow Lab for a walk and glanced up at the large clock over our fireplace. It should have read eight o'clock. Instead, the hands had stopped—at 12:44.

Father's Day. Tanner was with his dad. I was home alone listening to Celine Dion's "Because You Loved Me," the song we'd played at Max's funeral. I felt agitated. I wandered into the library, full of Max's books. I randomly pulled one from the shelf. An envelope fell to the floor. On the front was a woman's handwriting. It was a card from Max's mother from Father's Day the year before. "I've never seen you this happy in your life," she'd written. "It's because you have a family."

I could explain any one of these things, but all of them together? I decided to keep a list of every odd incident, weird feeling, and comforting coincidence. Maybe if I saw everything on paper, I'd begin to make sense of them.

I gave away most of Max's possessions, because that was what he had wanted, but it felt like giving away parts of him. His albums and books I donated to the library. His clothes and shoes I gave to Goodwill, saving a few favorite ties and shirts for Tanner. The least important things were the hardest to deal with. His round, tortoiseshell glasses, his worn, black-leather wallet, a tiny hairbrush that he used every morning. They seemed to bear his imprint, his touch. I was beginning to forget what it felt like back when his hands were still strong, when he held mine in his.

Tanner and I didn't plan anything for the first anniversary of Max's death. Just a quiet day at home. We sat at a table in the backyard; I caught up on work, Tanner read a book. After a while,

I went inside to make us a snack. On the way to the kitchen, I paused at the doorway of the guest bedroom suite. Something drew me inside. I turned toward the bathroom and flipped on the light.

On the mirror was a handprint.

It was no ordinary handprint. Not something revealed by the steam of a shower or left behind by someone's greasy fingers. It was made of a soft, powdery substance and perfectly formed. I could see every fingerprint, every crease, the life line and the love line. It showed all the facets of bone structure, like an X-ray. I'd combed my hair in front of that mirror just hours before. The hand hadn't been there.

I shouted for Tanner. He came running. "What's wrong, Mom?" He saw it too. It wasn't just my imagination.

"You didn't do this, did you?" I asked.

"No," he said. He held his hand up to the mirror. It was so small in comparison. "Where did it come from?"

I didn't have an answer, any reasonable explanation. But I knew whose hand it was. The same hand I'd held a year earlier, except this was the way I preferred to remember it. The hand that had once pressed the keys of a piano and thumbed through the books in our library. Max's hand.

I got my camera and took a picture, afraid the image would fade. But it didn't. It remained until that Wednesday, when Helen came to clean the house. "Do you want me to leave it there?" she asked, astounded.

I did, but it was time to say good-bye. Max had already given me enough to hold on to, just as he'd promised—if only we were willing to see.

Buxtehude

DONNA SWONKE

Growing up, my two boys, Chase and Shaun, spent a lot of time with their German grandfather, Opa. He would welcome them to his house with a twinkle in his eye and the promise of adventure. He might take them fishing, hiking, bird-watching—they never knew. "Where are we going today, Opa?" they'd beg to be told.

"Buxtehude!" he would practically shout.

In real life, Buxtehude is a pretty town that sits on the Este River in northern Germany, but for generations in my family, its name has symbolized a kind of wonderland. "Buxtehude is where dogs bark with their tails," Dad told me when I was little. I pictured a magical place where dogs frolicked and joy abounded. A bit like heaven, I guess, to a little girl.

But as the boys got older, the idea of Buxtehude faded, as if obscured by darkening clouds. My younger son, Chase, broke his neck in a high-school lacrosse game. The resulting paralysis left him in a wheelchair. He still had some movement in his arms but little in his hands. Chase was determined to stay active. He still believed in Buxtehude, I suppose. He joined a wheelchair users' group that went fishing and did other outdoor activities together. He took college classes and even had a truck specially outfitted so he could drive.

One morning Shaun, a volunteer firefighter at the time, woke my husband and me before dawn. "My chief is downstairs," he said, his voice quavering. "Chase was in a wreck. He didn't make it."

I felt a part of me die just then too. Chase had held on so tightly to life after his injury. As if a defense mechanism had kicked in, I threw myself into practical details: notifying friends and family, making sure we donated Chase's organs, arranging the funeral. The telephone had rung right after Shaun had given us the terrible news, but we hadn't picked up. Hours later, my husband checked our voice mail. The message was only a few seconds long, but when he listened, his jaw dropped. "What is it?" I asked.

He handed me the phone.

It was Chase's voice. Chipper. Excited, even. He said only one word, one beautiful word: Buxtehude.

PART 7

Ask and You Shall Receive

And my God shall supply all your need according to His riches in glory by Christ Jesus.

PHILIPPIANS 4:19

Not Tomorrow, Today!

CHRISTY CALDWELL

*B*eans and rice again. Can't really blame the kids for not cleaning their plates, I thought, scraping off the dishes into the sink. I was sick and tired of having the same thing night after night too. It was cheap and filled our bellies, but each sad supper made me feel emptier inside.

"Lord, we're really struggling here," I prayed. "I want some real food. Not tomorrow, Lord. Today!"

Five years earlier my husband had gotten a job in the oil fields and we had moved from Kentucky to Texas with our three children. Then the oil boom went bust, and there were mass layoffs. We were trying to get by on the hourly wages my husband made doing maintenance work.

I didn't know anyone I could turn to for help. I'd started going to church and joined a prayer group, but it had been only a few weeks.

Will things ever get better? I was tired of waiting. Frustrated, I plunged the plates into the soapy water. "Lord, real food. Not tomorrow, today. Please!"

That was silly, I thought. What was it they said in church? All in God's time, not when we want it.

Just as I finished the dishes, there was a knock at the door. I glanced at the clock. Almost nine. Who would be visiting this late?

It was Tico, the husband of Elvira, a woman I'd met at the prayer group. In his hands was a big platter wrapped in foil. "I'm sorry for bothering you so late," he said.

I told Tico it wasn't a problem.

"We were having a cookout at our daughter's house down the street," he explained. "A lot of food was left over, and we thought maybe you could use some of it."

He loosened the foil. There had to be four pounds of barbecued brisket, plus fresh, sliced tomatoes, lettuce, and bread.

My eyes went wide. "Thank you! You have no idea how much I needed this tonight."

"I thought we should wait until tomorrow to bring this over to you, late as it is," Tico replied. "But Elvira insisted. She said, 'No, not tomorrow. Today.'"

The Wrong Turn

MARK ANDREWSKY

L eft or right? A dizzying flurry of snowflakes danced in my headlights, blanketing the road in either direction. I strained to make out the double yellow lines and the edges of the pavement. I hadn't even left the parking lot of the wine shop where I worked, and already I worried about getting stuck. *I should have stayed home*, I thought. *Should have listened to the warnings.*

It was January 2014. All the weather guys had talked about lately was the "polar vortex," whatever that was. Normally, the snowstorms that blew off Lake Ontario into Prince Edward County didn't faze me. A native of Montreal, I knew how to get around in a blizzard.

That Saturday was my day to open and run the wine shop by myself, and I didn't want to let down my boss. I left home well before 9:00 a.m., but my usual route, cutting through fallow farmland via Benway Road, was already covered in snow and ice. My ten-minute drive turned into a nerve-racking half-hour odyssey.

All day not a single customer came in. Snow piled up outside. I thought I could distract myself with my cell phone, but I'd forgotten it at home. Dumb.

With no customers in sight, I called my boss on the landline. He told me to head home right away. At 2:00 p.m., I closed up shop, trudged across the parking lot through the deepening snow, and climbed into my SUV.

Left or right? The way I'd come or the parkway? I blasted the heater while I weighed my options. By now, the back roads would be impassable. The parkway wasn't the shortest route, but it was the only road I could depend on to be plowed. I wasn't taking any unnecessary risks. I put on my right blinker.

I looked both ways. No other cars were on the road. I tightened my grip on the steering wheel, eased my foot off the brake, and tapped the gas. The back tires skidded, the SUV swerved forward, and I turned the wheel—to the left.

Left? I wanted to go right. What was going on? Did the car turn itself? Left would take me to the back roads, not the parkway. Right, not left. Making a U-turn now, though, on the snow-packed road would be way too risky. I could get stuck. Before I knew it, I'd reached the turn onto Benway Road.

Through the windshield, I saw nothing but a white field ahead. There was no clear indication of where the road was, only a few spots here and there where a scraggly bush poked through. I inched forward. The snow swallowed my SUV's tires. A few more meters, and I shook my head. Even all-wheel drive was no match for this. I knew the parkway was the only way. Why had I turned left? Dumb.

I put the car in reverse and hit the gas. The SUV lurched backward, then stopped. I shifted into drive and tried to rock forward. The car didn't budge. I hit the gas once more, really gunned it. The tires just spun.

I was stuck. And in a terrible spot. These farms were practically abandoned this time of year. It would be a long walk to find help. *I have to dig myself out.*

I zipped my jacket tight against the freezing wind and waded out into the drifting snow. I crouched by each of my tires and, with my gloved hands, scooped out the snow packed tightly around the wheel wells.

After finishing the last tire, I stood up, exhausted and breathing heavily. I stared across the featureless white landscape, featureless except for one thing. There was a dark object in the distance. It couldn't be a bush—it was right in the middle of the road. A stray scarf? Something that had fallen out of someone's pickup? Maybe it was just a garbage bag.

The warm SUV beckoned. But my curiosity wouldn't let me go. I sensed by its shape that the object was something substantial. I stumbled through the snow, my eyes trained on the spot.

Once I was closer, I made out buttons and pockets. Someone's lost winter coat. I took the last few steps and bent down, then jumped back in horror. It was a winter coat all right, only someone was inside. Frantically, I brushed the snow away.

The pale face of an elderly man stared up at me.

"Are you okay?" I asked. The man's skin was nearly as white as the snow, but he was still breathing.

"I fell," he said, his voice raspy. "I didn't think anyone would come."

He was on his way home from getting supplies, he told me, when his car got stuck. He tried to walk the rest of the way but slipped on the ice and injured his hip. He was in rough shape.

I tried to lift him. He was too heavy. I ran to my SUV, grabbed an extra blanket, and wrapped it around his shoulders.

"I'll be back for you, I promise," I said, silently berating myself for leaving my cell phone at home. "Just hang on!"

I ran back to the SUV and hopped in. *Don't get stuck, don't get stuck.* I hit the gas, and the tires gripped the road. I was off.

I returned to the store, unlocked it again, and called 911, giving the old man's location. Then I drove back to Benway Road.

The snow was even deeper than before, but I made it all the way to the man without getting stuck. I sat and held him while we waited for the ambulance to arrive.

Twenty minutes later, a snowplow rumbled up the road, the paramedics following behind.

"He's going to be all right," one medic told me as they lifted the man into the ambulance. "He's lucky you found him."

"No kidding," said the plow operator. "I wasn't planning to come out here until after dusk. No one else is out on these roads. Nothing's worth driving for in this."

That's what I'd thought too. Then I'd turned left. As it turned out, for a good reason.

An Apartment for Rent

GINGER LLOYD

Ever since my husband, Ricardo, had lost his job and we'd lost our home, I'd said the same prayer every day. *Lord, help us find an apartment.* I wanted an apartment with lots of light, a new kitchen, and a clean, fully tiled bathroom. Outdoor space, like a balcony, would be nice too, but I knew that was asking way too much. A decent place would do.

Ricardo didn't believe in prayer. But he didn't have any other answers. We were renting part of a rundown house in Rockford, Illinois, not ideal conditions to raise our eight-year-old son. It was dark and cramped, the floors cold and bare. The kitchen appliances were constantly breaking down, and there was no storage for our things. The shared bathroom was filthy. But there was nothing else in the area that we could afford. Then I found mouse droppings and roaches. I'd had it. Walking back from doing errands one day, dreading returning to our squalid little space, I cried, "Lord, we can't live like this! Where is the apartment I've been praying for?"

Turn here and go up two blocks.

The voice popped into my head so suddenly, so strongly that I didn't question the thought. I turned and walked. At the end of the second block, the voice spoke again. *Turn right and go up three more blocks.* I obeyed.

The house I came to was nothing special, but that urgent voice commanded me, *Walk up to the door. Ask about the apartment.*

What apartment? I didn't see a for rent sign. But I'd come this far. I knocked, and a young woman answered.

"Do you know where I can find an apartment for rent?" I asked.

Her eyes widened. "How did you know? We didn't even list it yet." From inside, her husband asked who was at the door. "Someone about the apartment," she said. The man appeared, puzzled, but offered to show it to me.

Light cascaded through the windows and across the carpeted floor. Brand-new appliances gleamed in the kitchen. There were plenty of closets. The tile in the bathroom sparkled. "How much is the rent?" I asked tentatively.

"How much can you afford?" the man asked. I told him. "That'll do."

Ricardo couldn't believe it. "You found it how?" I told him about the voice, the commands, how the apartment had every detail I'd prayed for. With each thing I mentioned, the expression on his face shifted from disbelief to a dawning belief—especially when I added, "Actually, it has more than I asked for. There's even a balcony."

Surprise at Sunrise

BETTY HEAD

From far away came a terrifying noise. As I realized it was the alarm, I groaned. How could it be four o'clock already?

It was Easter morning, and I was in charge of the outdoor sunrise service at our church, Emmanuel Methodist. My long-suffering husband and I bundled our three small sons into the car and drove to the church.

A pantomime of the events between the Last Supper and the resurrection was quite an undertaking, involving a cast of almost thirty teenagers and young adults and tons of props. Two months of rehearsal were behind us. I was so tired that the back of my neck felt like fire. I knew the others were just as tired.

What if no one comes? I wondered as I entered the dark building. *What if the choir doesn't show up? What if* . . . I stopped myself. I closed my eyes and whispered for the last time the brief prayer that had been repeated by all of us in the past few weeks.

"Father, just use us. Let the people see *your* hand in this."

I heard laughter outside, and two teenagers came in, reporting they had forgotten their thongs. Then everyone seemed to come in a rush. I went from group to group, going over their cues.

Somewhere in this confusion, we discovered that no one had been asked to supply the sound effects when it came time for the cock to crow. Panic-stricken, I searched out each cast member, begging for someone to imitate a rooster. Under different circumstances, those rooster auditions would have been hilarious. But now they were merely frustrating. The only passable crower in the group was a choir member who would be in full view of the audience.

I sneaked a peek outside. The churchyard was full. An audience like that, and no rooster!

I saw the minister taking his place as narrator. This was his first church, and he was as nervous as I. He motioned for the cast to take their positions. Too late now to find a rooster. The young man who was to portray Christ passed me. He was a new convert, and his face was as white as his robe. I tried to smile, the service started, and the rooster was forgotten.

I watched from behind the church door as the characters began to move silently in accordance with the passage of Scripture being read. Somehow in the first light from the sun, the words took on a new reality. The stillness felt actually holy.

When the boy portraying Peter bent to warm his hands at our small fire, I remembered the rooster. I hoped fervently that the minister would not pause at the passage. The words came clearly: "And immediately, while he yet spake, the cock crew" (Luke 22:60 KJV).

The young minister's rich voice faltered, his hands holding the Bible shook, and even the crowd caught its breath when it happened. Faintly, yet ever so distinctly, from the direction of the city limits, came the crow of a rooster heralding the dawn. Into the silence came the cry—once, twice, three times!

The cast members were stunned. The minister recovered and went on. There was no time to speak to one another, but there was an awareness in the air, like electricity. Had God performed a little miracle just for us?

The rest of the service was like a dream. Each actor who came off whispered, "Did you hear the rooster?" As the closing hymn died away, the audience began to buzz, "Did you hear the rooster?"

During the following week, the word spread throughout the community. "You should've been at the sunrise service. When the preacher came to the verse where the rooster crowed, one did—three times! It was . . . well . . . like a miracle."

With all the gigantic problems and needs of our world, this experience may seem trivial. But I wonder, doesn't God work in small as well as in big events? I think he does, for exciting things have happened to people in our church. As for me, I have come to look for God's hand in the little things of each day.

My Hidden History

DIANE GOSHEFF

My eyes scanned the faces on page after dusty, yellowed page. Stacks of yearbooks lay open in front of me on a large oak table at the Washington Memorial Library in Macon, Georgia. No sign of the man I was looking for. Thud. The head librarian dropped off another stack and adjusted his wire-frame glasses. "I warned you what you were up against," he said. I'd driven five hours from Florida to this library for what, exactly? To find my biological father . . . or to make up for not finding my mother before it was too late?

For most of my life, I didn't even know their names. The adoption records were sealed, and my parents, the ones who raised me, never really talked about it. I didn't know the details until 1982, when I was thirty-eight years old and married, with children of my own. Mom decided it was time to show me the adoption decree. There it was: Martha Smith, my birth mother's name. My father was still unknown.

I made phone calls, dug around, contacted the hospital in Miami where I had been born. But Martha Smith was a pretty common name. I was at a loss, and raising my family took all my time.

Fourteen years later, I looked up—the kids were grown, life was manageable. Now was the time to find my birth mother. A friend at church had a son who was a private investigator. He tracked down my Martha Smith in two days.

Just like that, I had her number. She lived in Hampton, Georgia, with a daughter. I took a deep breath before dialing, going over the questions I'd rehearsed since I'd first learned I was adopted. A woman answered with a raspy "Hello?"

My words tumbled out. "I think you're the woman who gave me up for adoption on November 16, 1944, in Miami. Am I correct?"

It was an eternity before she spoke. "Oh, honey! The Lord has let me live long enough to hear from you."

I'd written all my questions on a yellow legal pad, the things I'd always wanted to know. But Martha's health was failing. Her answers were slow and sapped her energy. I was on her mind a lot these days, she said. So was Curtis, my biological father. I put down the legal pad and listened.

They met in 1943 at a USO dance in Miami. "Curtis grew up on a farm outside Macon," she said. "And, oh, Diane, he was the nicest man in the world. I loved him so much." But they weren't meant to be. Martha was married to another soldier fighting overseas.

They kept the pregnancy a secret and broke off the relationship after I was born. They hadn't spoken since, but she'd heard he still lived in Georgia. She promised to tell me more the next time we talked.

We never did. Martha died shortly after that phone call. I hadn't even asked my father's last name.

My half sister, Maddie, invited me up to Hampton to help sort through our mother's belongings. It felt strange to handle the things she'd cherished without having met her. Tucked away in her desk, I found a worn, sepia-colored photograph of a soldier.

Maddie had no idea who it was, but I did. His crescent-shaped eyes matched my own.

I'd been too late to meet one of my parents. I couldn't make that mistake again. My private investigator friend showed the photograph to every veterans' group in central Georgia but came up empty.

Undaunted, I looked up a library in Macon and called to test the waters—how hard would it be to track down someone with just a first name and a photograph? "Impossible," the librarian said. "There are hundreds of men named Curtis in the state. The few details you have are not nearly enough."

I filed the photo away. Every so often a voice would implore me, *Find him. Find him now.* I kept resisting with a three-word refrain of my own: *It's too late.* After six years, the voice reached a crescendo. I'd uncovered no new information. Who knew if he was still alive? But the voice wouldn't give way. *Find him now. Find him now.* On my drive to work, in church, at the dinner table, those three words played over and over like a song stuck in my head.

Now here I was in this library, searching old yearbooks, hoping to find a photo that matched the one I had of my father. The librarian left me to look through the new stack but stopped back around lunchtime to check my progress. He had a young man with him.

"I'd like you to meet Chris, one of our assistants," the librarian said. "His family has lived in Macon for decades. I thought he could help."

Chris picked up the photograph of my father. Studied it. "I'll make a copy and ask around," he said.

That night in my hotel room, I tried to psych myself up for another day on the hunt. There were four other libraries in Macon. The thought of more dust and disappointment made my head spin. *C'mon, Curtis. Where are you?*

The phone rang. It was Chris from the library.

"Diane, I hope you're sitting down," he said. "My dad recognized the soldier in the photograph—Curtis Jackson, a cousin. I guess that makes us related."

The next morning at ten o'clock sharp, I drove to the last address Chris's dad had for Curtis. I'd waited more than fifty years to meet him. I couldn't wait any longer.

I knocked on the door. Nothing. I walked to a neighbor's house. No one seemed to be home. How could I turn back when I was so close? I remembered seeing the name Jackson on a mailbox at the house down the road. I drove there and knocked. A middle-aged woman answered.

"I'm looking for Curtis Jackson," I said. "I'm an old family friend. Do you know where I might find him?"

"Well, yes, ma'am, he's right in there," she said, pointing inside the house. "I'm his daughter-in-law. He's staying here while he recovers."

Curtis had been the picture of health until a few months before, she explained. Now he went for dialysis three times a week. "He's been holding on," she said.

She led me to the family room. He was sitting in a blue recliner. So different from the man in the photograph. So frail.

He looked up. His face was weathered. But his eyes? They lit up.

I knelt beside his chair. "My name is Diane. I was born in 1944 in Miami. Martha told me about you. . . . I've waited a very long time to meet you."

His eyes filled with tears. Then he reached for my hand and held on tight.

"I've been waiting for you too."

The Only Brother I've Got

LINDA SILFIES

The telephone jolted me awake. It took me a few seconds to gather my wits. I'd been sitting at my computer watching an episode of my favorite show, *CSI*, but I must've dozed off.

I glanced at the clock. Midnight. *Who would be calling me at this hour?* I wondered.

I grabbed the phone. "Hello?" I said. Too late. The caller had hung up.

According to the caller ID, it was a Pennsylvania cell phone, one I didn't recognize. Probably a misdial.

I sat back down in my chair to shut off my computer, but I couldn't stop thinking about that call. *Should I call back?* I wondered. I decided to look in my address book to see if the number belonged to anyone I knew.

Finally, I found a match—my brother, Pete.

Pete and I hadn't spoken in almost a year. Not since our mother's funeral. There hadn't been any falling out between us, but we'd never been that close, and our lives were so different.

My brother was a long-haul truck driver and loved being on the road, traveling all throughout the Northeast. I was more of a homebody, living in Jacksonville and pursuing a journalism degree.

"Call your brother," Mom always urged me. "Keep in touch. You know he's the only brother you have."

"Well, what about *him*?" I'd respond. "He can call me too."

"Two wrongs don't make a right," was Mom's retort.

Mom had died exactly one year ago, I realized. Maybe that's why my brother was calling. Tentatively, I dialed the number.

My brother picked up right away. "Oh, I was just going to call you back," he said.

"Call me back?" I asked. "But I didn't call you. You called me!"

"That's impossible," Pete insisted. "I stepped away from the truck for a moment and left the phone on my seat. When I came back, I had a missed call from you."

We had a lot of catching up to do. We talked for a long time . . . so long that Pete's arm fell asleep holding the phone to his ear. "I have to go," he said, "but I'm glad we spoke."

"So am I," I said. "You're the only brother I've got. Let's talk more often."

And we have. It's what Mom would have called for.

The Problem of the Barn

KATHIE KANIA

I t was one of those gorgeous summer weekends on my parents' western New York farm. As I sat sipping coffee and looking out the kitchen window, my eyes went from porch to tree, bush to garden, as I remembered little childhood hiding places and play areas. Myriad emotions tugged me in different directions as I stared out at those childhood hideaways. For one thing, I was making mental plans for my upcoming wedding—delightful plans for colors and flowers and duplicate toasters. But then my eyes rested on the barn, and I felt that sick feeling again. Was I *really* going to walk out of my parents' lives at a time like this?

"What are you sitting here worrying about?" Mom came up behind me and gave her worrier a warm hug. She always knew thinking from worrying somehow.

"Oh . . . that barn," I said.

"I knew it," she shook her head in sympathy. "Well, let's not trouble ourselves on this beautiful day. The Lord will help us think of something. Why don't you have a piece of this cake? I want you to take some back to your apartment too."

270

Wasn't that just like Mom! Leave everything to the Lord, set aside things that need to be struggled with, and make sure everyone has cake.

That barn! It stood a dizzying three stories high. It had been designed well over a hundred years ago to accommodate livestock and hay and for fruit storage. But since my parents were no longer working the farm, they used it only to store machinery and tools. And the many winters and springs—the howling, rainy winds and snowstorms—had taken their toll on the barn despite Dad's attempts to patch and repair. Seeping water had caused the old stone-and-concrete foundation to begin moving and crumbling away from the wooden walls, leaving gaps. Frayed wiring provided electricity to the barn, the yellowed bulbs shining upon stored papers and junk. And the firetrap stood uncomfortably close to the house.

Yet how difficult to think of the barn as a hazard when I could remember so well the smell of the sun-warm boards of this, my haunted castle, my dance studio, my Kentucky stables. I had watched Dad build things in that barn with his treasure of shining tools and evil-sounding machines. I had drawn with chalk on the great sliding doors, painted my bike red on the west step. In the loft, I'd even composed a love song that now caused me to blush. But the usefulness of my barn-friend for play or for work had ended. It perched on its precarious points, waiting.

Dad came into the kitchen, blinking and sniffing deeply. He knew that the time had come for the barn to go. As I sat down across from him, I felt an aching sadness. So much was changing—even Dad. Something in me tried to force into my mind the image of Dad as he used to be: muscular, jet-black hair, large-featured handsomeness; a rider of motorcycles, a builder of things, an inventor. There was so much for me to be wildly proud of as a child—and I was still proud of him. But the graying man before me seemed smaller, older somehow.

"Dad," I began carefully, "what do you suppose it would cost to hire someone to take that barn down for you?"

"More'n I've got," he quipped. (I already knew the direction this conversation was going.)

"How about if we got some men from the church to help us do it?"

"I don't want anyone getting hurt on that thing."

"What about you?" I demanded. "I don't want you to get hurt either!"

"I haven't broken my neck on the Ark yet." Dad chuckled and settled back into his chair as if to close the subject. He had taken to calling the aging barn "the Ark." And a more stubborn Noah, I mused, there never was.

"Dad, I could help with the money. We could hire someone . . ."

"No!" He sat bolt upright now. "I got a certain way I want it done. The top beams can't be sawed or broken. I'm going to use them on the new garage I'm going to build. I know how wrecking crews like to do things. No, by ginger!"

"But, Dad . . ."

"Me and the Lord can take down the Ark." I knew by the way he sat back and looked away that the subject was very much closed.

"I'm going to come home every weekend and help 'you and the Lord,' Dad," I informed him. I didn't know how though. One of us was a thin office girl with a built-in fear of heights.

That next Saturday I arrived early, and Dad met me at the porch door. He had to smile at my work clothes and determined expression.

"I figure we'll start taking things out today," he said. We spent the weekend sifting through dusty objects. There were books, bottomless chairs, chicken feeders, rusty veterinary objects. We laughed at old feed bag designs, argued over what was or wasn't an antique, and told stories connected with some of the curios we found, such as the cougar-shaped lamp an uncle had won at the carnival.

After two weekends of sifting and sorting, we had the shed full of salvageable things and a great heap to be burned. The two tractors and their attachments had been placed in an easily accessible area just inside the barn's basement door. Much equipment still remained inside; we had barely scratched the surface, even though most of the valuable things had been removed. But we still faced the main goal of getting the old barn torn down.

That Sunday evening I again stood staring at the looming structure. Mom and Dad were an acre away, walking arm in arm, checking on their fruit trees. They had begun to call this "taking the tour." I could hear them arguing coyly and good-naturedly about how the apple trees should be trimmed, a topic on which they never agreed. They seemed totally oblivious to the problem of the barn. As I watched their distant forms move on to the next group of trees, I felt as if I were the mother hen and they—these parents whom I loved so fiercely—were the wandering, curious chicks, wobbling into misfortune before I could see and intervene. Often, lately, I was annoyed with them for neglecting themselves, for not eating better, for growing older.

I sat on the grass feeling helpless. I would be getting married in less than two months. Soon after the honeymoon, I would be leaving for the West, where my husband would finish college. How would this leveling of the barn ever get done? Shouldn't I be where I was really needed? And yet what good would my frail presence be on a job such as this? It all seemed so hopeless.

In the weeks that followed, I got caught up in the commotion of preparing for a wedding. When I wasn't busy with lists and errands, I would pause and think happily of the wonderful, tall, blond landscape architect who was making it all possible: Michael. Together we reveled in the great heap of bridal shower gifts (he complained to me that fishing equipment was never a present—just kitchen stuff). We made plans and occasionally retreated to the movies.

I put the barn problem aside for the most part, remembering it occasionally and then following Mom around, whining about what could happen. She would shake her head, admitting that she had no answers for me. She simply said, "Let's leave it with the Lord."

The wedding day came and went in a joyous, kaleidoscopic blur. We were off, then, on a carefree, monthlong honeymoon, camping like gleeful gypsies around the perimeter of Nova Scotia. Swept away by the patchwork landscape of eastern Canada and my brand-new husband, tan and tousled from walking the warm beaches, I admit I gave not one fleeting thought to the barn.

Soon it was time to begin the drive back home. I could hardly wait to tell the folks of clam digging and the day we'd made clam chowder in a bucket, of ferry rides and people we'd met—like John and Alex, the coal miners who had sung for us at our campfire.

Finally, we reached the town of Ripley. One by one we passed the friendly old landmarks: the stately school, Rice's Hardware Store, State Street's tracks.

As we rounded the curve of our tree-lined driveway, my eyes saw the sight, but my brain reeled with disbelief. There, where the huge barn had towered, was a flat, squatty pile of rubble with the roof on top of it all. Dad was grinning from atop that roof when we drove in, and he hopped to the ground with welcoming shouts.

Mom hurried out, a damp dish towel in her hands, and soon we were hugging and kissing. In the midst of it all, I couldn't help but marvel at how Dad had managed to get the barn down.

"Had a big windstorm last week," he said. "The Lord decided to take 'er down without my help. And lookit there . . ." I gazed in wonder as he pointed to the peaked portion of the roof that had gently protected the tractors when the structure had collapsed. "Not only is the equipment okay, but look at those roof beams."

I walked over to see that not one beam had been broken in the fall. Dad could disassemble them while standing barely four feet off the ground. And yet the happy expressions on my parents' faces were not ones of awe but of faithful satisfaction. And that was how they smiled at me now as I stood with Michael's arm gently around my shoulder.

"Funniest thing is," Dad said, lowering his head and scrunching up his shoulders like a mischievous little boy, "she never made much of a sound when she went! We slept right through the whole thing!"

And little wonder. If the Lord took this good of care of my trusting parents, he surely wouldn't wish to disturb their sleep.

The One I Prayed For

TERRIE BRADSTREET

I'd never met the child. Our lives had barely touched. But years later, I still thought about that poor kid—and remembered the prayer I'd sent up when I'd learned about the tragic accident.

I was a stay-at-home mom with an eighteen-month-old daughter, Laura, and was pregnant with my second child. It was a Friday in November, the day before Veterans Day, a cool afternoon—I'm famous for remembering little details like that. We lived outside Rochester in Penfield, New York. Laura was playing with her toys; I was getting dinner ready. My husband, Cliff, wouldn't be back until around four o'clock after a doctor's appointment.

At three, I heard Cliff come home. "You didn't forget about your appointment, did you?" I called.

Cliff came into the living room. "Dr. Seaford canceled his appointments today," he said. "His nurse, Kathy, was in a car wreck."

"Is everything okay?" I asked.

"It doesn't sound good," Cliff said.

Kathy was taking her kids out for ice cream when a garbage truck ran a red light and smashed into her van. Her daughter was fine, but Kathy had sustained some serious injuries, and her four-year-old son was in critical condition.

"He might not survive," Cliff said.

I looked at Laura playing with her toys. I put my hands on my belly, feeling the swell of the baby inside me. *If something happened to either one of them . . .* I couldn't even bear to think about it. All I could do was pray that Kathy's little boy would be okay.

The following week we heard that Kathy's son had survived but was paralyzed from the chest down.

That little boy stayed in the back of my mind for years to come. My daughter Mary-Kate was born—healthy—the following March. As both my girls grew up without the challenges that boy faced, I hoped he'd find happiness despite his circumstances. When Mary-Kate was six, our family moved to Walworth, a town out in the country, and adopted horses. Mary-Kate blossomed into a girly girl, but she loved riding with Laura and pitching in at the stables. From time to time, I'd look at the girls and thank God for our blessings, wondering what had happened to the boy and his family who had suffered so tragically.

It had been nearly twenty years since the accident when we moved back to Penfield into a smaller house. The girls were grown. That's when Mary-Kate came home from college to finish her business degree remotely. One day she announced that she'd signed up to volunteer at a sports camp.

"It's called SportsNet," she said. "It's a rec program for kids and adults with disabilities."

Mary-Kate really enjoyed it. She kept mentioning a fellow volunteer she'd befriended named Josh. They began to spend a lot of time together. I wanted to meet this young man.

"Why don't you invite him over one night?" I asked. "I'll make my macaroni and cheese."

"I don't know, Mom," she said. "It's hard for him because he's in a wheelchair."

"I'm sorry," I said. "I had no idea."

Mary-Kate explained that he'd been in an accident. "A truck ran a red light and hit his mom's van," she said. "He was only four years old."

A lightbulb went on. Truck . . . ran a red light . . . four years old . . . "Is Josh's mom a nurse?" I blurted. "Is her name Kathy?"

Mary-Kate eyed me suspiciously. "Yeah. How . . ."

"Did the accident happen in November?"

"I don't know," Mary-Kate said. "Why? Mom, you're weird-ing me out."

"I prayed for Josh," I said, "on the day of his accident. I was pregnant with you."

My memories of that day were so detailed that she had to believe me. And when Josh came over for macaroni and cheese a few weeks later, I felt an instant connection. He'd grown up to be a witty, smart young man with a sunny outlook on life. I could see why my daughter put so much time into this new friendship.

It was more than that, I discovered. Josh and Mary-Kate were in love. They dated for two and a half years before the beautiful day Kathy and I witnessed them taking their vows. Yes, that little boy I prayed for? He's now my son-in-law.

All Our Needs

PAULINE SMITH

Yet another cheery holiday tune was playing over the radio at the thrift store. I cringed. "Santa's on His Way" by George Strait: "Christmas is always my favorite time of year!" Not mine. Not now. I gripped the red plastic handle of my empty shopping basket in one hand and my gift list in the other and stared at the cracked snow globes and chipped mugs among other castoffs cluttering the shelves. What did I expect to find? This wasn't Toys R Us. It wasn't even Walmart. This was my last resort.

God, I'd prayed on the drive there, *give us only what we need. That's all I ask for Christmas.*

December 23, and I still didn't have a single present to put under the tree for my seven-year-old son, Joseph. How was I ever going to find—let alone afford—the brand-name craft set he and all his friends were going crazy over? When I'd dropped him off at school one morning, Joe had pointed out the beaded thingamabobs his friends had designed and melted together with the kit. He'd put it at the top of his list.

"I know Santa will get it for me," he told me. "I've been a good boy all year." How could I explain that sometimes even good boys didn't get what they asked for from Santa?

My husband, Jerry, an auto mechanic, had gone on temporary disability leave months earlier, so I had become our family's bread-winner. It couldn't have come at a worse time. I worked as an IT technician at a software-development company, but my boss had cut back my hours.

I'd scraped and saved every penny, but I still had only enough for a few secondhand gifts. I hoped I could at least find my son a new backpack for school. Maybe a wooden chess set so he and his dad could play. And a nice picture frame for my parents, one that would hold Joe's new first-grade pictures.

But the sorry state of everything in the thrift store dimmed my hopes. Clearly, I had a lot to learn about bargain hunting.

Santa's on his way? Yeah, right! Maybe for you, George Strait.

I took a deep breath and walked down another aisle. There was a doll that looked as if it had been run over by a truck. A set of colored pencils—half of them worn down to tiny nubs. More junk. I found a bunch of frames but none that would fit Joe's school photos. I stopped at a display of board games and stared at a beat-up box of Monopoly leaking play money. *Lord, if only those beige hundreds were real!*

I felt plain worn-out. It was hard to have faith that things would turn around for us, even if, deep down, I knew that without hope and faith I'd have nothing.

Just then I noticed something poking out from behind the box. I slid Monopoly to the side. A wooden chess set? It was in mint condition, never even opened. *What a find!* I thought. Odd that it would be hiding there. I dropped it in my basket.

In the next aisle, I spotted a backpack. It was bright green, Joe's favorite color. Behind it was an action figure in its original packaging from one of Joe's favorite animated shows and a brand-new computer game for three dollars. I swapped out my basket for a shopping cart. This was better than Toys R Us.

Maybe I just hadn't been looking hard enough, looking with hopeful eyes. I returned to the place where I'd seen the colored pencils. Sure enough, on the bottom shelf, I spied an unopened box with beads on the cover. The brand-name craft-supply set Joe had asked for . . . at only half the original retail price! I grabbed it and practically ran to the checkout.

I stopped at two more thrift stores and checked off just about everything on my list. At the last shop, something on a table by the register caught my attention. A picture album lying facedown. Someone had decided not to get it and had dropped it there, I guessed. I opened it up. The slots inside were just the right size for Joe's school photos, and the pages were decorated with fruit, blossoms, and bumblebees, perfect for my mom, a dedicated gardener.

I turned the album over. Inscribed on the front cover was a Bible verse from Philippians: "God shall supply all your need" (4:19).

PART 8

The Hidden Hand of God

Remember the former things of old; for I am
God, and there is no other; I am God, and
there is none like me, declaring the end from
the beginning and from ancient times things
not yet done, saying, "My counsel shall stand,
and I will accomplish all my purpose."

ISAIAH 46:9–10 ESV

Block 11

DANIEL KESSEL

O ctober 1943. Auschwitz-Birkenau concentration camp. Three gaunt men huddled together inside a pitch-black, airless cell in block 11. Narrow concrete walls, scuffed with the desperate scratches of previous prisoners, seemed to close in around them. In hushed tones, they discussed the only thing that mattered now—escape. But even if they found a way out, their fate was unclear. One thing was certain: the executioner would come for them.

Menachem Rosensaft sat in his office on the Upper East Side in New York City on a brisk January afternoon and stared at the book he held in his trembling hands. *Tehomot u-shehakim* read the Hebrew title—*From the Depths of the Skies*—the biography of an Auschwitz survivor named Zeev "Yumek" Londner. Menachem's stomach clenched as he imagined that dark, cramped cell, yet he could not get the image out of his head. A week earlier he had never heard of Zeev's biography. Now it was a precious key to his past: Zeev had been one of the three prisoners in the cell. Another was Menachem's father.

Block 11, a stark, brick building at Auschwitz, was known as the Death Block, where defiant prisoners were brought to be tortured and killed. According to camp records, Josef Rosensaft entered on September 30, 1943, and exited five days later. This much Menachem had known for most of his life. But what happened during those five days? How did his father manage to escape?

From a young age, Menachem had overheard his parents and their friends, many of whom were also Holocaust survivors, discuss their experiences during the Shoah, absorbing the adult conversation even when he couldn't understand every word. Concentration camp. Unterkapo. Block 11.

When Menachem was old enough, his father had sat him down and told him some of the stories, vivid, gripping accounts that seemed to come from another world.

Like the story of Josef's first escape. He was thirty-two years old in 1943 when the SS gathered his family and other Jews from the Bedzin ghetto in Poland and crammed them into a train bound for Auschwitz. He waited for an opportunity to flee. When the guards weren't looking, Josef slipped through an open window in the train compartment and dove into the freezing Vistula River. Swimming for his life, he was hit three times by German bullets but somehow escaped and walked, bleeding and barefoot, back to Bedzin.

Only later did he discover that virtually all the Jews on that train had been sent directly to the gas chambers. Not long after his return to Bedzin, the SS liquidated the ghetto entirely, and once again Josef was sent to Auschwitz. That time he couldn't break away, though he certainly tried.

"Never forget," Josef told his son, as if Menachem had lived through the Shoah himself. Remember the evil so it doesn't rise again. Remember the strength that overcame it, and never let it wither. Remember the faith that sustained the Jewish people.

Menachem always thought he would have more time with his father, more chances to ask about the past and fill in the details. But in September 1975, at age sixty-four, one year younger than Menachem was now, Josef Rosensaft died from a sudden stroke.

With his father's words in mind, Menachem told the stories to his daughter and hoped to share them with his grandchildren someday too. He had grown up to become general counsel to the World Jewish Congress, an organization protecting the rights of Jews worldwide, and taught law school courses on the topics of genocide and war crimes. He had just begun editing a manuscript, a collection of essays by the children and grandchildren of Holocaust survivors, another way to honor his parents' legacy.

He was born 103 years ago this month, Menachem thought a few days before his father's birthday as he sat at his desk sorting through the stories he'd collected. The gripping narratives told of courage in the face of unfathomable terror. He opened up his email and found a new message from an old friend, Hannah, who was living in Israel. "I came across something you'd like to read, a book written in Hebrew and only available here. It has to do with block 11 and your father. I'm sending you a copy!"

Block 11? Menachem could hardly believe it. After all these years, would this book finally shed light on the missing story? Within a week, Menachem received his copy. He sat in his office and flipped to the page Hannah had marked for him.

"Rosensaft did not stop thinking about escaping," Menachem read. His father. He leaned back in his chair and turned to the beginning of the chapter. Zeev Londner and his brother were only in their twenties when they found themselves in Auschwitz in September 1943. They made close friends there with an older man—Josef Rosensaft.

Menachem's heart raced. Josef was not just a brief mention in the chapter—he was the chapter. And in typical Josef Rosensaft

287

fashion, he had crafted a plan to escape. In October of that year, he told the brothers he knew a German doctor in Katowice, a city near Bedzin, a non-Jew who had offered to hide him before. The three of them would duck away from their work detail, hide in a deserted tunnel until the Germans stopped looking for them, and then make their way to the doctor's house.

But the wrong person overheard Josef's plan: an unterkapo, one of the Jewish inmates coerced by the Nazis—through a perverse system of threats and incentives—to supervise and spy on fellow prisoners. He brought the three men to the camp's officials, exposed their plan to escape, and shared the address in Katowice that they had been planning to flee to. A young SS officer named Otto Klaus seized Josef and the Londner brothers.

Josef knew that the punishment for plotting to escape was death. The three Jews would be sent to block 11, Officer Klaus explained, while the authorities decided whether they would be shot or hanged. Since it was a Thursday, and executions took place on Mondays, the men would spend the Sabbath in block 11. They were jammed into the cramped cell with two other prisoners and awaited their fate.

On Monday morning, they could hear other prisoners being dragged from their cells, followed by gunshots. Josef bade his friends good-bye. "May we meet again in the next world," he said. A minute crawled by. Then an hour. Still no one came for them. Finally, the officer in charge of block 11 appeared at their cell. "Nothing will happen to you, not today," he said. He unlocked the cell door and had them taken back to their barracks.

Menachem's eyes flew over the Hebrew writing. According to the book, questions about what had happened—what saved the three men—stayed with Zeev long after he, his brother, and Josef were separated and sent to different camps. He finally learned the truth two years after liberation in a displaced-persons camp in Germany when Josef located him and told him the rest of the story.

Menachem held his breath as he turned the page, closer to the answer he had sought for so many years.

Josef weighed hardly more than seventy-five pounds when he was liberated from the notorious Nazi death camp in April 1945. When he was strong enough, one of the first things he did was track down his doctor friend from Katowice. He told the doctor about his foiled attempt to escape from Auschwitz with the two brothers and their inexplicable release from block 11.

"I know what happened," the doctor responded. That October he'd received an unexpected visitor at his door: SS officer Otto Klaus.

Armed with the address in Katowice, Officer Klaus had ridden his motorcycle to the Polish town, planning to expose and arrest the traitor who was willing to harbor three runaway Jews. But when the door opened, he stared at the doctor in disbelief.

He knew the man.

More than twenty-five years earlier, during World War I, the doctor had saved the officer's father's life. In fact, the two families had remained friends. Officer Klaus had a decision to make: take the doctor into custody and turn him in or cover up the incident.

That day Officer Klaus returned to the camp and made his report: his investigation had not revealed any scheme to escape, he said. He vouched for Josef and the brothers and said they should be let go. On Monday, the three men returned to camp. Their ordeal was far from over, but they would live another day.

Menachem finished the chapter and closed the book, feeling as though he had just been given a miraculous gift, as if he himself had been liberated somehow. He was sitting at the dining room table again, listening to another of his father's stories, receiving a new lesson he was meant to remember and pass on to his daughter and future generations. In the middle of the deepest horror humankind had ever known, a spark of humanity had survived, powerful enough to move the heart of a Nazi officer and to deliver Josef Rosensaft from a dark prison cell back into the light.

Missing?

ELLIE VETTER

Lost: one irreplaceable ring given to me by my mother.
Suspect: an untrustworthy college roommate.

Problem: how to tell Mom the ring was missing while I was home on summer break.

I was a wreck. Dad gave Mom the ring way back when they were dating, a delicate white-gold band with a gorgeous emerald-cut ruby and a small diamond in the center. Mom entrusted it to me when I went off to college in Des Moines. I didn't wear it much because the ruby was loose in its setting and I didn't want anything to happen to that ring. Then one day I couldn't find it.

I tore through my room in a panic. "Has anyone seen my ring?" I asked my roommates. I must have looked like I was about to have a nervous breakdown. They all just shook their heads. Except one. "Ring?" she said. "What ring?"

Many things had "gone missing" since she had moved in, but my other roommates and I could never prove anything. We couldn't just accuse her. So I stopped looking for the ring and started praying.

Now came the moment of truth. I'd been home in Belle Plaine for a day. Mom and her coffee-club pals were waiting in the kitchen for me to tell them all about my college experience. I hadn't said a peep about the ring. Sooner or later Mom would ask, probably even wonder why I wasn't wearing it now.

Just then my best friend, Carol, dropped by. Her mother was one of the ladies in the kitchen.

"Am I glad to see you!" I said, steering her into the living room. I needed the moral support. That's when I saw it. Right there on her finger. The ring.

"Where did you get that?" I said with a gasp.

"Like it? Mom gave it to me. Here, try it on."

The ruby wiggled in its setting.

How did the ring get to Belle Plaine all the way from Des Moines?

"I was in Des Moines on business and did a little antiquing," Carol's mom explained after we burst into the kitchen and told the story. "I saw the ring in a pawnshop—caught my eye right away. How did your ring end up there?"

I had a pretty good idea. How it could come back to me? That was the amazing part.

The Case of the Flying Quilt

DANIEL KESSEL

The quilt on Lenice Hansen's guest bed really brought the room together. Something about the cheerful floral pattern, the fine hand-sewn stitches, and that deep ruby-red border felt homey and welcoming. It invited you to curl up and get cozy with a book and a hot cup of tea or simply take a catnap. But the quilt didn't belong to Lenice. It had ended up at her home in the oddest way—it had flown there.

On February 5, 2008, an F4-category tornado cut a 122-mile-long swath of destruction from Atkins, Arkansas, to just past Highland, where Lenice lived. It was the longest-lasting tornado ever to touch down in Arkansas—and among the most devastating. The recovery would take years, both physically and emotionally.

The day after the twister hit, Lenice checked in with her sewing group at church. The tornado hadn't touched her home—but not everyone had been so lucky. The members of the group got together and talked about how entire neighborhoods had been uprooted. Survivors had stumbled out of storm shelters to find that their houses had been flipped upside down and shaken out. Their most precious possessions—photo albums, baby books, cards and letters, priceless keepsakes—had been destroyed or lost forever, scattered to the winds or buried beneath debris in other people's yards. Was there some way the sewing group could help?

The women gathered around one item dropped off by another member of their church, Mark Hoosier, manager of the ALCO store in town. He'd gone to take a look at the debris that had settled on the store property. One thing had caught his eye immediately. A quilt.

It was filthy from the storm, still damp, and a tree branch had torn a small hole in it—but Mark couldn't throw it away. If someone restored it, the quilt could be quite beautiful. Perhaps the sewing group at his church could fix it up and send it overseas for its quilt-donation program.

Lenice had been making quilts all her life, a skill her grandmother had taught her. She knew a fine hand-sewn quilt when she saw one. "Someone loved this quilt," Lenice said to the group. "We can't send it overseas." Everyone agreed. Lenice offered to clean it up, mend its snags, patch the hole, and hold on to it until its rightful owner could be found.

"The flying homeless quilt"—that's what the group called it in an ad they placed in the *Villager Journal*, a local newspaper with a circulation of twenty-three hundred: "There's no way to know how far this patchwork of fabric pieces traveled before landing in our small community. After surviving such a journey, it deserves to find its way back home."

Lenice posted a photo of it—black-and-white, so she could test any caller claiming it was theirs; the true owner would know the quilt's colors. But no one called. Lenice put the ad in the lost-and-found section of *Country* magazine, a publication with a much larger reach. Several people called, but none knew the right colors.

It seemed more and more unlikely that the sewing group would find the owner. They couldn't afford to keep running ads. Lenice put the quilt on the guest bed, and there it remained. Someday maybe someone would come for it.

Around the first anniversary of the tornado, Highland was hit hard by another storm—an ice storm. The quilt helped keep Lenice and her family warm all week as they were stuck indoors without power.

The minute electricity was restored, the phone rang. "I believe you have my grandma's quilt," the female caller said. "I saw your ad."

"What is the quilt like?" Lenice asked.

"Well, it's made of floral squares, has a cream-colored backing, and it's all hand-stitched," she said. "Oh, and the border is ruby red."

Lenice and her daughter spent the next day preparing for the owner's arrival. They made sure the quilt was clean, and Lenice labored over a pot of chicken soup for lunch. One question nagged at her: How, after all this time, had the owner discovered that Lenice had the quilt? Her ad hadn't run in months.

"You don't know how happy I am to get this quilt back," the woman said when she arrived. "A year ago, my husband and I lost just about everything. The house, my husband's mechanic shop. We could rebuild those things, but I'd never be able to re-create my grandmother's quilts.

"All the quilts were special, but there was one I treasured most. The first one Grandma taught me to make. She sat in a chair at the quilting frame and sewed a stitch on top, then passed the needle down to me, sitting on the floor. I'd take care of the stitch underneath and pass the needle back up. It was this quilt. My grandmother chose the color of the border to match my name, Ruby.

"I stumbled on your ad by chance. I don't normally read the *Atkins Chronicle*, but my husband had a copy on his desk."

The *Atkins Chronicle*? The sewing group had never run an ad there. Why would they? The town was 140 miles away, a three-hour drive. Lenice had never even heard of that small-town paper. Ruby showed her the page: "Last week, several *Chronicle* readers brought us a feature from *Country* magazine. The picture of the quilt accompanied this story . . ." Lenice's ad was reprinted below the article.

None of Lenice's friends had any idea who passed along the year-old advertisement. It was as unfathomable as the quilt arriving practically unscathed from 140 miles away. But there was something about this quilt that brought everyone together. A grandmother and her granddaughter. A church sewing circle. Readers across the state of Arkansas. And the communities of Highland and Atkins. Each patch had been chosen, each stitch made with love. Strong enough to survive even the most powerful storm.

Fleeing for Our Lives

MARTA GABRE-TSADICK

Why did I snatch up such unusual things to take with me on that terrible night?

When you're under pressure, you do strange—and mysterious—things.

And I was under terrible pressure.

Our whole family had lived under the threat of death for almost a year. We'd been afraid ever since communists had taken over our country, Ethiopia, in September 1974. Our longtime emperor, Haile Selassie, had been arrested, and sixty-two of the country's leading officials had been shot. Our land teemed with ruthless Marxists and fanatic radicals intent on eliminating people such as us: I was a government loyalist who had served as a senator in the emperor's parliament; my husband, Deme, was a prosperous businessman who had once headed several government departments for the emperor.

There was another reason our family was in peril: my husband and I were outspoken Christians.

Now it was the fourth day since we'd learned that our emperor had died. With his death had come a new wave of arrests. To save our lives, it seemed to us that our only hope was to flee south across the border into Kenya, a trip of some five hundred miles, leaving our home in Addis Ababa and all our possessions behind.

For an exorbitant sum, we found a driver and a guide who would transport us in their ancient Land Rover. It was a trip that seemed impossible, for we knew we'd have to detour via farm fields and river gorges to avoid police roadblocks and cross forbidding terrain—yet we were ready to trust in God's promise: "But my God shall supply all your need according to his riches in glory by Christ Jesus" (Phil. 4:19 KJV).

We'd hoped to have a day or two to plan for our trip. But now, on August 31, 1975, we felt compelled to leave immediately. Later, we learned that an order for our arrest was being processed in police headquarters that very day.

There wasn't a moment to spare. Since informers were everywhere, we pretended we were going on a picnic. I hurried our three sons who were still with us in Ethiopia—Lali, nine, Beté, fifteen, and Mickey, twenty-two—into the vehicle. There was some fried chicken in the refrigerator; I had our cook pack it in a pan of aluminum foil and put it into a cooler. What else? We couldn't take too much in case we were stopped; it would look too suspicious.

Hurry, hurry! my heart whispered. I grabbed four cans of tomato juice and a bottle of water and climbed into the vehicle. The driver started the motor.

"Wait!" I said. I dashed back into the house, wondering, *What am I doing?* A roll of cloth adhesive tape had been left on a chair. I stuffed it into my purse. And there on a shelf was a jar of Vaseline. I made sure we took that too.

"Marta, please!" my husband pleaded. I climbed back aboard, and at eight o'clock, we drove off into the night.

We held our breath as we passed police barricades. Then, as we drove through the dark countryside past sleeping villages, I grieved for my fellow countrymen. What would happen to them in the hard times ahead?

My melancholy thoughts were interrupted when the old Land Rover broke down. The fuel pump had given out. But in the morning, we found a mechanic to fix it.

Later, as we rested beneath some acacia trees, we ate the cold chicken and drank the tomato juice. I started to dispose of the aluminum foil pan and the empty juice cans, but something stopped me. Without knowing why, I thrust them back into the cooler.

Already far behind schedule, we pressed on that evening to the town of Arba Mench, a Marxist stronghold. We prayed our way through the crowded streets and were on our way out of town when Deme looked behind us.

A police car was chasing us!

Our driver accelerated and switched off our lights. We veered off the road into the bush, lurching over the rough terrain, swerving to miss boulders and trees. We eventually shook off our pursuers! But in the bush, a thorny tree branch had ripped open the protective canvas cover on the Land Rover. Cold night air poured in around us.

"If only we had something to repair the canvas with," Deme muttered as we shivered in the cold.

"But we do!" I exclaimed, reaching into my purse for the cloth tape.

As we repaired the top, our driver said, "You were smart to think about bringing that with you."

"But I didn't think of it," I said. "The Lord made me pick it up."

He grunted. "You really think that Allah is interested in such little things?"

"The Lord is always watching over us," I answered softly.

On the third night, we had to follow a dry riverbed to bypass a dangerous town. The Land Rover groaned and squealed as it bounced off rocks. Then, with a terrible jolt, it lurched to a halt.

We climbed out to look and were instantly engulfed by a whining cloud of stinging insects. As we beat the air to ward them off, we discovered that a wheel had fallen off; its lug nuts had loosened and were lost in the dark forever. Deme suggested we take two lug nuts from each of the other wheels, and we used them to put the fallen wheel in place once again. But that was just the beginning of our wheel troubles.

Our next hurdle was the town of Yaballo, where the road crews were on the alert for escapees. There was a rise in the road before town, and we figured our best chance was to coast silently down the hill and through town just before dawn, when people would be sleeping their soundest.

Thank God it worked.

Then we faced the most dangerous place of all—Mega, a city near the border where all traffic was funneled through a police checkpoint. Deme, the driver, and the guide hoped they would look like a road crew. The boys and I hid on the floor in the rear of the Land Rover. Slowly we drove past the police guard. Since most of the crews drove Land Rovers, the police waved us on. Deme and I breathed a prayer of relief.

To avoid highway patrols, we again turned off the road and followed a dry riverbed. But just as we were beginning to breathe easier, the Land Rover's rear slammed onto the gravel with a bone-jarring jolt. We climbed out to find that the back wheel had broken away from the axle. Deme examined it.

"Powder," he groaned. "The wheel bearings have been ground to powder."

Now escape looked hopeless.

We waited fitfully through the night. As the light rose over the rolling hills, I raised my hands. "Thank you, Lord, for watching over us," I said. "Thank you that we broke down here instead of in a town. Thank you for providing this day for us."

Deme knelt at the wheel.

"Can you fix it?" I asked.

He shook his head. "Not unless we had new wheel bearings or . . ." He jumped up. "Or we had something to fill up the space in place of the bearings."

He began rummaging through the truck, then opened the cooler. "This just might work!" he exclaimed. Taking the aluminum foil, he folded it into tight strips. Then, fitting them into the wheel, he said, "Marta, we need grease. Do you have any cosmetics? Any cold cream?"

I reached into my purse and held up the jar of Vaseline—the jar the Lord had prompted me to retrieve as we left.

By Friday noon, the fifth day of our flight, the Land Rover limped slowly along. We'd had no water for a day and a half; our throats were parched and our tongues swollen. That evening our vehicle shuddered and collapsed. The back wheel had fallen off again. The foil bearings had been chewed away.

Have we come this far, I wondered, *to die here in the midst of nowhere?*

Deme slipped down against the Land Rover and, as if in prayer, sighed. "What do we have left? One wrench, half a jar of Vaseline, four empty tomato juice cans, and seven people dying of thirst."

Suddenly, he leaped up. "That's it," he exclaimed. "The tomato juice cans!"

As the sun rose on Saturday, Deme stomped the cans flat, shaped them into a metal tube around the wheel shaft, and applied the last of the precious Vaseline.

By noon that day, we faced the desert. Grim and foreboding, it undulated endlessly before us. Hour after hour we drove into charcoal-gray nothingness; even the sky had turned that sickly shade.

The Land Rover's metal was searing hot. I looked anxiously at our son Beté. He was in a stupor, dehydrated.

301

"Deme, we must find water for Beté!"

My husband buried his face in his hands, then looked up to heaven. Suddenly, his face lit up. "There is water here. In the radiator. I saw the mechanic fill it with plain water."

I worried as we drained the steaming rust-brown water into our one remaining glass. I tried to strain it through a tissue, then handed the glass to Beté.

"Don't drink it," I cautioned. "Just rinse your mouth." He grabbed it and gulped it down. Mickey and Lali did the same. Their thirst was quenched—and the liquid didn't seem to harm them.

As we rode on into the blazing afternoon, we began to see hills in the distance. Then, near 6:00 p.m., we saw a cluster of houses ahead where a dozen handsome Kenyans stood waiting for us.

We had found sanctuary.

However, now we faced the unknown. Destitute, where would we go? What would we do? Moreover, as I glanced back at the gray desert, my heart cried out for the countrymen I had left behind.

For a moment, deep sadness for the past and fear of the future gripped me. Then I looked at Deme. He smiled and took my hand. I knew what he was thinking: we had the most valuable thing of all—our faith.

Surely God would do as much with that as he had done with a roll of tape, a piece of aluminum foil, four tomato juice cans, and a jar of Vaseline.

Love Note

PAUL GRACHAN

How do you know when you've met the love of your life? I couldn't stop thinking about Esther. I laughed whenever we were together. My spirit soared at the sight of her. But we'd only been on a few dates! Was I really going to take her to dinner that weekend and ask her to be my girlfriend? I knew she liked me, but I was still nervous.

On my lunch break, I ran into a deli for a sandwich and pulled some bills that I had received as change earlier in the day from my wallet to pay for it. I glanced at them as I handed them to the cashier. Something was written on one of the dollars. I snatched it back and took a closer look. In pencil, right next to George Washington, was the word *Esther*. What were the chances?

No way would I let go of that dollar. Heading back to the office, I had a funny idea. I ducked into a drugstore, bought a small frame, and put the dollar inside. *I'll give it to Esther on Friday night*, I thought, chuckling to myself. *She'll get a kick out of this.*

At dinner, Esther told me she'd love to be my girlfriend. While we basked in the glow of our new relationship status, I pushed a box wrapped in pretty paper across the table. "I have a present for you."

"Aw, how sweet!" Esther said. She tore off the paper, opened the box, held up the frame, and stared at it.

"It was the craziest thing," I said, telling her how I had discovered it. She just kept staring at the dollar bill. Finally, she looked at me—but not with a smile. She appeared shocked, confused, disturbed maybe. I couldn't tell. It definitely wasn't the reaction I was hoping for.

"I thought you'd laugh," I said. "Isn't it wild?"

Esther wouldn't meet my gaze. "Remind me to tell you something later," she said, slipping the framed bill into her purse. She seemed so out of sorts I didn't want to press her about it.

It was a rare awkward moment between us. A year later, I was ready for the next step. I hired a mariachi band to serenade Esther outside her window and asked her to marry me. She looked stunned for a moment, then shouted, "Yes!"

About two years after I had given her the dollar, we moved into a new apartment together. While unpacking, I came across the framed bill. I didn't even know she'd kept it.

"Hey, you never told me about this dollar," I said, bringing it over to Esther. "You acted so strange when I gave it to you."

This time as Esther took the frame she smiled. "I thought if I told you the story behind it you would feel too pressured. After all, we'd only been on a few dates when you gave it to me."

"What do you mean the story behind it?" I asked.

"A few years before we met, I was working as a cashier at a copy shop downtown, dating someone who just didn't feel right. I started thinking, *How do you know when you've met the love of your life?* I got this nutty idea. I wrote my name on some dollar bills and gave them out when I had to make change. I said a prayer that somehow one would end up with the man I'd marry."

As it turns out, I'd hit the one-dollar jackpot! Now we have three great kids and are approaching our sixteenth anniversary. And I still consider myself lucky to be married to the love of my life.

Nineteen Bibles

JOHN KEITH

I'd had a long day of teaching psychology. All I wanted to do now that I was home was go in, have dinner with my wife, and unwind. But something blocked my front door. A large UPS box addressed to me. *Odd. I didn't order anything.* The label said it was from the American Bible Society.

I hefted the box through the door. "Honey, you know anything about this?" She didn't. I cut it open. Well, no surprise—Bibles. A bunch of them. But no bill, no indication of who had ordered them.

The mystery nagged at me even as my wife and I caught each other up on our day. I told her about handing out the midterm grades. After twenty-five years at the Community College of Southern Nevada, I still enjoyed seeing those nervous looks on my students' faces disappear when they discovered they'd passed. Many of them struggled, either financially or academically; some were on their "second acts" in life. One, a woman in her late thirties, looked absolutely panic-stricken awaiting her grade—afterward, she couldn't contain her joy. "Thank you, Jesus!" she cried out, loud enough to draw laughter from the other students.

She was the wife of a pastor who'd moved to a rough neighborhood in Las Vegas to plant a church. She was in her first semester in the nursing program, hoping to get a job to help with her family's finances.

The next day I spied her in the cafeteria. I pulled up a chair and mentioned my odd delivery. "I don't know what I'm going to do with all those Bibles," I said. The woman's eyes lit up the way they had when she'd learned her midterm grade.

"My husband and I are trying to start a Bible study, but we can't afford Bibles for our new members and folks don't have money to spare," she said.

"How many do you need?" I asked.

"Nineteen," she said.

It would be weeks before an acquaintance finally confessed that she'd "been impressed" to donate the Bibles to me, convinced I'd know who to give them to. Why she'd sent nineteen—exactly nineteen—she couldn't quite explain.

One More Day

ROBERTA MESSNER

Sunday evening, seven thirty. That's when I would do it.

I sat on the edge of my bed and twisted the cap off my prescription pain medication. Normally, one tiny, white pill would help ease the pain. Not this time. I emptied the entire bottle into my palm and counted. Thirty-two pills. If I took them all at once, I'd stop breathing, go into cardiac arrest.

I wouldn't need to write a note for those I left behind. Everyone would know why.

It was a cruel irony, being a registered nurse with an incurable disease. Tonight I would finally cure it for good.

Thirty-two pills. One for each surgery I'd had in my sixty years on earth.

I suffered from an invasive form of neurofibromatosis: noncancerous tumors that grow from nerve cells. Large masses formed in my brain and nasal cavities. The only way to treat them was to cut them out, and they kept growing back. I lived with unrelenting pain.

Two things had always gotten me through: faith and writing. Over the years, I wrote many stories about my condition for *Guideposts*—both devotions and magazine articles. I tried to show how my trust in God lifted me up when all seemed hopeless. I always concluded with a positive message, hoping to encourage and inspire others.

This was why I suffered, I believed. So I could help others who were also suffering. It was why, even with the pain, I still worked all week at a hospital, tending to the needs of my patients.

After my thirty-second surgery, I wrote a prayer that became something I said to God daily: "Thank you, Lord, for taking care of your own . . . always." For that surgery, my doctor had prepared a platelet gel using my own blood cells and injected it into the place the tumor had been—a procedure that he believed would prevent the mass from growing back. He would never have to operate on me again!

The joy I felt was overwhelming . . . and dangerous. I took a vacation with my sister—the first one I'd been able to take in years—and banged my head in a clumsy fall. The swelling didn't subside. An MRI showed tumor number thirty-three in my eye socket.

A large hematoma soon disfigured the left side of my face. I looked like Frankenstein's monster. The symptoms got worse—pounding headaches around the clock, constant tingling, and an occasional sharp spike of dying nerves. All signs pointing to the fact that the tumor was growing. I begged the doctor to remove it, but he said it was too risky—I could die on the operating table. I had to live like this for the rest of my life.

Calls from my sister barely registered. I rarely went out anymore. I was too self-conscious about my appearance. When I had to go to work, I hid my face behind my hair and makeup, wore huge glasses, and avoided looking anyone in the eye. I sat in the back of the church so I wouldn't have to lie about being okay. I was tired of faking it.

Those words I'd written, about God taking care of his own . . . did I even believe them anymore? How could they be true?

I woke up early Sunday morning with a throbbing skull. I could barely make it through church. The hymns I loved were like a chorus of jackhammers. *Even here, Lord? Even here I can't escape?*

All the prayer meetings, the anointing sessions, and the healing services I'd attended over the years in hopes of a miracle—none of them had worked. There was nothing left to live for.

Seven thirty on the dot. I shifted the mound of pain pills in my palm and cupped my hand to my mouth, ready to throw my head back and swallow. Out of the corner of my eye, I saw the edge of my nightstand, and on top, the journal and pen I used for drafting my *Daily Guideposts* devotions. *You told your favorite patient you'd read a devotion to her on Monday.*

Why should that matter? What did anything matter now? But I lowered my hand. I'd made it through Friday without thinking it was my last day among my friends and patients. Should I go through one more day? To say good-bye? No one had to know what I was planning. The pills would be waiting for me when I came home from work.

One more day. Then it's over.

I took my usual dose and made sure to get every last pill back in the bottle. I screwed the top on tight and put the bottle away. I massaged my temples. *Maybe this tumor will take me out in the middle of the night.*

I dragged myself to my desk early Monday morning—eyes burning, head in a vise. One of my coworkers poked her head in my door. "The director wants to see you," she said.

I hauled myself out of my chair and walked down the hall. In the office was the director, along with the hospital's chief of staff and two women I didn't recognize.

What was going on? Who were they? Former patients with a complaint? Had I been so distracted by my pain that I'd done something wrong?

"Roberta, I'd like you to meet Linda Hudson and her daughter, Beth Rucker," the chief of staff said as I went in. "I'll let them tell you why they're here."

Linda stepped toward me and grabbed my hands. "We're from New Martinsville. It's a five-hour drive from here. Beth and I headed out just before sunrise this morning. We wanted to make the trip here to meet you."

"Meet me?"

"You're the woman who writes the *Daily Guideposts* devotions we love to read."

What? I'd had readers send letters and emails . . . but I'd never had any show up in person. "You came all this way," I said. I couldn't tell her the truth—that she'd almost come here for nothing.

"Well, it's the strangest thing," Linda said. "Beth and I had been putting the trip off for weeks. Then yesterday evening, around seven thirty, you fell so heavy on my mind. I started praying for you. I knew I had to see you. Not tomorrow, not next week, but today. I couldn't wait one more day."

The *Ryndam*

WILHELMINA FEDDEMA

The *Pride of Galveston* was docked in the Gulfport, Mississippi, harbor, the cruise ship's blue smokestack rising like a
dolphin's fin from its gleaming white decks. My husband, Willem, helped me up the gangway, a porter behind us carrying our
bags. We'd flown here from Canada to embark on a journey we'd
dreamed about for most of our forty-year marriage—a grand tour
of the Caribbean Islands. I couldn't help but recall the last time
I had been on a ship, my only voyage until now, a lifetime ago.

It was 1953. I was twenty years old, aboard the *Ryndam* on a
ten-day crossing from the Netherlands to Nova Scotia, leaving
my whole world behind. I'd bought a second-class ticket with the
money that Willem, then my fiancé, had saved from his meager
earnings as a farmhand in rural Ontario. All I had were the clothes
on my back and my wedding dress, packed in a small suitcase. I'd
bidden farewell to Amersfoort, a city still struggling to recover
from the ravages of war, and to my widowed mother and four
younger siblings.

I spent my days at sea pacing the *Ryndam*'s decks, the salt breeze
on my face, a prayer on my lips. *Lord, bless this journey. Be with*

Willem and me, always. Beyond sight of land, the entire world seemed to be water. I couldn't tell what lay behind me or what lay ahead. I felt completely adrift. Was I doing the right thing? Could I make a home so far from everything and everyone I knew?

Forty years had taken away those fears and answered my prayers. Willem built a successful cabinetmaking business. We raised four children, three daughters and a son. I'd grown to love my adopted country, even if our responsibilities left little time or money for vacations. This cruise was a celebration of all we'd accomplished, the life we'd created from scratch.

The *Galveston*'s captain greeted us on deck. "This brings back so many memories," I said, gazing up at the finlike smokestack once more. "The last time I was on a ship I was coming over from Holland."

"Ah, then you might be interested in this vessel's history," the captain said. "She once carried immigrants from Europe. Back then she wasn't known as the *Pride of Galveston*. She was built for the Holland America Line. They named her the *Ryndam*."

Who Was the Woman in the Picture?

NANCY BURGETT

The halls of the College of Pharmacy at the University of Oklahoma are lined with old photos. One always captivated me: a young coed with a crisp lab coat and curly hair, neatly rolling out pills. That's how pharmacists used to fill a prescription—measure the right powders, mix them with liquid, and roll them out, cutting each pill by hand, almost like cookie dough.

Every time I described this process to my pharmacy students, I thought of that woman in the photo. It must have been taken in the early 1940s. The field was dominated by men back then, and I could only imagine that she'd seized the opportunity presented by the war: Rosie the Riveter as a budding pharmacist. If only I could talk to her. I'd love to do a video interview with her for my students. But was she even alive? There was no name attached to the photo. She was just a compelling picture.

At the start of the fall semester in 2009, I welcomed my students and gave my introductory lecture. I always started on a lighter note to break the ice. "Look around you," I said. "Someone is going to fall in love with someone they meet here. It happens every year." The students laughed, but it was no joke. My class was like a love drug. Except for me. I'd left a bad marriage and devoted myself to teaching.

On the Monday of the third week of classes, a student handed me a copy of an article from a 1942 edition of the *Tecumseh Herald*. "It's about one of the first women pharmacists," she said. Aha! So something I'd said had registered. I glanced at the page and was stunned—the woman in several of the photos was that pretty, young coed in the hall! The article explained that she had been one of three female students at the college that year—Irene Klapp Burgett.

"How in the world did you find this?" I asked.

The student told me that her mom taught at a grammar school outside Tulsa where Irene's son was a fellow teacher. After her mom had mentioned her daughter's field of study, he had brought in the article.

That Thursday a man came to my office. "I hope you don't mind me dropping by," he said. "I've been meaning to talk to someone here about my mom. She was a grad from the forties." He held up the article from the *Tecumseh Herald*.

I held up my copy. "I think one of my students got this from you."

"She did," he said.

"Did you see the photo of your mom in the hall?" I asked.

"What photo?"

We talked while we walked. His name was John, and he was a physical education teacher. His grandfather had been a pharmacist, and his mother had followed in her dad's footsteps. "I guess I broke with tradition," he joked. He was thrilled to see the photo. Finally, I asked, "Is she still alive?"

"Yes," he said. Irene was in her late eighties but doing well.

315

"Could I interview her?"

"She'd like that." We made arrangements to meet at his house. "I'll cook dinner," he said.

Three weeks later, I went to John's house. Photos of his two sons, now grown, hung on the wall, but I noticed no one was around to help him with dinner while I interviewed his mom. I learned he was divorced and had raised his boys on his own.

At the dinner table, he bowed his head and said grace. My heart skipped a beat. The conversation was lively, and his mom was lovely. It was an unforgettable evening.

That might have been it, if it hadn't been for friends in my women's group at church. We were planning our annual Christmas dinner. "Why don't you invite that man whose mom you interviewed?" they said. "He sounded nice."

So I sent John an email and held my breath. "I'd love to come," he wrote back.

The rest is history—and you know how much I like history. That semester I was the lovestruck one in class. The student who'd connected us left at the end of the term to pursue another career, but that pharmacist from the photograph welcomed me into her son's life. John and I married in June a year and a half later.

The Case of the
Stained-Glass Windows

Evan Miller

For days on end, Taras Pavlovsky pored over the markings and symbols, an arrangement of tiny black dots and strokes that Slavic monks had set on paper hundreds of years before. It was musical notation, a guide to the chants the monks had sung every day to glorify God.

To most people, the markings were indecipherable. Few had ever figured out a translation. Why go to the trouble?

But what others saw as a pointless dive into obscurity, Pavlovsky saw as a fascinating quest. He was a musician himself—the bandura, a lute-like folk instrument, was his favorite—and after college, he had taken a job as a choir director, later a cantor, at a Ukrainian Orthodox church in New Jersey, a cathedral with icons illuminated by the light filtering through its leaded-glass windows. He loved the dissonance of the music from the old country. It was when he was getting his master's degree in musicology at Rutgers University that he found his passion for digging into the past, like an academic Indiana Jones, uncovering secrets and artifacts once thought to be unknowable, undiscoverable. Those marks made by the monks. Slowly the pattern emergèd. Not just notes but an entire story. The work became his master's thesis. A triumph. For Pavlovsky, nothing equaled the thrill of the hunt.

There was little of that in Pavlovsky's career eighteen years later, in 2005, as dean of the library at the College of New Jersey. He stared at his calendar—another day of meetings, calls, and reports. He definitely needed to review the details for the approaching grand opening of the new library building. So much to do, but he couldn't help but feel there was something missing in his life. He longed to lose himself in history, teasing out the answer to a question at once enigmatic and fascinating. But he was an administrator now. No time for an adventure into the past.

Pavlovsky reached into the in-box on his desk and pulled out a memo from Pat Beaber, the head reference librarian. It was attached to a faded news clipping from the school newspaper in 1939. The article announced that eight stained-glass windows had been transplanted from the old campus (once known as the Normal School, the state's first teacher training academy) and installed in the library.

Pavlovsky knew every inch of the library. There wasn't a pane of stained glass in it. What had happened to those windows?

A tingle ran down Pavlovsky's spine. It wasn't deciphering Slavonic chant notation, but it had all the ingredients. History. A puzzle to be solved. How amazing would it be to uncover even one of the school's windows, lost to time? It would be perfect to hang in the new library.

Pavlovsky and Beaber sifted through old editions of the school newspaper, microfilm, and dusty yearbooks. They discovered that the windows had been gifts to the college from the earliest graduating classes. They searched every nook of the school and interviewed nearly a dozen retired employees. The last time anyone remembered seeing the windows was in the 1960s. They'd been taken down during a renovation project.

Somebody recalled seeing one in an antique shop in Pennsylvania. Another person said they'd seen a stained-glass window in a New Jersey bar. Both were dead ends.

The new library opened, and the campus magazine ran an article about Pavlovsky's search. Everyone at the library knew how badly he wanted to find those windows. Finally, though, he and Beaber threw in the towel. They hadn't recovered the windows, but at least they'd recovered their memory. A replica of one, based on an old photo that Beaber had found, was commissioned for the new building.

Pavlovsky hated giving up. But it had always been a long shot. Stained glass is fragile, and the wrong kind of care can destroy the pigment. Most likely, he figured, they had been thrown away. Beaber retired, and the dedicated sleuths went their separate ways. Nine years passed, but Pavlovsky couldn't forget the windows. He'd walk past the replica and wonder, *Are they out there somewhere waiting for me?*

Twelve miles away, in Bordentown, New Jersey, the door to a musty basement creaked open. George Costantini flipped the light switch and trudged down the stairs. He'd put off this job as long as he could. It was early 2014, about a year since his father, a retired General Motors employee, had died at the age of ninety-six, leaving behind this room piled high with dusty antiques from a lifetime of collecting. Where to even start?

Costantini's hand brushed against a makeshift package—plastic foam wrapped tightly between pieces of plywood. He cut through the duct tape holding it together. The overhead light reflected off a stained-glass image, a woman with wings holding a swan. He opened the package beside it to find what seemed to be her twin, a goddess holding an owl, a star shining down on her. Costantini had no way of knowing they were replicas of frescoes by the Italian Renaissance artist Raphael titled "Hours of the Day and Night."

He had a faint memory of his father bringing the windows home back in the seventies and hanging them in the sunroom. Where had his dad said they'd come from?

Costantini needed someone who could point him in the right direction. A college a couple of towns over had a big library. Maybe someone there would know something about the windows. It was a long shot, he knew, but he emailed the reference desk anyway.

Pavlovsky stared in astonishment at the email that had been forwarded to him. He dialed the number and arranged to go to Costantini's to see the windows for himself. Once there he recognized them immediately. Costantini was happy to return them.

Pavlovsky had known they were out there, buried, meaningless to all but someone with a well-trained eye and a single-minded focus, like the mysterious marks of the medieval monks. He'd felt it in his bones, that hunger for discovery that had lain dormant for years. But even he couldn't have predicted this—the treasures he'd been searching for all those years were perfectly preserved. Ready to be displayed once more in a place of honor in the college library. Almost as if they were waiting for him, and only him.

Out of the Ruins

JIM HINCH

Germany, 1943. One week before Christmas. Fifteen-year-old Rosemarie Reichert pushed open the door of the tiny bookshop in Rüdesheim am Rhein, a picturesque village nestled at the base of some hills beside the Rhine River. The town was known for its vineyards and for the Ruine Ehrenfels, the remains of a medieval castle. A bell tinkled as Rosemarie stepped inside the store and took in the warmth and the comforting smell of old books.

It was a bleak time. The Nazis' mounting losses had ravaged the country, and Hitler's SS had accelerated its campaign to root out spies, traitors, and "undesirables." Rosemarie's family had been torn apart—but she didn't know why. Her father and his side of the family had been in France since before the start of the war, and when she asked about him, the grown-ups changed the subject. Rosemarie had returned home from boarding school to care for her mother, who had lymphoma and was in a hospital across the river.

"Rosemarie!" The shopkeeper clasped the girl's hand. "How is your mother?" Frau Richter was a prim elderly woman with dark-rimmed glasses and gray hair put up in a neat chignon. She and Rosemarie's mother had bonded over their love of books.

"Oh! You don't know," said Rosemarie. "She is in the hospital."

"My darling child," said the shopkeeper, looking stricken. "I am so sorry."

"I want to get her a special Christmas gift," said Rosemarie. "She often talked of an author named Thomas Mann. He won a Nobel Prize. I can't remember the name of his book though."

"Wait here," said Frau Richter, lowering her voice. She disappeared into the back of the shop and soon returned bearing a small, plainly bound hardback with a pale red stripe around the cover and a one-word title in blue ink: *Buddenbrooks*. She looked around, making sure no one was watching, before wrapping the book in newspaper and slipping it into Rosemarie's hands.

"Trust me, child," Frau Richter said, "your mother will love this book."

At home, Rosemarie tore off the newspaper. She leafed through the pages of old-fashioned Gothic script. Then she wrote a brief inscription inside—*Für Mama mit Lieben, Weihnachten, 1943* ("For Mama with love, Christmas, 1943")—and signed her name. She rewrapped the book, boarded a ferry to cross the river, and presented the gift to her mother at the hospital.

"Rosekind, this year I have no gifts for you," Rosemarie's mother said.

"Mama, it's all right. Please open yours."

Her mother unwrapped the book and gasped.

"Rosemarie, where on earth did you get this?" she asked in an urgent whisper. "It's a banned book!" She hurriedly stuffed it under the covers and lowered her voice even further. "You were only a small child in 1933 when the Nazis stormed into libraries and universities, even private homes, looking for books by Jewish authors and others they deemed to be against the party. Thomas

Mann's books were among those they burned. It is forbidden to own one."

"But . . . Frau Richter said you would love it," said Rosemarie.

"I do love it," Rosemarie's mother said. "It is a thoughtful gift. I wish I could keep it, but I cannot. The nurses will find it. You must take it away and tell no one you have it. Get rid of it if you have to. We live in such bad times." She embraced her daughter.

Frightened, Rosemarie boarded the ferry back home. She prayed for guidance. Frau Richter certainly knew the book was banned—yet she'd entrusted Rosemarie's mother with it. Rosemarie didn't want to throw the book away. Her mother said she loved it. It didn't make sense. Just like her father's disappearance. Like everything else in that troubled time.

Gazing across the river, Rosemarie glimpsed the old ruined castle, Ruine Ehrenfels, above the streets of Rüdesheim. It was a lonely but beautiful place where Rosemarie and her mother sometimes hiked to have a picnic. She had an idea: climb the hill to the ruins and bury the book in the courtyard. No one would find it. When the war was over, she would return and dig it up.

Rosemarie tucked the book inside an old metal cigar box, taking care to first rip out the page with her inscription—no identifying marks! On Christmas morning, she climbed through the vineyards to the castle. With a trowel, she began to dig by one of the stone walls. The soil was hard but not yet frozen. Her hands felt cold and stiff, but she wiped her face and blew her dripping nose, pressing on. *This is one book the Nazis will never burn*, she thought. She dropped the box inside the hole, covered it, and stomped the earth flat.

Rosemarie's mother died two months later. At the war's end, Rosemarie, evacuated to Bavaria, found work translating for American soldiers. English had been her favorite subject in school.

Her uncle Anton, Mama's family patriarch, finally revealed the truth about her father: he was Jewish. Keeping that a secret had protected Rosemarie and her mother from Nazi persecution. Rosemarie's father, however, despite fleeing Germany for France, had been betrayed by the Vichy regime and sent to a concentration camp, where he was killed.

Heartbroken and orphaned, Rosemarie resolved to emigrate to America. There was one thing she needed to do first. Had the book survived when so much else had not?

She told Uncle Anton her secret. Together, they returned to Rüdesheim and climbed the hill, creeping along the walls of the ruined castle. In the courtyard, they began to dig. The shovel struck something hard. The box! Rosemarie pulled it from the ground, brushed off the dirt, and opened it. The book was still inside, somehow looking just as it had the day she had buried it.

Later, Rosemarie read the book and knew why her mother had loved it, why Frau Richter had saved it. Mann wrote of a Germany that existed before the Nazis and of a family whose fall from grace mirrored the fall of the country. For Rosemarie, the book became a symbol of the place she was leaving behind.

Rosemarie lived a happy life in America. She married an Air Force officer, Edward McManus, and had three sons and six grandchildren. She and Edward enjoyed a long retirement in the house they had built by a lake in North Carolina near their children and grandchildren.

Only one thing marred her happiness. A hurricane had caused a flood that swamped the storage unit where they'd been keeping their things while waiting to move into their lakeside home. Rosemarie and Edward's beloved library—hundreds of books they'd collected over the years—had been ruined. *Buddenbrooks* had been lost. To Rosemarie, it was like losing her mother all over again. The Nazis had killed her father. Cancer had taken her mother. Only the book had survived. And now it was gone. Her act of defiance against the Nazis had saved nothing.

Then came the day Rosemarie and Edward were packing up their house, preparing to move into a retirement home. Their granddaughter Tessa finished packing a few new books Rosemarie and Edward had bought to rebuild their library. "Your books are in here, Omie," Tessa said, pointing to a small box. "I put them with some other old things." Rosemarie smiled and thanked her, though it was hard watching a lifetime's memories pared down and packed away in boxes.

On the final days before the move, Rosemarie found herself thinking back over her life. Wartime Germany. Her evacuation to Bavaria. Her travels with Edward. She sat in the living room watching television, feeling vaguely sad. She thought of the box of books Tessa had packed. Rosemarie could still picture the one book she really wished she had, the small, plainly bound hardback with the pale red stripe around the cover, lost a decade earlier in the flood.

As if moved by some unseen force, Rosemarie sprang out of her chair and hurried to the small book box. She cut through the packing tape and opened the flaps. She reached inside.

There, wedged between several brand-new books, was a volume that appeared to be nearly falling apart. Brittle with age, water-spotted, with some pages stuck together. Gently, Rosemarie pulled it out. She saw the pale red stripe around the cover. The title in blue letters. And the place where she'd torn out the page with her inscription: *Für Mama mit Lieben, Weihnachten, 1943*.

Every other book from the flood had been dumped, ruined beyond recognition. Not *Buddenbrooks*. Once buried, never burned, never destroyed, it was a symbol of something indestructible that no evil could ever erase.

The Surprising Saga
of the Chained Prince

RICK HAMLIN

In 1781, an Irish doctor with a taste for adventure and only one eye left his ship to go hunting along the coast of West Africa. He got separated from his party and, instead of making his way to shore, wandered farther inland to a region where few Europeans before him had ever traveled. Half-starved, disoriented, lame in one leg from the bite of a poisonous worm, Dr. John Cox walked for days, finally collapsing. The local people who found him carried him to their ruler, their almami, a man named Sori.

Sori examined the wound and urged Cox to stay until he recovered, offering him a house and a nurse. By all accounts, Dr. Cox, an easygoing, good-natured soul, was happy to stay for six months as the guest of Muslim royalty in the city of Timbo. He was impressed by Sori's family, especially the favored son, nineteen-year-old Ibrahima.

Ibrahima was both scholar and warrior. He'd gone to Timbuktu for his studies, learning math and geography and Arabic, so he could read the Koran, committing long passages to memory. As

326

a soldier, he had recently won an important battle for his father, bringing peace to the realm. He enjoyed Dr. Cox's company and even acquired a bit of English.

Finally, well enough to travel, the doctor was given a new set of clothes and some gold for expenses. He was accompanied by fifteen warriors for protection. At the coast, he was able to find the same ship he'd come on, and he returned to his native land full of stories of the Muslim prince and his generous family.

Back in Africa, Ibrahima was given greater command in his father's army. In 1788, at age twenty-six, he led his troops into battle and was captured. He pleaded with his captors to ransom him, claiming he would be worth more than one hundred head of cattle and a man's weight in gold, but they opted to sell him to slave traders for a mere pittance—gunpowder, muskets, tobacco, and rum. The African prince was clapped in chains and shipped to America. There he was taken up the Mississippi River to Natchez and sold to Thomas Foster, a tobacco farmer his own age.

Even after months of humiliation and a hellish journey crammed in a slave ship where he couldn't stand upright, Ibrahima retained his dignity. He explained to his master that he was a prince and that his father would pay untold amounts for his freedom. Whether Foster believed him or not, he needed a slave for his farm. His only concession was to give Ibrahima the name Prince.

Compared with his fellow slave owners, Foster was relatively kind. He allowed Ibrahima to marry a young slave woman, Isabella, and did not sell their children out from under them. He gave Ibrahima key positions on the growing plantation and let the couple market their own produce in town and keep the money for themselves. But while Ibrahima was allowed a great deal of freedom, he was not free. He was certain he would never see his homeland again. Prince—he hated the name. It was a mockery.

Ibrahima attempted to run away when he first came under Foster's ownership. He yearned for home and liberty. But his rebellion didn't last long. He quickly sized up his fate and sacrificed his pride, although, as Terry Alford's excellent biography, *Prince among Slaves*, notes, he did not sacrifice his dignity.

So how did his story come to light? Why is his name not lost to memory, just another of the millions of slaves brought to America? Other slaves claimed to have noble backgrounds, and their stories died with them. Such is the horrific nature of slavery—it robs a person of their identity.

Ibrahima had no time to read or study, and he wasn't allowed books anyway. Most slaves were illiterate, as were many of their masters (Foster's wife and mother couldn't read). But sometimes Ibrahima was seen to trace Arabic characters in the sand when there was a break in the work—a word or two of sacred verses, recalling his study of the Koran.

Then one day in 1807, Ibrahima was sent to town to sell some produce. A white man on horseback approached him. Ibrahima offered him sweet potatoes. The man on horseback studied Ibrahima's face with his one good eye. "Where are you from?" he asked.

"From Africa," Ibrahima answered.

"You came from Timbo?" the white man asked. Yes, he came from Timbo. Yes, his name was Ibrahima. And did he know whom he was speaking to? Yes, he knew very well; it was Dr. Cox, the Irishman who had stayed with his family, recovering from his illness, who had even taught him some English. Twenty-six years after they had first encountered each other, fifty-five hundred miles away, the two happened to meet in a dusty Mississippi town, the African prince and the man who owed his very survival to the prince's father.

Dr. Cox hastened to meet Thomas Foster and did all he could to buy Ibrahima's freedom, offering huge sums, money he could ill afford to part with because, truth to tell, life had not been easy for him. He'd been in a couple of shipwrecks, emigrated to the United States, practiced medicine on the frontier, lost money in bad investments, and come to Mississippi to start over. No matter what he offered, Foster would not accept it. He needed his slave—now his overseer—too much. He couldn't do without Ibrahima.

The good doctor died before he could buy Ibrahima's freedom—but his efforts brought the matter to the attention of abolitionists and the United States government. Secretary of State Henry Clay, a slave owner himself, was moved by the story of Dr. Cox and Ibrahima and finally bought Ibrahima's freedom. By then Ibrahima was an old man, although hardly broken in spirit. In 1828, he launched a lecture tour across the country, trying to raise money for his children's freedom, and the following year he returned to Africa, to the new country of Liberia, founded as a home for freed American slaves.

Tragically, Ibrahima never made it back to his homeland. He passed away only months after his return to the continent. However, more than a century later, the legacy of his unlikely encounter with Dr. Cox lives on in his descendants. Dr. Artemus Gaye, Ibrahima's seventh-generation grandson, left Liberia after that country's civil war and is now a professor of ethics at Garrett-Evangelical Theological Seminary in Illinois. He only recently learned of his princely ancestor when he began digging into his genealogy. "The story sounded impossible," Dr. Gaye said to me. "For anyone to escape the evil of slavery was a tremendous struggle. Ibrahima could have been another one of the forgotten, erased from history. Instead, here I am to tell his story and carry on his name."

#149 DTG

CINDY HOLLAND

It was 1970. My husband, Barry, was on his second tour of duty in Vietnam. All I wanted was for him to come home safely. I wrote him a letter every day, and on the back of each envelope, I noted how many days to go (DTG) until we would be together again.

But one day I lost it. I was sick and tired of missing Barry, of tiptoeing around the house, of not being able to live my own life. The army wouldn't let spouses stay in military quarters during deployments, so I'd taken our toddler son and moved back in with my parents. There I was, thirty-eight weeks pregnant, trying to corral my rambunctious twenty-month-old plus a German shepherd in heat and keep them quiet all day so my parents, who worked nights, could sleep.

My stress and frustration boiled over. "I don't want to be an army wife anymore," I wrote. I detailed all the reasons I was miserable. I stuck the letter in an envelope, sealed it, and wrote "#149 DTG" on the back, my pen digging in so furiously it almost ripped the paper. One hundred forty-nine days to go. One hundred forty-nine days I would no longer have to wait. I handed the letter to the mailman with a feeling of sullen satisfaction.

By the time I came to my senses, it was too late to get the letter back. I pictured my husband in the jungle getting shot at, not knowing if he'd see me or our son again, if he'd ever get a chance to hold our baby. I wrote him again. "Please disregard my last letter. Forget it even existed." I told him how sorry I was, how I couldn't wait for him to come home. "No matter what, remember I love you."

I heard back sooner than I expected. To his credit, Barry didn't write one word about #149 DTG. He just told me he was safe, that he missed me and loved me. But I still beat myself up about that letter. It must have crushed him.

A few weeks later, the mailman knocked at the door. "Mrs. Holland," he said, his expression grave. "I'm sure that your husband is okay. This must be some kind of mistake."

He handed me a crinkled envelope, a muddy tire track smeared across the front. Below it someone had written, "Address Unknown, Person Not Found."

I turned the envelope over. #149 DTG.

I assured the mailman, "My husband is fine." So is our marriage. We'll celebrate our fiftieth wedding anniversary this year.

PART 9

Animals— God's Special Messengers

The wolf also shall dwell with the lamb, the leopard shall lie down with the young goat, the calf and the young lion and the fatling to-gether; and a little child shall lead them.

ISAIAH 11:6

Shadow

DIANA AYDIN

Tranquil Acres in Decatur, Alabama, is a neighborhood that lives up to its name—comfortable homes and spacious lawns, but not so spacious as to keep neighbors from being friends. That's what kept Bill Hughes and his family in the area even after his kids were grown, and why retirees Ronald and Carolyn Harris moved there to grow their prizewinning roses. For a rambunctious mutt named Shadow, however, Tranquil Acres was more than a place to call home. It was his calling.

He arrived through the classified section of the *Decatur Daily* newspaper. Becky Hughes, Bill's youngest daughter, was a college student living at home. One morning at breakfast, she flipped through the paper and an ad caught her eye—"FREE puppies to a good home!" *A puppy? That's what I need*, Becky thought. She'd grown up with four sisters and three brothers, but they'd moved out and started families of their own. Her friends had gone away for school. It was just her and her parents in the big house, and she was feeling a bit lonely. Wouldn't it be nice to have a furry friend to greet her when she came home from class late at night?

335

Becky went to look at the litter of puppies. One little guy stood out from the rest—he nearly jumped out of the box. He wasn't the cutest of the bunch, but there was something about his big, soulful eyes. His fur was the color of midnight lightening to blond, especially in the back, like a shadow had been cast across half his body.

"You sure you can take care of him?" Becky's parents asked their daughter, eyeing the pup skeptically when she returned.

Their skepticism was justified. Shadow would run off as soon as Becky went to classes. But invariably, when her car came up the drive at 8:00 p.m., he would reappear. He'd hop up on the porch, wagging his tail, waiting for Becky to throw her arms around him. Bill had no idea what Shadow was up to all day, but when Becky was home, the dog didn't leave her side.

Shadow had just turned five when Bill took a fall at work and had to have hip surgery. The doctor recommended walking every day to speed his recovery. Bill dreaded it. He was shaky on his feet; even getting around the house exhausted him. He stepped outside, and the driveway looked a mile long. He'd never make it. Then Bill heard a bark. Shadow. The dog scampered up beside him as if to say, "Let's go."

Shadow accompanied Bill every morning, bounding a few steps ahead. Now and then he'd turn to check on Bill and patiently wait for him to catch up.

Becky was glad Shadow and her father had bonded. She was about to finish school. Soon she'd be moving out. It felt almost like Shadow wasn't her dog anymore. He was Bill's. The neighbors grew accustomed to the tap-tap of Bill's walking stick against the asphalt and the sight of his ever-present Shadow.

Ronald and Carolyn Harris often waved at the duo trotting by while they were outside tending to their rosebushes. They'd raised two sons of their own and had dreamed of a quiet retirement in the country. That's how they'd ended up on a three-acre plot half a mile down the road from Bill.

Carolyn had never been a dog person. But there was something wonderful about the way Shadow walked with Bill, as much companion as pet.

"I'll tell you something," Carolyn said to Ronald one morning. "If ever I'm on my own, I'd want a dog just like that by my side, a real devoted dog."

She had no reason to think anything would happen to Ronald. While he'd had some heart trouble in his fifties, he'd been in good health ever since. They were still young and active. But three days later, Carolyn was getting ready for bed when Ronald began gasping. He suffered a massive heart attack and died en route to the hospital. Just like that, he was gone.

All of Tranquil Acres rallied around Carolyn, attending Ronald's funeral, filling the house with flowers and comfort food. Their sons came up for a spell, but they couldn't stay forever. Soon enough, Carolyn found herself alone. She'd never been alone. It was deeply unnerving. What was life without her beloved Ronald?

On a misty night, a week after Ronald's death, Carolyn glanced into the backyard and spied a dark shape hovering in the shadows. Her heart hammered until the figure came closer to her deck.

What was Bill Hughes's dog doing there at nine o'clock at night?

"Shoo!" Carolyn said. "Go home!"

The dog stayed put. Carolyn picked up the phone and dialed Bill.

"Your dog is at my house," she told him. "He doesn't want to leave."

"Don't you worry about that," Bill said. "He'll come home on his own. If he doesn't, I'll get him in the morning."

Really? In the morning? Still, she couldn't bring herself to invite Shadow in. She checked on him several times that night. He was still there. In the morning, she fed him some scraps and gave him a bowl of water out on the deck. Around 10:00 a.m., Bill stopped by as he made his regular turn around the cul-de-sac. Shadow dutifully followed Bill. Carolyn felt a bit sad to see him go. It'd been nice to have company, even if it was just a neighbor's dog hanging out in her yard.

Half an hour later, though, Shadow was back. He bounded up her driveway, Bill giving chase. Carolyn stepped out her front door. "Leave poor Mrs. Harris alone," Bill called. But Shadow planted himself at Carolyn's feet and refused to budge.

"It's fine," Carolyn said. "I don't mind him being here."

He stayed all day and through the night once again.

Shadow was busy. He still walked with Bill every morning. He still met Becky when she came home from school. The rest of the time he took up residence on Carolyn's deck. Carolyn called the Hughes family, apologetic. She felt like she'd stolen their dog.

"I just can't get him to leave," she told Becky.

"Mrs. Harris," Becky said, "is Shadow a bother?"

"Not at all, dear," Carolyn said. "He's such a comfort to me."

"Then I won't force him to come home," Becky said. "Invite him in. That's what he wants. Shadow knows where he needs to be and who needs him to be there. Always has."

Becky eventually got married and moved away from Decatur. Shadow remained behind. He was a fixture in Tranquil Acres. He belonged there, roaming the subdivision, finding people who needed him, following like a shadow until each mission was complete.

The Leopard

ERICA KAGGWA, AS TOLD
TO DANIELLE ELISKA LYLE

Fear and pain do strange things to one's sense of time. I do
not know how many days and nights I huddled in that pit. It
was dug for a latrine but never used, and I had thought it could be
my hiding place. If I stayed out of sight of the militants hunting
down my people, I might live.

But this was not living, lying pressed against the earth, light-
headed from machete wounds on my body and from hunger that
gnawed at my insides. The sun beat down on me by day, and insects
crawled across my flesh. At night, the eyes of predatory creatures
hovered. I felt hardly better than those animals, scuttling out of
the pit after dark to scavenge from nearby gardens.

One night I could not bear it any longer. I pleaded with God
to let me die. It was the only way I would see everything and
everyone I loved again.

My country, Rwanda, is known as the Land of a Thousand Hills.
My family lived in Kigali, the capital. Although it was a thriving
city, it had the feel of the countryside—built among ridges and
valleys rich with trees, bushes, and flowers.

I was the third-born of four children. My brother Emmanuel and my sister, Elyse, came before me, my brother Claude after. We were a happy, God-fearing, middle-class family. The four of us children felt so loved and protected by our parents. Ours was a beautiful life.

But it all came to a terrible, sudden end. On the night of April 6, 1994, Rwanda's president, Juvénal Habyarimana, was assassinated, his plane shot down as it approached the Kigali airport. Years of simmering tensions between his tribe, the Hutu, the majority in Rwanda, and the Tutsi people erupted into brutal violence. The killing frenzy—the genocide—began. Hutu militia set up roadblocks and went from house to house slaughtering Tutsis. Moderate Hutus who opposed the killing were themselves killed.

My parents knew the militia was coming for us. "We are in the hands of God," my father said. That night, April 7, as we were preparing for bed, men with guns and machetes invaded our house. They demanded our money. "Please don't hurt my children," my mother begged, tears falling from her eyes as my father handed over all we had.

The pleas and the money were not enough. My father died in front of us, felled by a machete. Then my brother Emmanuel. Elyse, Claude, and I raced out the back door, my mother behind us. I was the first to the fence around our garden. Partway up, I turned and reached back to help my mother climb. "Mama, come . . ."

"No, Erica, don't help me," she cried, urgency flaming in her eyes. She pushed me over the fence. "Go! Run away from here!"

I ran. So many were fleeing and being cut down, not only by the militia but also by civilians pressured to turn against their neighbors. The lush green hills and valleys of Kigali were stained with the blood of thousands. I kept running. I found myself in a part of the city I did not know and ran right into the hands of militants.

They herded a group of us into a church. I looked for my mother, my sister, my brother. They were not there. We prisoners were lined up and forced to walk out of the church one by one. I watched those in line before me be executed, beheaded by machete.

Then it was my turn to go out. The soldier swung his machete. I heard the blade slicing through the air. It hit not my neck but my hand. I fell to the ground among the bodies of the dead.

There I lay, scarcely daring to breathe until the men with machetes left. I got up, and again I ran, searching desperately for someplace safe. The pit was my last resort.

Days and nights at the bottom of the hole blurred together. After so much time in the pit, I'd lost all hope. My wounds had clotted but still burned like fire. My heart was heavy with sorrow for my lost family, for my lost country. Where was God? Had he abandoned us? Why?

Life could never be good again, I decided one night. Not after this, not after what I had witnessed. *This is not living, God. Let me die*, I pleaded. *Let me be with my family again.*

Yet hunger overrode that desire. I climbed out to forage for food. I dug a cassava out of someone's garden. I was returning to my hiding place when I heard a shout. Militants. Their machetes glinted in the moonlight.

I couldn't make it back to the pit. Still, I ran. I came upon a large bush, its branches long and thick. A place to hide! As much as I wanted to die, I feared the machete cleaving my flesh. *Please, God, not by the blade . . .*

I parted the branches and gasped. A pair of eyes stared back. A leopard crouched in the underbrush. It crept toward me, its gaze steady, its sleek body low to the ground, shoulders shifting as if to pounce. Had God sent it to kill me before the men could?

The leopard paused. I glanced back. The militants were almost upon me when they stopped short, nearly falling over one another.

I looked at the leopard. It was staring at the men. The great spotted wildcat stalked toward them, growling. The militants turned on their heels and ran.

The leopard lay down. It gazed at me for a long moment with its beautiful amber eyes, then rested its chin on its paws. I climbed into a space in the bush, branches sheltering me like a cocoon.

All night the leopard kept vigil. Under its watchful eyes, my mind cleared, my fear and despair faded. It never approached, never bared its teeth at me. I stayed in the bush for three days, counting each sunrise, in awe of my silent protector, who remained nearby. On the third morning, the militia moved on. I no longer heard gunshots or rioting. Only then did the leopard disappear back into the wilderness. I left the bush not knowing where I'd end up but knowing I was protected.

I eventually made my way to a refugee camp, then a children's home where I met another orphan, a young Ugandan man named Daniel. Today we're married and parents to seven. Daniel is a pastor, and our ministry finds adoptive homes for orphans. It's the way we rebuild and heal. Of my family, only my sister, Elyse, survived. Not a day goes by that I don't grieve for my losses, for the losses of all. The hearts of some men, God can't reach. But in the midst of the horror, God sent his protector. He meant for me to live.

Guard Cat

LINDA KENNEDY-BLANTON

The snow was coming down hard when I pulled into the carport beside our double-wide and took out my groceries. I couldn't wait to get inside and warm up. But just as I started for the front door, my arms full, the stray cat I'd found several months earlier jumped down out of nowhere and planted herself on the steps right in front of me. "Move, Kitty, these bags are heavy," I said. "Scat!" But Kitty refused to budge.

I knew I shouldn't have kept that cat. I wasn't even a cat person.

Maybe because my husband and I lived on the outskirts of town, we'd found pets abandoned by their owners on more than one occasion. That's how we'd gotten our dog, Blackie, who'd turned up by our trailer a few weeks after we'd moved in. During the week, my husband was 125 miles away at college, so I was happy to have a companion. A dog—now, a dog was useful. A dog, especially a big one like Blackie, could keep me safe.

But what good was a cat, really? I'd found Kitty in a ditch, curled up in a tiny ball. My neighbor's cat had just had kittens, and I assumed she was one of the litter. But my neighbor said all his kittens were accounted for. I'd rescued Kitty, and now I was stuck with her.

Sighing, I set my groceries on top of the car, picked up the cat, and put her in her house under the carport. The second I turned to grab my bags, Kitty bolted up the steps and blocked my way again, meowing defiantly.

"Move! I'm warning you . . ." I gave Kitty the stare-down. That's when I saw a glint of something on the steps. Broken glass. I looked up. The window of our front door had been busted out.

Had someone broken in? Why wasn't Blackie barking? I backed away from our trailer, jumped in the car, and took off. When I got a safe distance down the street, I pulled over to call the police.

They found Blackie, who'd been knocked unconscious by a blow to the head. "The burglar ran out the back door when we arrived," the officer told me. "It's a good thing you didn't go inside."

Kitty brushed against my leg and looked up at me. Small enough to be overlooked by a burglar but big enough for the Lord's work.

Intruder

KATIE WHITE

I opened the door to our house tentatively, as had become my habit, as if some barrier were keeping me from crossing the threshold. My eight-week-old German shepherd puppy, Sascha, trotted inside ahead of me, his nails clicking on the tiles.

"Jeremy?" No answer.

Empty. I dropped my keys in my purse and checked the hallway. Hung up my coat. Checked out the kitchen. I crept up the stairs to the darkened landing and stopped, listening. What was that creak? A footstep? Or just the house settling? My heart sped up.

I pushed open the door to the bedroom. The curtains cast long, black shadows across the floor. What was I so scared of in my own home? It was frustrating that I had to live this way!

Something brushed my leg and made me jump. Only Sascha, wagging his tail. "Good boy," I said. "You're a great guard dog." Well, guard puppy. I went downstairs, turning on lights as I went. I sat at the kitchen table, Sascha at my feet. The two of us waited for my husband, Jeremy, to get home from work.

"You okay?" he asked when he got in an hour later.

"Sure," I said. How could I tell him the truth—our dream home had become a nightmare?

For most of our marriage, Jeremy and I had been apartment dwellers. But the Cape-style house with white pine cabinets in the kitchen and marble tile in the bathroom was exactly what we'd been saving for. The yard was beautiful. We were excited to move in. Our first few days there I just walked from room to room, barely able to believe all this was ours. It felt as much a miracle as a house.

Two weeks after we moved in, on an ordinary Wednesday afternoon, everything changed. I was at a friend's house when Jeremy called. "Come home quick," he said. "We've been robbed."

The police were waiting when I got there. Together we searched the place. Jeremy pointed to a shelf of DVDs. They were falling over, turned every which way. I pictured the thief rifling through them, picking out his favorites, and shuddered.

On the kitchen counter was a half-empty can of soda. He just helped himself! Jeremy opened the fridge. "All the soda's gone," he said.

I flushed with anger and revulsion. I didn't care about stolen soda, but the idea of someone going through the fridge, touching everything, making himself at home, in my home . . .

I was shaking by the time we headed up to the bedroom. I opened the dresser drawers. "Oh no."

All my delicates had been rifled through. It made my skin crawl. Then I saw the open space in the middle. My jewelry box—gone.

Numbly, I told the police what was inside it: my great-grandmother's locket. A pair of amethyst earrings Jeremy had given me for Valentine's Day. A silver bird pendant from my mother. The ring with an unusual topaz stone that I had worn on my wedding day for "something blue." Some of the pieces were worth money, like my mother's diamond ring—the one she had given to me when I graduated from college—but even the costume jewelry held sentimental value. As the only granddaughter, I'd inherited things passed down for generations. Now they were all in the hands of some awful stranger. Some . . . intruder.

The officers weren't optimistic about solving the crime. "It'd help if you had some idea who might have done it," one said. "Sometimes jobs like this are local. Someone who knows the house can watch to see when it's empty." I glanced nervously at the window. Was someone watching now? Planning another invasion?

"We've only lived here a few weeks," Jeremy said. "We have no idea who'd do something like this."

The cops said they would do their best, that something like this could happen anywhere. I knew we'd never find the perpetrator.

From then on, I compulsively checked for security risks. Neighbors seemed sinister. I dreaded being home alone but also dreaded leaving, knowing anyone could bust in while I was out. I lay in bed at night thinking of confronting strangers in the hallway or defending myself in the kitchen. Would I ever trust again?

We changed the locks. I wanted to install an expensive state-of-the-art security system, but Jeremy had other ideas. "Let's get a dog. You don't like being alone here. Dogs bark."

I'd never had a dog. I was a little nervous around them. But I agreed to give it a try. A puppy wasn't exactly what I'd had in mind though. Someday, maybe, Sascha might grow up to be intimidating. It was hard to imagine now; he was such a cuddly dog. Not that I didn't need that. He was a sweetheart. In a few days, he'd converted me into a true dog lover.

One afternoon I came home with Sascha in the car. He bounded out and darted for the sidewalk. I chased after him.

"You got a puppy!" someone squealed. The daughter of one of our neighbors came running up. "He's so cute. Can I pet him?"

Sascha wagged his tail furiously as the girl buried her fingers in his fur. I saw something sparkle. A ring. My ring. The diamond ring my mother had given me. I was so shocked I didn't know what to do. Not until Jeremy got home. We called the police.

A few hours later, two officers were at our front door with the girl, still wearing my ring. "My brother gave it to me," she said, sniffling. "He said he found it on the street. I swear!"

Her teenage brother soon confessed. An older man had enticed him to watch nearby houses and steal jewelry when their owners were out. The older man had a record, so he didn't want to risk getting caught himself. But he was going back to jail now. I hoped the teenage boy would make better choices. He got off with probation.

As for me, my dream home feels like a dream again—an even better one, thanks to Sascha. Jeremy and I have since adopted two more German shepherds—not for protection but because we love them. What I got back was more than just some stolen jewelry. I got back my sense of trust and my home.

The Disappearance

EVAN MILLER

In a backyard in Mount Pleasant, North Carolina, David Ginn, his head and neck covered with a mesh veil, wafted smoke into the entrance of his largest beehive. Just enough to pacify the ten thousand domesticated honeybees and keep them from sounding an alarm. He slowly lifted the top of the super, the white wooden box the size of a small filing cabinet that the bees called home. The yellow-and-black insects tirelessly constructed dense slabs of honeycomb like tiny engineers. The sound of their beating wings, a gentle buzz, filled the autumn air, music to David's ears, music that was in danger of being silenced by a mysterious malady spreading across the globe.

From the garden just beyond the hives, Teresa stopped picking lettuce and watched her soul mate at work. At first she'd been terrified of that sound and of being stung. Then she'd heard David talk about the bees and his devotion to them. They were crucial players in the circle of life. Everything in the world, he said, depended on these creatures to spread pollen among flowering plants. Without the bees, plants would fail to reproduce and bear fruit. David's job was to watch over this colony and three smaller ones like it, to protect the bees and ensure that they had everything they needed to carry out their mission. It was a responsibility handed down to him from his father fifteen years earlier.

The bees and the plants needed each other. Just like Teresa and David. She was drawn to his passion for nature. He needed her unfailing optimism. She loved this life they shared, the natural rhythm and harmony of it. They were, in so many ways, a perfect couple.

David searched for the queen, the mother of the hive. She looked healthy, active, surrounded by hundreds of nurse bees feeding pollen and honey to her larvae. Already, fatter bees populated the hive, girded for the oncoming winter. When the cold descended, they'd cluster together, still working, still buzzing to keep each other warm until spring.

Fall was a critical time for bees, when they were most susceptible to disease, the effects of pesticides and mite infestations. Bees around the world were dying off. Colony-collapse disorder it was called, a phenomenon that had baffled scientists and ravaged wild bee populations as well as domesticated ones. David was determined his colonies would not disappear.

He put the lid on the hive. He just needed to check the last three supers before he could help Teresa. He opened the first one. Then the second. Everything looked fine. He lifted the top to his smallest hive and . . .

Teresa heard David shouting for her to come. She ran to his side. No bees swarmed around him. She looked into the super. Not one bee was moving.

"I'm so sorry," Teresa said.

"I . . . I can't believe they're all dead."

Teresa struggled to find words to comfort him. "Maybe if we said a prayer."

David just stared down at the ground and shook his head.

Faith was the one thing that separated them. To David, God had set the circle of life in motion but had mostly stayed out of things since. There were rules that governed the universe. God wouldn't break them for any one person. Or any tiny creature. The colony's death was out of anyone's control.

"The hive can come back, can't it?" Teresa asked.

"No," David said. "Whatever killed them, it's in here. We can clean it, seed it with a new queen and new bees, but once destroyed, a colony doesn't come back."

They spent the afternoon scouring the super, scraping away thousands of dead bees and hosing it out. David inspected the bodies, looking for mites or any sign of what had killed them. Nothing stood out. There was no obvious cause.

"I've got to figure out some way to save the other bees," David said, steely determination in his voice.

Yet month after month, bees continued to die. Teresa could only watch helplessly as David refused to give up. Every few days he was out in the backyard checking on those who survived.

By spring, only the biggest hive was left. Even though the flowers were in bloom, David fed the bees sugary syrup to give them an extra boost.

They were going to make it. He felt sure of it. The hive was strong.

On the first Saturday in May, David and Teresa were outside working in the garden when it hit them: they hadn't seen any bees the entire morning. David ran to check the hive. There was no activity—not one bee was flying in or out of the entrance. He didn't bother with the smoker. He opened the super.

The bees had been dead for days, their carcasses covered with brown mold and ants feasting on the sticky remains.

The lid from the hive dropped from David's hand.

"I'll help you clean it," Teresa said.

"Just leave it," David said. "I'm done."

He pressed the lid down hard on top of the hive. Teresa slipped her hand into his. They slowly walked back to the house.

David scarcely spoke to Teresa. Scarcely spoke at all. Every so often she would ask if maybe he'd like to start over with a new colony. David just shook his head, certain those bees would die too. The hive sat, ignored, for the rest of the year.

The next spring, in early March, Teresa was ready to plant the garden. David wasn't. "I doubt it will amount to much," he said, "without the bees to pollinate it."

Teresa dragged him outside to the garden plot to help her figure out what they should plant where. She brushed something away from her arm. Then her face.

"That was a bee," she said.

"I don't think so," David said. Then he heard it. The buzz. It wasn't just by his ear. And it was louder than a single bee.

He nearly flew to the hive himself, Teresa right behind him. A steady stream of bees flew in and out of the entrance of the largest super. "That's impossible," David said. He stared as if he were in a trance, trying to make sense of the sight.

Teresa nudged him. "Get your hood and the smoker," she said.

Minutes later, David pried open the lid. His jaw dropped at the sight of thousands of healthy, industrious bees. A colony of wild honeybees had secretly moved in and set up shop, an occurrence most beekeepers will never see in a lifetime. "Bees just don't do this," David whispered. "It's impossible. Impossible."

Teresa stood watching David, the mesh veil over his head, his joy uncontainable. The two of them joined in a new understanding of the circle of life. David wasn't the only one watching over the bees. The bees weren't the only thing the world depended on.

The Moth

CHARLENE RUSSO

Every family has its own folklore and superstitions. In our big Italian Catholic family, it's said that the souls of the dead come back to visit us in the form of a moth. Crazy, huh? "That could be Aunt Ray!" Mom would say when one flew inside, and my younger brother, Charles, and I would laugh. We were twelve years apart but close. He always wore black and white. I teased him that they were the only colors he knew how to match. At twenty-three, Charles passed away suddenly in his sleep. Part of my world died too. I yearned for a sign that Charles was at peace. I finally understood my family's strange belief.

Three days after Charles died, Dad called. "Get over here!" he said, his voice urgent. I drove to my parents' house and found my family crowded by the front door. "Look!" my sister Natalie whispered. It was perched on the door handle. A moth with black-and-white-speckled wings . . . exactly like the pattern on the tie Charles had worn at our cousin's wedding, the last time we had seen him alive. We watched the moth until it vanished into the house. Dad found it the next morning on Charles's pillow, the very spot where he'd drawn his last breath. It stayed there for twelve hours, then flew away.

A year later, the entire family gathered at the cemetery for the anniversary of Charles's death. Natalie and I made a moth-shaped wreath out of white carnations and roses we'd dyed black. I laid it on his headstone. Afterward, we sat on the deck at my parents' house sharing "Charles stories." I tried to join in, but it was all too much. I got up from the table with my sister Connie and wandered over to the memorial garden Dad had planted in the backyard for Charles. "I miss him so much," I told Connie. She put her arm around me.

Just then I spotted something fluttering by the edge of the garden. I knelt down to take a closer look. A white moth! I pointed—and it leaped onto my finger. That's when I saw the white-and-black stripes on its legs. "You guys gotta see this!" I called to the rest of the family. They formed a circle around me, all wanting to pet the moth.

It was the oddest thing. The moth wasn't afraid at all. Connie squatted next to me, and it moved right onto her knee! There was a fourteen-year age difference between Connie and Charles, but they had always been as thick as thieves, especially after Connie's divorce. Charles would stop by her house to check up on her kids and make sure they weren't falling behind in school. On the weekends, he'd take Connie on mini road trips to keep her from feeling lonely.

The moth flew to my three-year-old niece, Ava, next. She squealed in delight. Charles had been close to all the kids in the family. But Ava—the baby of the bunch—was his favorite. She was spunky and mischievous, like him. He even had her photo as the background image on his phone. Ava was too young to understand the tragedy of his death, but she asked about her uncle Charlie and prayed for him every night before bed.

"Can I see?" my ten-year-old, Victoria, asked, and the moth hopped onto her index finger. The rest of us looked on in awe. This little creature was so friendly! Charles had been like a big brother to my three kids, a rock star who could do no wrong. They would hear his car pulling into our driveway and rush outside to greet him. Whenever he babysat for us, my husband and I would come home to find the house a mess, candy and toys everywhere.

Next the moth visited Fran, Charles's childhood friend. She had been his first love—his girlfriend from middle school to junior high. Even after they'd broken up, they'd remained close. In the months after his death, we all became friends with Fran. She'd check in on my parents, shovel the snow in front of their house, and call my sisters and me just to chat. She became like another sister. It made sense the moth wouldn't leave her out.

I loved the black-and-white stripes on the moth's legs. Totally Charles's style. He'd probably laugh at us all going crazy over a moth. But then again . . . Charles always made me smile. I couldn't think of any better way to lift our spirits than a visit from the object of family folklore. By the end of the evening, the moth had landed on every one of us. It flitted back to me and rested on my dress.

It was time to go home, but the moth wouldn't say good-bye. "Take it with you," Mom said, as if that were the most natural thing in the world. So that's what I did. I climbed into the car with the moth still on my shoulder. It stayed there the entire drive home. When it was time to get ready for bed, I carefully changed out of my dress and hung it up. The moth didn't budge.

I was disappointed the next morning to find that the moth had finally flown off. I sat on the edge of my bed, a little teary-eyed. Just as I was about to leave the bedroom, though, I saw a flutter of white wings. I held out my hand, and the moth landed on me again. It accompanied me downstairs for breakfast, much to the delight of my kids, who couldn't stop snapping pictures of the two of us.

The moth didn't stay forever. But the wonder and comfort of its visit linger with me and my family. And so does the message that one day we will see Charles again, a message delivered in a way that only God could have done.

Homage to Mkhulu

FRANÇOISE MALBY ANTHONY

I can still hear them. The rumbling that vibrated through the reserve that dry evening in March. Their moans filled with grief. The agitated movements of their ears. Those big brown eyes fixed on me and me alone. My husband, Lawrence, always said there were things in this world that cannot be explained by reason, cannot be seen. Deep roots that connect all living things, humans and animals alike. It wasn't until that night, two days after Lawrence died, that I truly understood.

This was a man who had somehow charmed me into leaving my native France for an old Dutch farmhouse out on the savannah of Zululand in South Africa. A man who had suddenly suggested we buy an old game reserve and transform it into Thula Thula, a lodge and an animal haven where leopards, zebras, and white rhinos could roam free. A man who, after watching a news report on the Iraq War, had sneaked into Baghdad in the midst of battle to rescue trapped zoo animals. And then, of course, there were the elephants.

Everyone called Lawrence the Elephant Whisperer. He earned the nickname in 1999 after adopting a herd of nine "delinquent" elephants about to be put to death. The herd was unstable, prone to escaping its protected habitat and rampaging through populated areas. Dangerous. Lawrence's mind was made up though. Maybe the elephants kept wandering because they weren't in the right home, he said.

He had no knowledge of wild African elephants. Yet night after night he camped out with them to earn their trust, a risky move that almost got him trampled. He sang to them, talked to them. People called him crazy. But it worked. Little by little the herd took him in. First the matriarch, Nana, then the rest. They forged a deep bond, one based on trust and respect. The elephants stopped escaping, made Thula Thula their home.

Sometimes I tagged along with Lawrence on his visits to the elephants deep in the bush. Nana would extend her trunk to him, caress his face, as if he were a member of the family. The herd had increased to twenty-one elephants, and our property had doubled in size over the years. But the bond remained. So did Lawrence's nickname, though he preferred to be called the Elephant *Listener*.

"I don't have a special talent," he told me. "The elephants talk to me if they want to. If they don't want to, I don't insist. I just listen."

I only wished he'd listen to me every now and then. Lawrence was physically strong, a robust six foot three. But lately, he'd been having heart trouble. In September, at the age of sixty-one, he'd suffered his second heart attack. He wasn't supposed to fly but insisted on traveling to Johannesburg for a weeklong business trip to help advance the mission of Thula Thula. "Françoise, I'll be fine," he said before he left. "There's no need to fret."

The call came at seven o'clock in the morning on Friday, March 2, 2012. I was up early, straightening up the house in preparation for Lawrence's return that night. On the phone was David,

Lawrence's right-hand man. He was sobbing. I caught only snippets. *Lawrence. Unconscious. Heart attack.*

"I'm . . . so . . . sorry . . . Françoise," he said. "He's gone."

I clutched the phone, hoping I'd misheard. "Impossible, impossible," I whispered. But deep down I knew it was true.

News of Lawrence's death hit Thula Thula like a bomb. Our staff of seventy was inconsolable. Lawrence wasn't just the boss. His Zulu name was Mkhulu, or "grandfather." That's how everyone saw him. I knew they needed me to be strong, to assure them that we'd be okay, even without Lawrence. But I couldn't think, couldn't speak. My head was somewhere else, lost in memories.

Like the memory of the first time we had met. We were both waiting for a taxi in London, where we had both gone on business. It was freezing, a mix of rain and snow coming down. I finally made it to the front of the line. The concierge asked if I'd mind sharing a ride with the man at the back of the line, who was also headed to the convention center. Lawrence was wearing a bright blue Windbreaker in the middle of January as if he were on safari. No way was I sharing a ride with *that guy.* "No, no," I said.

To my great surprise, I ran into him later at a Tube station. It was hard to miss that Windbreaker. This time I introduced myself, apologized for my rudeness. It was one of those moments orchestrated by that invisible force Lawrence believed in. We met for dinner and a jazz show. One year later, I left Paris, headed for South Africa, and never looked back. It was easy to face the unknown with Lawrence. He made me less fearful.

I didn't want to face the unknown without him. Didn't want to live in a world without his fierce spirit and generosity. I kept waiting for something to wake me from the nightmare. Life without Lawrence? Impossible, impossible!

Two days after Lawrence's death, a Sunday, I was still holed up in our bedroom. People passed in and out of the house, paying their respects. It made no difference to me.

"They're here!" someone said with a gasp. Who was here? The voice was followed by shouts. All kinds of commotion. What was going on?

I dragged myself downstairs and opened the front door. The staff was gathered outside, all staring in the same direction, eyes wide. On the other side of the fence on our property were twenty-one distinct gray shapes. The elephants. Lawrence's elephants.

Nana gazed at me. So did the rest. As if they were waiting for something. Or someone. They remained like that for more than an hour, then they marched up and down along the fence, rumbling. The same noise they'd always used to "talk" with Lawrence. They seemed edgy. Distressed. Finally, they lined up one by one and made their solemn procession back into the bush.

It's been nearly four years since Lawrence died. The work at Thula Thula continues, as my husband would have wanted it to. By now, most people have moved on. But an elephant never forgets.

A year after Lawrence's death, on March 4, 2013, the elephants returned, led by Nana in the same procession. The year after that, on March 4, they were back. And again on March 4, 2015. They mourn him like one of their herd.

How do they know? Who sent them? What does it mean? Some things in this world are beyond human understanding—cannot be explained by reason, cannot be seen.

Kash

DORIS RICHARDSON

Admittedly, the house had been quiet since my husband had died, but I didn't want a dog. I had enough responsibilities as an elementary school principal. Besides, no dog could ever replace Kash, my childhood best friend. I only went with my friend Dee to the animal shelter for pet adoption day because when she gets an idea, she's like, well, a dog with a bone. I figured she'd drop it once she saw I had no interest.

But one dog took an interest in me. He came right up and looked at me plaintively, imploringly. He was some sort of Cattle Dog mix, with reddish-brown fur and a white stripe that ran from the back of his head down to his salt-and-pepper muzzle. I gave him a pat and shooed him away.

He didn't go. When I tried to walk away, he followed, as if he was herding me. "I guess your dog found you," Dee said.

"Not hardly," I said. "He's not for me."

No dog ever would be after Kash. He was a mixed breed, the kind we called a Heinz 57 variety back in Opp, Alabama. Those were lean times, and my parents worked long hours. I would have been lonely without Kash. He watched me jump rope, listened as

I read from my schoolbooks, and sat with me by the dirt road, waiting for my folks to come home. He was smart and affectionate and made me laugh. It devastated me when he died. I vowed never to get another dog. This mutt though . . . no amount of coaxing could pry him from my side. He even barked at other dogs, keeping them away. "Come on, Doris, you can't say no," Dee begged.

"Try him for the weekend," the shelter worker said. "Bring him back Monday if things don't work out."

"Okay," I said to the persistent dog, "you get a weekend. No more."

The dog kept me company as I did my chores. I laughed, watching him surge through the piles of autumn leaves on a walk around the neighborhood. That first night he curled up by my side. And all at once I felt like we were a pair, like the house wasn't so empty anymore.

On Monday, I returned to the shelter—to finalize the adoption.

"Have you named him yet?" the worker asked. I admitted I hadn't.

"Well, if you're interested," she said, "his last owner called him Kash."

A Note from the Editors

We hope you enjoyed *Mysterious Ways*, created by the Books and Inspirational Media Division of Guideposts, a nonprofit organization that touches millions of lives every day through products and services that inspire, encourage, help you grow in your faith, and celebrate God's love.

Thank you for making a difference with your purchase of this book, which helps fund our many outreach programs to military personnel, prisons, hospitals, nursing homes, and educational institutions.

We also create many useful and uplifting online resources. Visit Guideposts.org to read true stories of hope and inspiration, access OurPrayer network, sign up for free newsletters, download free ebooks, join our Facebook community, and follow our stimulating blogs.

To learn about other Guideposts publications, including the bestselling devotional *Daily Guideposts*, go to ShopGuideposts. org, call 1-800-932-2145, or write to Guideposts, PO Box 5815, Harlan, IA 51593.

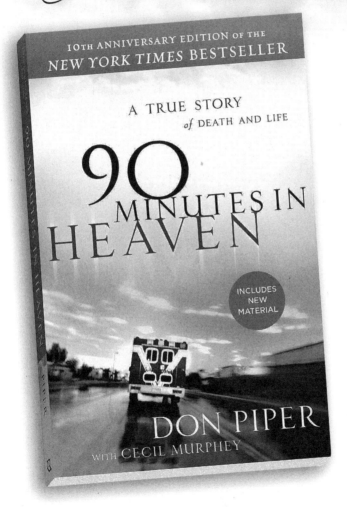

An ideal gift of *comfort and hope*

10TH ANNIVERSARY EDITION OF THE
NEW YORK TIMES BESTSELLER

A TRUE STORY
of DEATH AND LIFE

90 MINUTES IN HEAVEN

INCLUDES
NEW
MATERIAL

DON PIPER
with CECIL MURPHEY

TRUE STORIES OF HOPE AND PEACE AT THE END OF LIFE'S JOURNEY

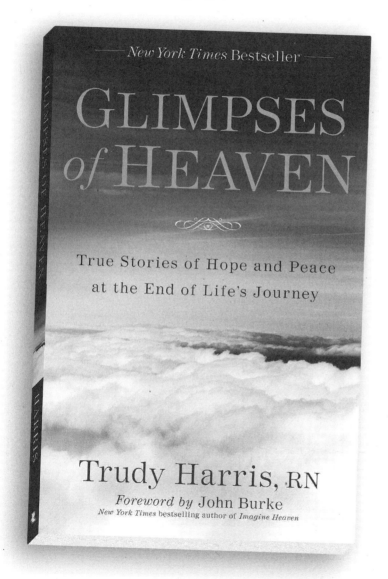

New York Times Bestseller

GLIMPSES *of* HEAVEN

True Stories of Hope and Peace
at the End of Life's Journey

Trudy Harris, RN

Foreword by John Burke
New York Times bestselling author of *Imagine Heaven*

Revell
a division of Baker Publishing Group
www.RevellBooks.com

—